Chapter 1
Managerial Accounting and the Business Environment

Exercise 1-1 (10 minutes)

1. Line
2. Directing and motivating
3. Budgets
4. Planning
5. Staff
6. Decentralization
7. Precision; Nonmonetary data
8. Managerial accounting; Financial accounting
9. Feedback
10. Controller
11. Performance report

Exercise 1-3 (15 minutes)

1. The characteristics of the JIT approach include the following:

   • Reducing the number of suppliers and requiring suppliers to make frequent deliveries of defect-free goods.

   • Creating a continuous flow of product through the plant, minimizing the investment in raw materials, work in process, and finished goods.

   • Making production operations more efficient by redesigning workstations and improving the plant layout by creating individual product flow lines.

   • Reducing setup time.

   • Reducing defects.

   • Cross training employees so that all are multiskilled and can perform all functions required at a particular workstation.

3. A successful JIT system requires suppliers who are willing to make frequent deliveries of defect-free goods in small quantities. This often requires weeding out unreliable suppliers and working intensively with a few, ultra-reliable suppliers.

Problem 1-5 (30 minutes)

1. See the organization chart on the following page.

2. Line positions would include the university president, academic vice-president, the deans of the four faculties, and the dean of the law school. In addition, the department heads (as well as the faculty) would be in line positions. The reason is that their positions are directly related to the basic purpose of the university, which is education. (Line positions are shaded on the organization chart.)

   All other positions on the organization chart are staff positions. The reason is that these positions are indirectly related to the educational process, and exist only to provide service or support to the line positions.

3. All positions would have need for accounting information of some type. For example, the manager of central purchasing would need to know the level of current inventories and budgeted allowances in various areas before doing any purchasing; the vice-president for admissions and records would need to know the status of scholarship funds as students are admitted to the university; the dean of the business faculty would need to know his/her budget allowances in various areas, as well as information on cost per student credit hour; and so forth.

Problem 1-5 (continued)

1. Organization chart:

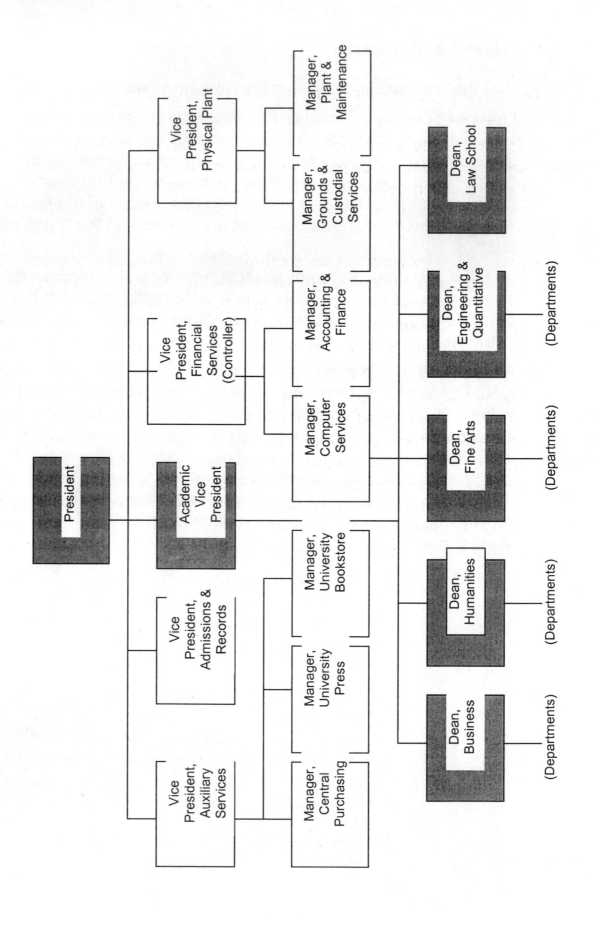

Problem 1-7 (30 minutes)

The following changes would have to be made in manufacturing procedures in order to follow JIT inventory practices:

- The company would have to focus on a few dependable suppliers who would deliver defect-free materials at specified intervals—perhaps even deliver on a daily basis. Warehousing of raw materials would be eliminated, as would the inspection of incoming materials.

- The company would have to break up groups of similar machines and organize all equipment into product flow lines. Thus, there would no longer be a Sewing Department, Cutting Department, or Assembly Department. Each flow line would contain "cells" within which various manufacturing tasks would be performed. Pieces of equipment on the flow line would be tightly grouped together. Having product flow lines would also eliminate the need for setups.

- The company would have to eliminate the "checkers" who are now inspecting products. Suppliers would be required to inspect material before shipment to ensure that it was defect free, and workers in each cell would be required to inspect their own work before transferring it to the next cell. An early warning system would need to be installed, which would stop a flow line if a defect was found in a partially completed football.

- The company would have to cross train its workers to perform multiple tasks in the production process. Workers would have to operate all machines in a cell, and perhaps all machines on the flow line. In addition, they would need to perform maintenance on these machines during slack periods.

- The company would have to operate under a "pull" approach, rather than a "push" approach, in manufacturing the products. Thus, products would be manufactured according to customer demand, with each cell responding to the "pull" exerted by the final manufacturing step.

Problem 1-7 (continued)

The sketch of the product flow line would be as follows:

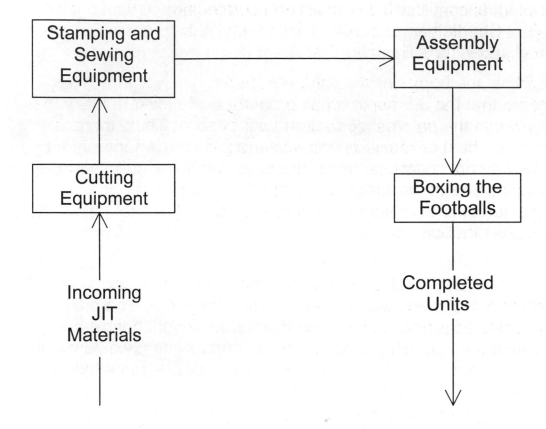

Problem 1-9 (30 minutes)

1. No, Charlie would not be justified in ignoring the situation. First, the standards of ethical conduct for management accountants states that the management accountant must "Avoid actual or apparent conflicts of interest and advise all appropriate parties of any potential conflict." If J.B. insists on continuing the relationship with A-1, Charlie has a responsibility to advise both the corporate counsel and WIW's Board of Directors.

   Second, as the company's controller, Charlie has a responsibility to ensure that the JIT approach is properly implemented. From the data given in the problem, it does not appear that A-1 Warehouse Sales is the best or most dependable supplier available. Orders are late and not complete, and there is no way to ensure proper quality since nearly all orders are shipped directly from the manufacturer. The present arrangement with A-1 negates most of the benefits that can accrue from JIT.

2. Charlie's first step should be to verify the accuracy of his information. He states that A-1's markup is 30 percent, but he does not indicate how he obtained this figure. Also, the adverse financial impact on WIW is dependent in part on the price it would have to pay directly to the manufacturers as compared to the price being paid to A-1. That is, can WIW purchase directly from the manufacturers for the same price as given to jobbers, who handle huge volumes of goods? If not, then the adverse financial impact of buying through A-1 may, in fact, be very small, since WIW may have to pay about the same price either way.

   Charlie's second step should be to discuss the potential legal ramifications on a confidential basis with WIW's corporate counsel. Before meeting with the corporate counsel, Charlie may wish to discretely determine if Tony, the purchasing agent, and J.B., the president, worked together in their prior employment. (Remember that both have been with WIW for five years.) Armed with the information obtained from the discussion with counsel, Charlie should review the situation again with J.B., explaining more directly his concerns about the apparent conflict of interest and ask that the Board of Directors approve the continued use of A-1 as a supplier.

Problem 1-9 (continued)

If J.B. refuses to follow this course of action, Charlie's only alternative is to submit a memorandum to the Board of Directors. J.B. should be notified of this action in advance. The memorandum should present only the facts. If the Board approves the continued relationship with A-1, Charlie may possibly conclude that his concerns about an apparent conflict of interest do not represent an actual conflict. This presumes that legal counsel has advised the Board that the arrangement with A-1 does not violate any laws and that the company has made adequate disclosures in its public filings. Only Charlie can make the decision as to whether or not he can continue at WIW under these circumstances.

Problem 1-11 (30 minutes)

The financial statements provide a useful opportunity to review basic financial reporting. The extent and detail of discussions obviously depends on the needs of students.

The required concentrates on some additional types of information that could be useful to management. The following are some suggestions:

1. costs by type of product
2. revenue and costs by customers
3. details of receivables and payables
4. budgets
5. delivery times for suppliers

6. on time delivery for customers

Chapter 2
Cost Terms, Concepts, and Classifications

Exercise 2-1 (15 minutes)

1. Product; variable
2. Conversion
3. Opportunity
4. Prime
5. Sunk
6. Period; variable
7. Product; period; fixed
8. Product
9. Period
10. Fixed; product; conversion

Exercise 2-3 (15 minutes)

1. a. Batteries purchased 8,000
        Batteries drawn from inventory... 7,600
        Batteries remaining in inventory 400
        Cost per battery .... x $10
        Cost in Raw Materials Inventory at April 30.......................... $ 4,000

    b. Batteries used in production (7,600 – 100)........................... 7,500
        Cars completed and transferred to Finished Goods
          (90% x 7,500 = 6,750).. 6,750
        Cars still in Work in Process at April 30............................... 750
        Cost per battery .... x $10
        Cost in Work in Process Inventory at April 30 .... $ 7,500

    c. Cars completed and transferred to Finished Goods (above) .. 6,750
        Cars sold during the month (70% x 6,750 = 4,725) 4,725
        Cars still in Finished Goods at April 30................................. 2,025
        Cost per battery .... x $10
        Cost in Finished Goods Inventory at April 30 .... $20,250

    d. Cars sold during the month (above) 4,725
        Cost per battery .... x $10
        Cost in Cost of Goods Sold at April 30................................. $47,250

    e. Batteries used in salespersons' cars 100
        Cost per battery .... x $10
        Cost in Selling Expense at April 30 .... $ 1,000

2. Raw Materials Inventory—balance sheet
    Work in Process Inventory—balance sheet
    Finished Goods Inventory—balance sheet
    Cost of Goods Sold—income statement
    Selling Expense—income statement

Exercise 2-5 (20 minutes)

1.

MASON COMPANY
Schedule of Cost of Goods Manufactured

Direct materials:		
Raw materials inventory, beginning...............	$ 7,000	
Add: Purchases of raw materials...................	118,000	
Raw materials available for use....................	125,000	
Deduct: Raw materials inventory, ending	15,000	
Raw materials used in production		$110,000
Direct labour...		70,000
Manufacturing overhead:		
Indirect labour	30,000	
Maintenance, factory equipment	6,000	
Insurance, factory equipment	800	
Rent, factory facilities	20,000	
Supplies	4,200	
Depreciation, factory equipment...................	19,000	
Total overhead costs		80,000
Total manufacturing costs		260,000
Add: Work in process, beginning......................		10,000
		270,000
Deduct: Work in process, ending......................		5,000
Cost of goods manufactured		$265,000

2. The cost of goods sold section of Mason Company's income statement:

Finished goods inventory, beginning	$ 20,000
Add: Cost of goods manufactured	265,000
Goods available for sale....................................	285,000
Deduct: Finished goods inventory, ending........	35,000
Cost of goods sold	$250,000

Exercise 2-7 (10 minutes)

1. Direct labour cost: 31 hours × $10.......................$310
   Manufacturing overhead cost: 9 hours × $10........ 90
      Total cost $400

2. Direct labour cost: 48 hours × $10.......................$480
   Manufacturing overhead cost: 8 hours × $5.......... 40
      Total cost $520

3. A company could treat the cost of fringe benefits relating to direct labour workers as part of manufacturing overhead. This approach spreads the cost of such fringe benefits over all units of output. Alternatively, the company could treat the cost of fringe benefits relating to direct labour workers as additional direct labour cost. This latter approach charges the costs of fringe benefits to specific jobs rather than to all units of output.

Problem 2-9 (30 minutes)

Req. 1

Name of the Cost	Variable Cost	Fixed Cost	Product Cost Direct Materials	Direct Labour	Mfg. Overhead	Period (Selling and Admin.) Cost	Opportunity Cost	Sunk Cost
Rental revenue foregone, $30,000 per year							X	
Direct materials cost, $80 per unit	X		X					
Rental cost of warehouse, $500 per month		X				X		
Rental cost of equipment, $4,000 per month		X			X			
Direct labour cost, $60 per unit	X			X				
Depreciation of the annex space, $8,000 per year		X			X			X
Advertising cost, $50,000 per year		X				X		
Supervisor's salary, $1,500 per month		X			X			
Electricity for machines, $1.20 per unit	X				X			
Shipping cost, $9 per unit	X					X		
Return earned on investments, $3,000 per year							X	

Req. 2 Knowledge of cost behaviour is an asset for managers in strategic planning because it helps provide information on what will happen to costs under alternative volume levels. Volume decisions are something that represents a key component of strategic decisions. Also cost leadership is a key component to strategic decisions. Cost behaviour knowledge would assist in providing managers with the implications of various strategic production or sales options involved in cost leadership decisions.

Problem 2-11 (30 minutes)

1. Total wages for the week:

Regular time: 40 hours × $10..................	$400
Overtime: 6 hours × $15	90
Total wages	$490

Allocation of total wages:

Direct labour: 46 hours × $10..................	$460
Manufacturing overhead: 6 hours × $5 ...	30
Total wages	$490

2. Total wages for the week:

Regular time: 40 hours × $10..................	$400
Overtime: 8 hours × $15	120
Total wages	$520

Allocation of total wages:

Direct labour: 45 hours × $10..................		$450
Manufacturing overhead:		
Idle time: 3 hours × $10	$ 30	
Overtime premium: 8 hours × $5..........	40	70
Total wages		$520

3. Total wages and fringe benefits for the week:

Regular time: 40 hours × $10..................	$400
Overtime: 10 hours × $15	150
Fringe benefits: 50 hours × $3	150
Total wages and fringe benefits	$700

Allocation of wages and fringe benefits:

Direct labour: 48 hours × $10..................		$480
Manufacturing overhead:		
Idle time: 2 hours × $10	$ 20	
Overtime premium: 10 hours × $5........	50	
Fringe benefits: 50 hours × $3	150	220
Total wages and fringe benefits		$700

Problem 2-11 (continued)

4. Allocation of wages and fringe benefits:

Direct labour:

Wage cost: 48 hours × $10......................	$480	
Fringe benefits: 48 hours × $3.................	144	$624

Manufacturing overhead:

Idle time: 2 hours × $10...........................	20	
Overtime premium: 10 hours × $5	50	
Fringe benefits: 2 hours × $3...................	6	76
Total wages and fringe benefits............		$700

Problem 2-13 (40 minutes)

1.

Cost Item	Cost Behaviour		Selling or Administrative Cost	Product Cost	
	Variable	Fixed		Direct	Indirect
Factory labour, direct	$118,000			$118,000	
Advertising		$ 50,000	$ 50,000		
Factory supervision		40,000			$40,000
Property taxes, factory building		3,500			3,500
Sales commissions	80,000		80,000		
Insurance, factory		2,500			2,500
Depreciation, office equipment		4,000	4,000		
Lease cost, factory equipment		12,000			12,000
Indirect materials, factory	6,000				6,000
Depreciation, factory building		10,000			10,000
General office supplies	3,000		3,000		
General office salaries		60,000	60,000		
Direct materials used	94,000			94,000	
Utilities, factory	20,000				20,000
Total costs	$321,000	$182,000	$197,000	$212,000	$94,000

2. Product Costs:

Direct $212,000
Indirect 94,000
Total $306,000

$306,000 ÷ 2,000 sets = $153 per set

Problem 2-13 (continued)

3.   The cost per set would increase. This is because the fixed costs would be spread over fewer units, causing the cost per unit to rise.

4. a. Yes, the president may expect a minimum price of $153, which is the average cost to manufacture one set. He might expect a figure even higher than this to cover a portion of the administrative costs as well. The brother-in-law probably will be thinking of "cost" as including only materials used, or, at best, materials and direct labour. Materials alone would be only $47 per set, and materials and direct labour would be only $106.

   b. The term is opportunity cost. The full, regular price of a set might be appropriate here, since the company is operating at full capacity, and this is the amount that must be given up (benefit foregone) in order to sell a set to the brother-in-law.

5.   Knowledge of cost behaviour would help in volume decisions, pricing decisions, and production/sales decisions all of which represent key components of strategic planning. Such cost behaviour knowledge is critical in understanding what happens to cost if various alternatives are undertaken.

Problem 2-15 (20 minutes)

1.

Name of the Cost	Variable Cost	Fixed Cost	Product Cost Direct Materials	Direct Labour	Mfg. Overhead	Period (Selling and Admin.) Cost	Opportunity Cost	Sunk Cost
Staci's present salary, $2,500/month							X	
Building rent, $500/month		X			X			
Clay and glaze, $2/pot	X		X					
Wages of production workers, $8/pot	X			X				
Advertising, $600/month		X				X		
Sales commission, $4/pot	X					X		
Rent of production equipment, $300/month		X			X			
Legal and filing fees, $500		X				X		X
Rent of sales office, $250/month		X				X		
Phone for taking orders, $40/month		X				X		
Interest lost on savings account, $1,200/year							X	

2. The $500 cost of incorporating the business is not a differential cost. Even though the cost was incurred in order to start the business, it is a sunk cost. Whether Staci produces pottery or stays in her present job, she will have incurred this cost.

Problem 2-17 (50 minutes)

1.

SWIFT COMPANY
Schedule of Cost of Goods Manufactured
For the Month Ended August 31

Direct materials:		
Raw materials inventory, August 1	$ 8,000	
Add: Purchases of raw materials......................	165,000	
Raw materials available for use......................	173,000	
Deduct: Raw materials inventory, August 31 ...	13,000	
Raw materials used in production		$160,000
Direct labour..		70,000
Manufacturing overhead:		
Indirect labour cost...	12,000	
Utilities (60% × $15,000)	9,000	
Depreciation, factory equipment......................	21,000	
Insurance (75% × $4,000)	3,000	
Rent on facilities (80% × $50,000)...................	40,000	
Total overhead costs		85,000
Total manufacturing costs		315,000
Add: Work in process inventory, August 1		16,000
		331,000
Deduct: Work in process inventory, August 31		21,000
Cost of goods manufactured		$310,000

Problem 2-17 (continued)

2.

SWIFT COMPANY
Income Statement
For the Month Ended August 31

Sales...		$450,000
Less cost of goods sold:		
Finished goods inventory, August 1.............	$ 40,000	
Add: Cost of goods manufactured	310,000	
Goods available for sale............................	350,000	
Deduct: Finished goods inventory,		
August 31	60,000	290,000
Gross margin		160,000
Less operating expenses:		
Utilities (40% × $15,000)	6,000	
Depreciation, sales equipment	18,000	
Insurance (25% × $4,000)	1,000	
Rent on facilities (20% × $50,000)	10,000	
Selling and administrative salaries	32,000	
Advertising	75,000	142,000
Net income..		$ 18,000

3. In preparing the income statement for August, Sam failed to distinguish between product costs and period costs, and he also failed to recognize the changes in inventories between the beginning and end of the month. Once these errors have been corrected, the financial condition of the company looks much better and selling the company may not be advisable.

Problem 2-19 (15 minutes)

1. The controller is correct in his viewpoint that the salary cost should be classified as a selling (marketing) cost. The duties described in the problem have nothing to do with the manufacture of a product, but rather deal with movement of *finished units* from the factory to distribution warehouses. As stated in the text, selling costs would include all costs necessary to secure customer orders and get the finished product into the hands of customers. Coordination of shipments of finished units from the factory to distribution warehouses would seem to fall into this category.

2. No, the president is not correct; from the point of view of the reported net income for the year, it does make a difference how the salary cost is classified. If the salary cost is classified as a selling expense all of it will appear on the income statement as a period cost. However, if the salary cost is classified as a manufacturing (product) cost, then it will be added into Work In Process Inventory along with other manufacturing costs for the period. To the extent that goods are still in process at the end of the period, part of the salary cost will remain with these goods in the Work in Process Inventory account. Only that portion of the salary cost which has been assigned to finished units will leave the Work In Process Inventory account and be transferred into the Finished Goods Inventory account. In like manner, to the extent that goods are unsold at the end of the period, part of the salary cost will remain with these goods in the Finished Goods Inventory account. Only that portion of the salary which has been assigned to finished units *that are sold during the period* will appear on the income statement as an expense (part of Cost of Goods Sold) for the period.

Problem 2-21 (40 minutes)

1.

VISIC COMPANY
Schedule of Cost of Goods Manufactured

Direct materials:		
Raw materials inventory, beginning............	$ 20,000	
Add: Purchases of raw materials...............	480,000	
Raw materials available for use.................	500,000	
Deduct: Raw materials inventory, ending ..	30,000	
Raw materials used in production		$470,000
Direct labour..		90,000
Manufacturing overhead:		
Indirect labour	85,000	
Building rent (80% × $40,000)	32,000	
Utilities, factory.......................................	108,000	
Royalty on patent ($1.50 × 29,000 units) ..	43,500	
Maintenance, factory	9,000	
Rent on equipment:		
$7,000 + ($0.30 × 29,000 units)	15,700	
Other factory overhead costs	6,800	
Total overhead costs..............................		300,000
Total manufacturing costs		860,000
Add: Work in process inventory, beginning ..		50,000
		910,000
Deduct: Work in process inventory, ending ..		40,000
Cost of goods manufactured		$870,000

Problem 2-21 (continued)

2. a. To compute the number of units in the finished goods inventory at the end of the year, we must first compute the number of units sold during the year.

$$\frac{\text{Total sales,} \quad \$1,300,000}{\text{Unit selling price,} \quad \$50} = 26,000 \text{ units sold.}$$

Units in the finished goods inventory, beginning	–0–
Units produced during the year	29,000
Units available for sale	29,000
Units sold during the year (above)	26,000
Units in the finished goods inventory, ending	3,000

b. The average production cost per unit during the year would be:

$$\frac{\text{Cost of goods manufactured,} \quad \$870,000}{\text{Number of units produced,} \quad 29,000} = \$30 \text{ per unit.}$$

Thus, the cost of the units in the finished goods inventory at the end of the year would be: 3,000 units × $30 per unit = $90,000.

3.

VISIC COMPANY
Income Statement

Sales		$1,300,000
Less cost of goods sold:		
Finished goods inventory, beginning	$ –0–	
Add: Cost of goods manufactured	870,000	
Goods available for sale	870,000	
Finished goods inventory, ending.................	90,000	780,000
Gross margin		520,000
Less operating expenses:		
Advertising	105,000	
Entertainment and travel	40,000	
Building rent (20% × $40,000)......................	8,000	
Selling and administrative salaries	210,000	
Other selling and administrative expense....	17,000	380,000
Net income...		$ 140,000

Chapter 3
Systems Design: Job-Order Costing

Exercise 3-1 (10 minutes)

a. Process costing	g. Job-order costing
b. Job-order costing	h. Process costing*
c. Process costing	i. Job-order costing
d. Process costing	j. Process costing*
e. Process costing	k. Job-order costing
f. Job-order costing	l. Job-order costing

* Some of the companies listed might use either a job-order or a process costing system, depending on how operations are carried out. For example, a chemical manufacturer would typically operate with a process costing system, but a job-order costing system could be employed if products were manufactured in relatively small batches. The same thing might be true of the tire manufacturing plant in item "j."

Exercise 3-3 (20 minutes)

1. a. Raw Materials Inventory............................. 210,000
         Accounts Payable   210,000

   b. Work in Process... 178,000
         Manufacturing Overhead...........................   12,000
         Raw Materials Inventory..........................   190,000

   c. Work in Process... 90,000
         Manufacturing Overhead........................... 110,000
         Salaries and Wages Payable   200,000

   d. Manufacturing Overhead........................... 40,000
         Accumulated Depreciation   40,000

   e. Manufacturing Overhead........................... 70,000
         Accounts Payable   70,000

   f. Work in Process... 240,000
         Manufacturing Overhead...........................   240,000
         30,000 MH × \$8 per MH = \$240,000.

   g. Finished Goods... 520,000
         Work in Process..   520,000

   h. Cost of Goods Sold................................... 480,000
         Finished Goods..   480,000

      Accounts Receivable 600,000
         Sales...   600,000
         \$480,000 × 1.25 = \$600,000.

2.

Manufacturing Overhead			
(b)	12,000	240,000	(f)
(c)	110,000		
(d)	40,000		
(e)	70,000		
		8,000	
		(Overapplied overhead)	

Work in Process			
Bal.	42,000	520,000	(g)
(b)	178,000		
(c)	90,000		
(f)	240,000		
Bal.	30,000		

Exercise 3-5 (15 minutes)

1. Item (a): Actual manufacturing overhead costs for the year.
   Item (b): Overhead cost applied to work in process for the year.
   Item (c): Cost of goods manufactured for the year.
   Item (d): Cost of goods sold for the year.

2. Cost of Goods Sold 70,000
       Manufacturing Overhead................................   70,000

3. The underapplied overhead will have to be allocated to the other accounts on the basis of the overhead applied during the year that is in the ending balance in each account:

Work in process	$ 19,500	5%
Finished goods	58,500	15
Cost of goods sold	312,000	80
Total cost	$390,000	100%

Using these percentages, the entry would be as follows:

Work in Process (5% × $70,000)......................	3,500	
Finished Goods (15% × $70,000)....................	10,500	
Cost of Goods Sold (80% × $70,000)..............	56,000	
Manufacturing Overhead.............................		70,000

Exercise 3-7 (15 minutes)

1. Cutting Department:

$$\frac{\text{Estimated overhead cost, } \$360,000}{\text{Estimated machine-hours, } \quad 48,000} = \$7.50/\text{MH}$$

Finishing Department:

$$\frac{\text{Estimated overhead cost, } \quad \$486,000}{\text{Estimated direct labour cost, } \$270,000} = \frac{180\% \text{ of direct}}{\text{labour cost}}$$

2.

	Overhead Applied
Cutting Department: 80 hrs. × $7.50 per hr.	$600
Finishing Department: $150 × 180%	270
Total overhead cost applied	$870

3. Yes; if some jobs required a large amount of machine time and little labour cost, they would be charged substantially less overhead cost if a plantwide rate based on direct labour cost were being used. It appears, for example, that this would be true of job 203 which required considerable machine time to complete, but required only a small amount of labour cost.

Exercise 3-9 (20 minutes)

1. a. Raw Materials... 325,000
        Accounts Payable.................................... 325,000

   b. Work in Process 232,000
       Manufacturing Overhead 58,000
          Raw Materials... 290,000

   c. Work in Process 60,000
       Manufacturing Overhead 120,000
          Wages and Salaries Payable.................... 180,000

   d. Manufacturing Overhead 75,000
       Accumulated Depreciation......................... 75,000

   e. Manufacturing Overhead 62,000
       Accounts Payable..................................... 62,000

   f. Work in Process 300,000
       Manufacturing Overhead 300,000

   $$\frac{\text{Estimated overhead cost,}\quad \$4,800,000}{\text{Estimated machine-hours,}\qquad 240,000} = \$20/\text{MH}$$

   15,000 MH × $20 per MH = $300,000.

2.

Manufacturing Overhead			Work in Process		
(b)	58,000	300,000 (f)	(b)	232,000	
(c)	120,000		(c)	60,000	
(d)	75,000		(f)	300,000	
(e)	62,000				

3. The cost of the completed job would be $592,000 as shown in the Work in Process T-account above. The entry would be:

   Finished Goods.................................... 592,000
      Work in Process............................... 592,000

4. The cost per unit on the job cost sheet would be:

   $592,000 ÷ 16,000 units = $37 per unit.

Exercise 3-11 (20 minutes)

1.

	Harris	Chan	James
Designer-hours..........................	120	100	90
Predetermined overhead rate....	× $90	× $90	× $90
Manufacturing overhead applied	$10,800	$9,000	$8,100

2.

	Harris	Chan
Direct materials	$ 4,500	$3,700
Direct labour............................	9,600	8,000
Overhead applied......................	10,800	9,000
Total cost (a)	$24,900	$20,700

Completed Projects*	45,600	
Work in Process		45,600

* $24,900 + $20,700 = $45,600.

3. The balance in the Work in Process account will consist entirely of the costs associated with the James project:

Direct materials	$ 1,400
Direct labour...	7,200
Overhead applied...	8,100
Total cost in work in process	$16,700

4. The balance in the Overhead account can be determined as follows:

Overhead			
Actual costs	30,000	27,900	Applied costs
Under-applied	2,100		

As indicated above, the debit balance in the Overhead account is called underapplied overhead.

Exercise 3-13 (30 minutes)

1.

	Job 1010	Job 1020	Job 1030
Machine-hours	1,200	1,000	900
Predetermined overhead rate	× $9	× $9	× $9
Manufacturing overhead applied...	$10,800	$9,000	$8,100

2.

	Job 1010	Job 1020
Direct materials	$ 4,500	$ 3,700
Direct labour	9,600	8,000
Manufacturing overhead applied...	10,800	9,000
Total cost (a)	$24,900	$20,700
Number of units (b)	4,000	3,600
Cost per unit (a) ÷ (b)	$6.225	$5.75

3.

Finished Goods*	45,600	
Work in Process		45,600

*$24,900 + $20,700 = $45,600.

4.   The balance in the Work in Process account will consist entirely of the costs associated with job 1030:

Direct materials	$ 1,400
Direct labour	7,200
Manufacturing overhead applied.........	8,100
Total cost in work in process	$16,700

Exercise 3-13 (continued)

5. The balance in the Manufacturing Overhead account can be determined as follows:

Manufacturing Overhead			
Actual costs	30,000	27,900	Applied costs
Under-applied	2,100		

6. Looking at completed jobs only, Job 1010 had a unit cost of $6.225 while Job 1020 had a cost of $5.75. The largest cost element was overhead. Overhead was driven by machine hours. Job 1010 had 0.3 hours per unit while 1020 had 0.28 per unit. Thus 1010 appears to be the more costly. Direct labour per unit is also higher for Job 1010.

Exercise 3-15 (15 minutes)

Method 1:

Special finished goods inventory	4,160	
Finished goods inventory		4,160

To credit the recovery expected to the costs of the good product.
400 m * ($18 + $3 + $5) * .40 = $4,160

Method 2:

Manufacturing overhead...	10,400	
Finished goods inventory		10,400

To charge the defects to overhead.
400 m * ($18 + $3 + $5) = $10,400.

Special finished goods inventory	4,160	
Manufacturing overhead		4,160

To credit the expected recovery to the cost of the defects.
400 m * ($18 + $3 + $5) * .40 = $4,160

Problem 3-17 (45 minutes)

1. a. Raw Materials 170,000
      Accounts Payable   170,000

   b. Work in Process.................................... 144,000
      Manufacturing Overhead.......................... 36,000
      Raw Materials   180,000

   c. Work in Process.................................... 200,000
      Manufacturing Overhead.......................... 82,000
      Salaries Expense 90,000
      Salaries and Wages Payable   372,000

   d. Manufacturing Overhead.......................... 65,000
      Accounts Payable   65,000

   e. Advertising Expense 100,000
      Accounts Payable   100,000

   f. Manufacturing Overhead.......................... 18,000
      Insurance Expense 2,000
      Prepaid Insurance................................   20,000

   g. Manufacturing Overhead.......................... 153,000
      Depreciation Expense 27,000
      Accumulated Depreciation   180,000

   h. Work in Process..................................... 350,000
      Manufacturing Overhead......................   350,000

      $200,000 actual direct labour cost x 175%
      = $350,000 overhead applied.

   i. Finished Goods..................................... 700,000
      Work in Process...................................   700,000

   j. Accounts Receivable 1,000,000
      Sales...   1,000,000

      Cost of Goods Sold................................ 720,000
      Finished Goods....................................   720,000

Problem 3-17 (continued)

2.

Raw Materials							
Bal.	32,000	180,000	(b)
(a)	170,000		
Bal.	22,000		

Finished Goods				
Bal.	48,000	720,000	(j)
(i)	700,000		
Bal.	28,000		

Work in Process				
Bal.	20,000	700,000	(i)
(b)	144,000		
(c)	200,000		
(h)	350,000		
Bal.	14,000		

Manufacturing Overhead				
(b)	36,000	350,000	(h)
(c)	82,000		
(d)	65,000		
(f)	18,000		
(g)	153,000		
Bal.	4,000		

Cost of Goods Sold		
(j)	720,000	

3. Overhead is underapplied by $4,000 for the year. The entry to close this balance to Cost of Goods Sold would be:

Cost of Goods Sold	4,000	
Manufacturing Overhead		4,000

4.
ALMEDA PRODUCTS, INC.
Income Statement
For the Year Ended March 31

Sales...		$1,000,000
Less cost of goods sold ($720,000 + $4,000)...		724,000
Gross margin		276,000
Less selling and administrative expenses:		
Salary expense	$ 90,000	
Advertising expense......................................	100,000	
Insurance expense..	2,000	
Depreciation expense....................................	27,000	219,000
Net income..		$ 57,000

Problem 3-19 (30 minutes)

1. Molding Department predetermined overhead rate:

$$\frac{\text{Estimated overhead cost, } \$602,000}{\text{Estimated machine-hours, } 70,000} = \$8.60 \text{ per machine-hour.}$$

Painting Department predetermined overhead rate:

$$\frac{\text{Estimated overhead cost, } \$735,000}{\text{Estimated direct labour cost, } \$420,000} = 175\% \text{ of direct labour cost.}$$

2. Molding Department overhead applied:

110 machine-hours × $8.60............................	$ 946
Painting Department overhead applied:	
$680 direct labour cost × 175%..........................	1,190
Total overhead cost...	$2,136

3. Total cost of job 205:

	Molding Dept.	Painting Dept.	Total
Direct materials..........................	$ 470	$ 332	$ 802
Direct labour	290	680	970
Manufacturing overhead applied..	946	1,190	2,136
Total cost	$1,706	$2,202	$3,908

Cost per unit for job 205:

$$\frac{\text{Total cost, } \$3,908}{50 \text{ units}} = \$78.16 \text{ per unit}$$

4.

	Molding Dept.	Painting Dept.
Manufacturing overhead incurred..............	$570,000	$750,000
Manufacturing overhead applied:		
65,000 machine-hours × $8.60 per machine-hour	559,000	
$436,000 direct labour cost × 175%		763,000
Underapplied (or overapplied) overhead ...	$ 11,000	$ (13,000)

Problem 3-21 (60 minutes)

1. a. Materials and Supplies 690,000
      Accounts Payable 690,000

   b. Films in Process...................................... 560,000
      Production Overhead 140,000
         Materials and Supplies 700,000

   c. Production Overhead 90,000
         Accounts Payable 90,000

   d. Films in Process...................................... 1,300,000
      Production Overhead 230,000
      Salaries Expense 650,000
         Salaries and Wages Payable 2,180,000

   e. Advertising Expense 800,000
         Accounts Payable 800,000

   f. Production Overhead 60,000
      Insurance Expense 10,000
         Prepaid Insurance 70,000

   g. Production Overhead 520,000
      Depreciation Expense 130,000
         Accumulated Depreciation 650,000

   h. Production Overhead 360,000
      Rent Expense 40,000
         Accounts Payable 400,000

   i. The company's predetermined overhead rate would be:

$$\frac{\text{Estimated production overhead,} \quad \$1,350,000}{\text{Estimated camera hours,} \qquad\qquad 15,000} = \$90 \text{ per camera-hour}$$

   The overhead cost applied to production would be:

   16,500 camera hours x $90 per camera-hour = $1,485,000.

   The entry to record this application follows:

   Films in Process.. 1,485,000
      Production Overhead 1,485,000

Problem 3-21 (continued)

j.	Finished Films	3,400,000	
	Films in Process		3,400,000
k.	Accounts Receivable	6,000,000	
	Sales Revenue		6,000,000
	Cost of Films Sold	4,000,000	
	Finished Films		4,000,000
l.	Cash	5,400,000	
	Accounts Receivable		5,400,000
m.	Accounts Payable	2,500,000	
	Salaries and Wages Payable	2,200,000	
	Cash		4,700,000

2. See the T-accounts on the following pages.

3. Production overhead is overapplied for the year. The journal entry would be as follows:

Production Overhead	85,000	
Cost of Films Sold		85,000

4.

FILM SPECIALTIES, INC.
Income Statement
For the Year Ended April 30

Sales revenue		$6,000,000
Less cost of films sold ($4,000,000 − $85,000)		3,915,000
Gross margin		2,085,000
Less operating expenses:		
Salaries expense	$650,000	
Advertising expense	800,000	
Insurance expense	10,000	
Depreciation expense	130,000	
Rent expense	40,000	1,630,000
Net income		$ 455,000

Problem 3-21 (continued)

5.   Job costing provides cost information for specific jobs which in turn assists in pricing, assessing competitive position and determining overall performance for the company. Such information along with the capacity utilization evident from the under- or overapplied overhead enables management to have a basis from which they can set new plans for the future. This history provides a record of past results in these various areas which supports the decision processes necessary for management to decide what they wish to undertake in the future.

Problem 3-21 (continued)

2.

Cash			
Bal.	60,000	4,700,000	(m)
(l)	5,400,000		
Bal.	760,000		

Accumulated Depreciation		
	1,990,000	Bal.
	650,000	(g)
	2,640,000	Bal.

Accounts Receivable			
Bal.	210,000	5,400,000	(l)
(k)	6,000,000		
Bal.	810,000		

Accounts Payable			
(m)	2,500,000	700,000	Bal.
		690,000	(a)
		90,000	(c)
		800,000	(e)
		400,000	(h)
		180,000	Bal.

Prepaid Insurance			
Bal.	90,000	70,000	(f)
Bal.	20,000		

Salaries & Wages Payable			
(m)	2,200,000	35,000	Bal.
		2,180,000	(d)
		15,000	Bal.

Materials and Supplies			
Bal.	130,000	700,000	(b)
(a)	690,000		
Bal.	120,000		

Capital Stock		
	2,500,000	Bal.

Films in Process			
Bal.	75,000	3,400,000	(j)
(b)	560,000		
(d)	1,300,000		
(i)	1,485,000		
Bal.	20,000		

Retained Earnings		
	1,400,000	Bal.

Sales		
	6,000,000	(k)

Finished Films			
Bal.	860,000	4,000,000	(k)
(j)	3,400,000		
Bal.	260,000		

Cost of Films Sold		
(k)	4,000,000	

Studio and Equipment	
Bal.	5,200,000

Problem 3-21 (continued)

	Production Overhead		
(b)	140,000	1,485,000	(i)
(c)	90,000		
(d)	230,000		
(f)	60,000		
(g)	520,000		
(h)	360,000		
		85,000	Bal.

	Depreciation Expense	
(g)	130,000	

	Insurance Expense	
(g)	10,000	

	Advertising Expense	
(e)	800,000	

	Rent Expense	
(h)	40,000	

	Salaries Expense	
(d)	650,000	

Problem 3-23 (30 minutes)

1. Research & Documents predetermined overhead rate:

$$\frac{\text{Estimated overhead cost, } \$840,000}{\text{Estimated research hours, } 24,000} = \$35 \text{ per hour.}$$

   Litigation predetermined overhead rate:

$$\frac{\text{Estimated overhead cost, } \$360,000}{\text{Estimated direct attorney cost, } \$900,000} = 40\% \text{ of direct attorney cost.}$$

2. Research & Documents overhead applied:

26 hours × $35	$ 910
Litigation overhead applied: $5,700 × 40%.............	2,280
Total overhead cost...	$3,190

3. Total cost of case 418–3:

	Departments Research & Documents	Litigation	Total
Legal forms and supplies	$ 80	$ 40	$ 120
Direct attorney cost	350	5,700	6,050
Overhead cost applied	910	2,280	3,190
Total cost	$1,340	$8,020	$9,360

4.

	Research & Documents	Litigation
Departmental overhead cost incurred.........	$870,000	$315,000
Departmental overhead cost applied:		
26,000 hours × $35	910,000	
$750,000 × 40%		300,000
Underapplied (or overapplied) overhead	$ (40,000)	$ 15,000

Problem 3-25 (50 minutes)

1. a. $\dfrac{\text{Estimated manufacturing overhead cost, } \$840{,}000}{\text{Estimated direct labour cost,} \qquad\qquad \$600{,}000} = $ 140% of direct labour cost.

b. $\$9{,}500 \times 140\% = \$13{,}300.$

2. a.

	Fabricating Department	Machining Department	Assembly Department
Estimated manufacturing overhead cost (a)............	$350,000	$400,000	$ 90,000
Estimated direct labour cost (b)...........................	$200,000	$100,000	$300,000
Predetermined overhead rate (a) ÷ (b)	175%	400%	30%

b. Fabricating Department:
   $2,800 × 175%.................................... $4,900
   Machining Department:
   $500 × 400%...................................... 2,000
   Assembly Department:
   $6,200 × 30%..................................... 1,860
   Total applied overhead......................... $8,760

3. The bulk of the labour cost on the Koopers job is in the Assembly Department, which incurs very little overhead cost. The department has an overhead rate of only 30% of direct labour cost as compared to much higher rates in the other two departments. Therefore, as shown above, use of departmental overhead rates results in a relatively small amount of overhead cost being charged to the job.

Use of a plantwide overhead rate, however, in effect redistributes overhead costs proportionately between the three departments (at 140% of direct labour cost) and results in a large amount of overhead cost being charged to the Koopers job, as shown in Part 1. This may explain why the company bid too high and lost the job. Too much overhead cost was assigned to the job for the kind of work being done on the job in the plant.

Problem 3-25 (continued)

On jobs that require a large amount of labour in the Fabricating or Machining Departments the opposite will be true, and the company will tend to charge too little overhead cost to the jobs if a plantwide overhead rate is being used. The reason is that the plantwide overhead rate (140%) is much lower than the rates would be if these departments were considered separately.

4. The company's bid price was:

Direct materials	$ 4,600
Direct labour	9,500
Manufacturing overhead applied (above)..........	13,300
Total manufacturing cost..............................	27,400
Bidding rate..	× 1.5
Total bid price	$41,100

If departmental overhead rates had been used, the bid price would have been:

Direct materials	$ 4,600
Direct labour	9,500
Manufacturing overhead applied (above)..........	8,760
Total manufacturing cost..............................	22,860
Bidding rate..	× 1.5
Total bid price	$34,290

Note that if departmental overhead rates had been used, Teledex Company would have been the low bidder on the Koopers job since the competitor underbid Teledex by only $2,000.

5. a.
Actual overhead cost	$864,000
Applied overhead cost ($580,000 × 140%)	812,000
Underapplied overhead cost	$ 52,000

Problem 3-25 (continued)

b.

	Fabricating Department	Machining Department	Assembly Department	Total Plant
Actual overhead cost	$360,000	$420,000	$84,000	$864,000
Applied overhead cost:				
$210,000 × 175%	367,500			
$108,000 × 400%		432,000		
$262,000 × 30%			78,600	878,100
Underapplied (overapplied) overhead cost	$ (7,500)	$ (12,000)	$ 5,400	$ (14,100)

Problem 3-27 (120 minutes)

1. a. Raw Materials.................................... 200,000
      Accounts Payable.............................. | 200,000
   b. Work in Process 185,000
      Raw Materials.................................... | 185,000
   c. Manufacturing Overhead 63,000
      Utilities Expense................................. 7,000
      Accounts Payable.............................. | 70,000
   d. Work in Process 230,000
      Manufacturing Overhead 90,000
      Salaries Expense 110,000
      Salaries and Wages Payable.............. | 430,000
   e. Manufacturing Overhead 54,000
      Accounts Payable.............................. | 54,000
   f. Advertising Expense............................. 136,000
      Accounts Payable.............................. | 136,000
   g. Manufacturing Overhead 76,000
      Depreciation Expense 19,000
      Accumulated Depreciation................... | 95,000
   h. Manufacturing Overhead 102,000
      Rent Expense..................................... 18,000
      Accounts Payable.............................. | 120,000
   i. Work in Process 390,000
      Manufacturing Overhead .... | 390,000

$$\frac{\text{Estimated overhead cost, Nkr 360,000}}{\text{Estimated DLH,} \qquad\qquad 900} = \text{Nkr 400 per DLH.}$$

975 actual DLH x Nkr 400 per DLH = Nkr 390,000.

   j. Finished Goods................................... 770,000
      Work in Process................................. | 770,000
   k. Accounts Receivable 1,200,000
      Sales.. | 1,200,000
      Cost of Goods Sold............................ 800,000
      Finished Goods................................. | 800,000

Problem 3-27 (continued)

2.

Accounts Receivable				Sales		
(k)	1,200,000				1,200,000	(k)

Raw Materials					Cost of Goods Sold		
Bal.	30,000	185,000	(b)	(k)	800,000	
(a)	200,000					
Bal.	45,000					

Work in Process				Manufacturing Overhead			
Bal.	21,000	770,000	(j)	(c)	63,000	390,000	(i)
(b)	185,000			(d)	90,000		
(d)	230,000			(e)	54,000		
(i)	390,000			(g)	76,000		
Bal.	56,000			(h)	102,000		
						5,000	Bal.

Finished Goods				Advertising Expense		
Bal.	60,000	800,000	(k)	(f)	136,000	
(j)	770,000					
Bal.	30,000					

Accumulated Depreciation				Utilities Expense		
		95,000	(g)	(c)	7,000	

Accounts Payable				Salaries Expense		
		200,000	(a)	(d)	110,000	
		70,000	(c)			
		54,000	(e)	Depreciation Expense		
		136,000	(f)	(g)	19,000	
		120,000	(h)			

Salaries & Wages Payable				Rent Expense		
		430,000	(d)	(h)	18,000	

Problem 3-27 (continued)

3.   FROYA FABRIKKER A/S
            Schedule of Cost of Goods Manufactured

Direct materials:
  Raw materials inventory, beginning............... Nkr 30,000
  Purchases of raw materials 200,000
  Materials available for use............................ 230,000
  Raw materials inventory, ending 45,000

Materials used in production		Nkr 185,000
Direct labour		230,000
Manufacturing overhead applied to work in process..		390,000
Total manufacturing costs.................................		805,000
Add: Work in process, beginning		21,000
		826,000
Deduct: Work in process, ending		56,000
Cost of goods manufactured............................		Nkr 770,000

4. Manufacturing Overhead	5,000	
Cost of Goods Sold..		5,000

Schedule of cost of goods sold:

Finished goods inventory, beginning..................	Nkr 60,000
Add: Cost of goods manufactured......................	770,000
Goods available for sale	830,000
Deduct finished goods inventory, ending	30,000
Unadjusted cost of goods sold...........................	800,000
Deduct: Overapplied overhead	5,000
Adjusted cost of goods sold	Nkr 795,000

Problem 3-27 (continued)

5.

FROYA FABRIKKER A/S
Income Statement

Sales		Nkr 1,200,000
Less cost of goods sold		795,000
Gross margin		405,000
Less selling and administrative expenses:		
Advertising expense	Nkr 136,000	
Utilities expense	7,000	
Salaries expense	110,000	
Depreciation expense	19,000	
Rent expense	18,000	290,000
Net income		Nkr 115,000

6. Direct materials	Nkr	8,000
Direct labour		9,200
Manufacturing overhead applied		
(39 hours × Nkr 400 per hour)		15,600
Total manufacturing cost		32,800
Add markup (60% × Nkr 32,800		19,680
Total billed price of job 412	Nkr	52,480

Problem 3-29 (30 minutes)

(a)
	Debit	Credit
Raw and In-Process Inventory — Cell C	150,000	
— Cell R	75,000	
Accounts payable		225,000

(b)
	Debit	Credit
Overhead — Cell C (290,000 + 88,000)	378,000	
— Cell R (210,000 + 76,000)	286,000	
Cash (290,000 + 210,000)		500,000
Various credits (88,000 + 76,000)		164,000

(c)
	Debit	Credit
Cost of Finished Construction — Cell C	384,800	
— Cell R	294,300	
Overhead — Cell C		384,800
— Cell R		294,300

Overhead rates

	C	R
Estimated	$390,000	$270,000
Hours	15,000	10,000
Rate	$ 26	$ 27
Applied		
Hours	14,800	10,900
Amount	$384,800	$294,300

(d)
	Debit	Credit
Overhead — Cell C	6,800	
— Cell R	8,300	
Cost of construction — Cell C		6,800
— Cell R		8,300

To close overhead amounts for under- and overapplied amounts.

Problem 3-31 (45 minutes)

1. (a) Inventory—raw materials 6,000
         Accounts Payable 6,000

   (b) Inventory—work in process 6,500
         Inventory—raw materials 6,500
         1201 $ 800
         1202   700
         1203   3,000
         1204   2,000
                 $6,500

   (c) Inventory—work in process 6,500
         Cash 6,500
         1107 $ 300
         1201   700
         1202   2,000
         1203   2,500
         1204   1,000
                 $6,500

   (d) Overhead—Supervision............................ 2,000
         Cash 2,000

   (e) Overhead—Depreciation—p & e 2,000
         Depreciation—vehicle............................. 1,000
             Accumulated Depre—p & e.................... 2,000
             Accumulated Depre—vehicle 1,000

   (f) Overhead—Insurance 150
         Prepaid Insurance................................. 150
   (g) Overhead—Maintenance........................... 500
         Cash 500

Problem 3-31 (continued)

(h)	Inventory—work in process		5,850		
	Overhead—applied			5,850	
	1107	$ 270			
	1201	630			
	1202	1,800			
	1203	2,250			
	1204	900			
		$5,850			
(i)	Bidding Expenses............................		800		
	Cash			800	
(j)	Administrative Salary		2,500		
	Cash			2,500	
(k)	Accounts Receivable		23,700		
	Construction Revenue...................			23,700	
	1105	$ 2,000			
	1107	5,000			
	1201	2,500			
	1202	4,200			
	1203	10,000			
		$23,700			
	Cost of Finished Jobs		18,750		
	Inventory—finished jobs			800	(1105)
	Inventory—work in process			17,950	
	1107	$3,000 + $300 + $270 =	$ 3,570		
	1201	$800 + $700 + $630 =	2,130		
	1202	$700 + $2,000 + $1,800 =	4,500		
	1203	$3,000 + $2,500 + $2,250 =	7,750		
			$17,950		
(l)	Cash..		23,000		
	Accounts Receivable.....................			23,000	
(m)	Accounts Payable.............................		8,000		
	Interest Expense.............................		500		
	Cash			8,500	
(n)	Overhead—Rework wind storm		290		
	Inventory—raw materials			200	
	Cash			90	

Problem 3-31 (continued)

2.

Terry Construction Ltd.
Income—Jobs

	1105	1107	1203
Revenue	$2,000	$5,000	$10,000
Costs of finished jobs			
Material	800*	3,000*	3,000
Labour		300	2,500
Overhead		270	2,250
	800	3,570	7,750
Income per job	$1,200	$1,430	$ 2,250

*Prior period costs are not categorized

3.

Inventory—work in process	Job 1204
Materials	$2,000
Labour	1,000
Overhead	900
Total	$3,900

Wind damage is a normal cost and thus spread over all jobs through being charged to overhead.

Chapter 4
Systems Design: Process Costing

Exercise 4-1 (10 minutes)

Work in Process—Cooking	42,000	
Raw Materials Inventory		42,000
Work in Process—Cooking	50,000	
Work in Process—Molding	36,000	
Wages Payable		86,000
Work in Process—Cooking	75,000	
Work in Process—Molding	45,000	
Manufacturing Overhead		120,000
Work in Process—Molding	160,000	
Work in Process—Cooking		160,000
Finished Goods	240,000	
Work in Process—Molding		240,000

Exercise 4-3 (10 minutes)

FIFO Method

Units to be accounted for as follows:	Equivalent Units (EU)	
	Materials	**Conversion**
Work in process, beginning:		
30,000 units × 35%*..................................	10,500	
30,000 units × 70%*..................................		21,000
Started and completed during October	160,000**	160,000**
Work in process, ending:		
15,000 units × 80%	12,000	
15,000 units × 40%		6,000
Equivalent units of production......................	182,500	187,000

*Work needed to complete these units.
**175,000 − 15,000 = 160,000

Exercise 4-5 (15 minutes)

FIFO Method

Quantity Schedule

Kilograms to be accounted for:
Work in process, July 1 (all
materials, 30%
conversion cost added
last month)........................... 20,000
Started into production
during July 380,000
   Total kilograms 400,000

| | **Equivalent Units (EU)** | |
	Materials	**Conversion**
Kilograms accounted for as follows:		
Transferred to department 2:		
From the beginning inventory 20,000	—	14,000*
Started and completed this month 355,000**	355,000	355,000
Work in process, July 31 (all materials, 60% conversion cost added this month)........... 25,000	25,000	15,000
Total kilograms and equivalent units of production.........400,000	380,000	384,000

* Work required to complete these units: 100% - 30% = 70%.
70% x 20,000 kilograms = 14,000 kilograms.

** 380,000 kilograms started, less 25,000 kilograms in ending work in
process inventory, equals 355,000 kilograms started and
completed this month.

Exercise 4-7 (10 minutes)

FIFO Method

1. The number of tonnes completed and transferred out during the month would be the same regardless of the costing method used. Thus, as in Exercise 4-6, 180,000 tonnes would have been completed and transferred out. However, under the FIFO method we must break this figure down between the tonnes that were completed from the beginning inventory and the tonnes started and completed during the current period. This breakdown is shown in Part 2 below.

2. Tonnes to be accounted for:

Work in process, June 1 (90% materials; 80% labour and overhead added last month)	20,000
Started into production during the month	190,000
Total tonnes to account for	210,000

Tonnes accounted for as follows:
Transferred out during the month:

Tonnes from the beginning inventory	20,000
Tonnes started and completed during the month.	160,000*
Work in process, June 30 (60% materials 40% labour and overhead added this month)	30,000
Total tonnes accounted for	210,000

*190,000 – 30,000 = 160,000

Exercise 4-9 (20 minutes)

FIFO Method

1.

	Quantity Schedule
Units to be accounted for:	
Work in process, beginning (80% materials, 60% labour and overhead added last month)	5,000
Started into production.........	45,000
Total units	50,000

		Equivalent Units (EU)		
		Materials	Labour	Overhead
Units accounted for as follows:				
Transferred to the next department:				
From the beginning inventory......................	5,000	1,000*	2,000*	2,000*
Started and completed this month	37,000**	37,000	37,000	37,000
Work in process, ending (75% materials, 50% labour and overhead added this month)	8,000	6,000	4,000	4,000
Total units and equivalent units of production	50,000	44,000	43,000	43,000

* Work required to complete the beginning inventory.
** 45,000 – 8,000 = 37,000

Exercise 4-9 (continued)

2.

Cost to be accounted for:

	Total Cost	Materials	Labour	Overhead	Whole Unit
Work in process, beginning	$ 7,625				
Cost added during the month	106,550	52,800	$ 21,500	32,250	
Total cost (a)	$114,175				
Equivalent units of production (b)	—	44,000	43,000	43,000	
Cost per EU (a) ÷ (b)	—	$1.20 +	$0.50 +	$0.75 =	$2.45

Exercise 4-11 (15 minutes)

Weighted-Average Method

	Total Cost	Equivalent Units (EU)	
		Materials	Conversion
Cost accounted for as follows:			
Transferred to the next process (175,000 units x $2.298)	$402,020*	175,000	175,000
Work in process, May 31:			
Materials, at $0.298 per EU	2,980	10,000	
Conversion, at $2.000 per EU	6,000		3,000
Total work in process	8,980		
Total cost	$411,000		

*Actually, the amount is $402,150; the figure has been adjusted downward to avoid a discrepancy in the column totals. The discrepancy is due to rounding error.

Exercise 4-13 (20 minutes)

FIFO Method

	Total Cost	Equivalent Units (EU)	
		Materials	Conversion
Cost accounted for as follows:			
Transferred to the next process:			
From the beginning inventory:			
Cost in the beginning inventory	$ 5,000		
Cost to complete these units:			
Materials, at $0.30 per EU	—	—	
Conversion, at $2.00 per EU	6,000		3,000
Total cost	11,000		
Units started and completed this month: 170,000 units × $2.30........	391,000	170,000	170,000
Total cost transferred	402,000		
Work in process, May 31:			
Materials, at $0.30 per EU	3,000	10,000	
Conversion, at $2.00 per EU...........	6,000		3,000
Total work in process	9,000		
Total cost	$411,000		

Problem 4-15 (20 minutes)

Weighted-Average Method

1. The computation of equivalent units would be:

	Quantity Schedule	Equivalent Units (EU)		
		Materials	Labour	Overhead
Units accounted for as follows:				
Transferred to the next department	48,000	48,000	48,000	48,000
Work in process, June 30 (all materials, 40% labour and overhead added this month)	5,000	5,000	2,000	2,000
Total units and equivalent units of production..................	53,000	53,000	50,000	50,000

2. The cost reconciliation follows:

	Total Cost	Equivalent Units (EU)		
		Materials	Labour	Overhead
Cost accounted for as follows:				
Transferred to the next department:				
48,000 units x $1.28	$61,440	48,000	48,000	48,000
Work in process, June 30:				
Materials, at $0.65 per EU	3,250	5,000		
Labour, at $0.21 per EU	420		2,000	
Overhead, at $0.42 per EU	840			2,000
Total work in process	4,510			
Total cost	$65,950			

Problem 4-17 (45 minutes)

Weighted-Average Method

Quantity Schedule and Equivalent Units

	Quantity Schedule
Units to be accounted for:	
Work in process, June 1 (all materials, 75% conversion cost added last month)...................	20,000
Started into production.....................	180,000
Total units	200,000

		Equivalent Units (EU)	
		Materials	Conversion
Units accounted for as follows:			
Transferred to bottling:.....................	160,000	160,000	160,000
Work in process, June 30 (all materials, 25% conversion cost added this month)...................	40,000	40,000	10,000
Total units and equivalent units of production.......................................	200,000	200,000	170,000

Problem 4-19 (continued)

2.

	Total Cost	Materials	Conversion	Whole Unit
Work in process, April 1	$ 98,000	$ 67,800	$ 30,200	
Cost added during the month	827,000	579,000	248,000	
Total cost (a)	$925,000	$646,800	$278,200	
Equivalent units of production (b)	—	220,000	214,000	
Cost per EU (a) ÷ (b)	—	$2.94	+ $1.30	= $4.24

3.

Total units transferred	190,000
Less units in the beginning inventory	30,000
Units started and completed during April	160,000

4. No, the manager should not be rewarded for good cost control. The reason for the Blending Department's low unit cost for April is traceable to the fact that costs of the prior month have been averaged in with April's costs in computing the lower, $2.94 per unit figure. This is a major criticism of the weighted-average method in that the figures computed for product costing purposes can't be used to evaluate cost control or measure performance for the *current* period.

Problem 4-21 (45 minutes)

Weighted-Average Method

1. A completed production report follows:

Quantity Schedule and Equivalent Units

	Quantity Schedule
Kilograms to be accounted for:	
Work in process, May 1 (all materials, 1/3 labour and overhead added last month)........	18,000
Started into production	167,000
Total kilograms...........................	185,000

	Quantity Schedule	Equivalent Units (EU)	
		Materials	Labour & Overhead
Kilograms accounted for as follows:			
Transferred to mixing	170,000	170,000	170,000
Work in process, May 31 (all materials, 2/3 labour and overhead added this month)........	15,000	15,000	10,000
Total kilograms and equivalent units of production.......................	185,000	185,000	180,000

Problem 4-21 (continued)

Cost per Equivalent Unit

	Total Cost	Material	Labour & Overhead	Whole Unit
Cost to be accounted for:				
Work in process, May 1............	$ 21,800	$ 14,600	$ 7,200	
Cost added during May	360,200	133,400	226,800	
Total cost (a)	$382,000	$148,000	$234,000	
Equivalent units of production (b)	—	185,000	180,000	
Cost per EU (a) ÷ (b)...............	—	$0.80 +	$1.30 =	$2.10

Problem 4-21 (continued)

Cost Reconciliation

	Total Cost	Equivalent Units (EU)	
		Materials	**Labour & Overhead**
Cost accounted for as follows:			
Transferred to mixing:			
170,000 units × $2.10...........	$357,000	170,000	170,000
Work in process, May 31:			
Materials, at $0.80 per EU....	12,000	15,000	
Labour and overhead, at			
$1.30 per EU	13,000		10,000
Total work in process	25,000		
Total cost.........................	$382,000		

2. In computing unit costs, the weighted-average method mixes costs of the prior period in with current period costs. Thus, under the weighted-average method, unit costs are influenced to some extent by what happened in a prior period. This problem becomes particularly significant when attempting to measure performance in the current period. A good job of cost control in the current period might be concealed to some degree by the unit costs which have been brought forward in the beginning inventory. The reverse could also be true in that poor cost control during a period might be concealed somewhat (or entirely) by the costs of the prior period that have been brought forward and added in with current period costs.

Problem 4-23 (60 minutes)

Weighted-Average Method

1. The equivalent units would be:

	Materials	Labour	Overhead
Units completed during the year	900,000	900,000	900,000
Work in process, Dec. 31:			
300,000 units × 100%...................	300,000		
300,000 units × 50%....................		150,000	150,000
Total equivalent units (a).................	1,200,000	1,050,000	1,050,000

The costs per equivalent unit would be:

	Materials	Labour	Overhead	Whole Unit
Work in process, January 1	$ 200,000	$ 315,000	$ 189,000*	
Cost added during the year	1,300,000	1,995,000	1,197,000**	
Total costs (b)	$1,500,000	$2,310,000	$1,386,000	
Cost per EU (b) ÷ (a).	$1.25 +	$2.20 +	$1.32 =	$4.77

* $315,000 x 60% = $189,000
** $1,995,000 x 60% = $1,197,000

Problem 4-23 (continued)

2. The amount of cost that should be assigned to the ending inventories is:

	Work in Process	Finished Goods	Total
Work in process:			
Materials: 300,000 units × $1.25	$375,000		$ 375,000
Labour: 150,000 EU × $2.20	330,000		330,000
Overhead: 150,000 EU × $1.32	198,000		198,000
Finished goods: 200,000 units × $4.77		$954,000	954,000
Total cost that should be assigned to inventories	$903,000	$954,000	$1,857,000

3. The necessary adjustments would be:

	Work in Process	Finished Goods	Total
Cost that should be assigned to inventories (above)	$903,000	$ 954,000	$1,857,000
Year-end balances in the accounts	660,960	1,009,800	1,670,760
Difference	$242,040	$ (55,800)	$ 186,240

	Debit	Credit
Work in Process Inventory	242,040	
Finished Goods Inventory		55,800
Cost of Goods Sold		186,240

Problem 4-23 (continued)

4. The simplest computation of the cost of goods sold would be:

Beginning finished goods inventory	0
Units completed during the year	900,000
Units available for sale	900,000
Less units in ending finished goods inventory	200,000
Units sold during the year	700,000
Cost per equivalent unit (from part 1)	× $4.77
Cost of goods sold	$3,339,000

Alternative computation:
Total manufacturing cost incurred:	
Materials (part 1)	$1,500,000
Labour (part 1)	2,310,000
Overhead (part 1)	1,386,000
Total manufacturing cost	5,196,000
Less cost assigned to inventories (part 2)	1,857,000
Cost of goods sold	$3,339,000

Problem 4-25

ARB Chemicals Ltd.
Cost of Production Report
For the Month of November 2001

	Physical Flow	Materials	Conversion Costs
Beginning Inventory	15,000		
Units started during July	57,000		
	72,000		
Transferred to Finished goods	54,000	54,000	54,000
Normal spoilage	0	0	0
Abnormal spoilage	0	0	0
Ending inventory (.10,.20)	18,000	1,800	3,600
Equivalent units	72,000	55,800	57,600
Costs:	**Total**		
Beginning inventory	$ 64,000	20,000	$ 44,000
Current	186,190	26,400	112,190
	$ 182,590	$ 46,400	$156,190
Cost per equivalent unit	$3.5431	$0.8315	$2.7116
Cost accounted for:			
Transferred to finished goods (54,000 x $3.5431)			$ 191,327.40
Normal spoilage			0
			$191,327.40
Abnormal spoilage			0
Ending inventory, WIP (1,800 x $0.8315)+(3,600 x $2.7116)			11,258.46
Total (rounded)			$202,585.86

1. 15,000 units 20% complete = 3,000 equivalent units

2. materials = 55,800 equivalent units

   conversion costs = 57,600 equivalent units

3. $3.5431 (materials $0.8315 + conversion costs $2.711)

4. Finished goods values is $191,327.40
   Ending inventory of materials is $1,496.70
   Ending inventory of conversion costs is $9,761.76

5. $20,000 ÷ (20% x 15,000) = $6.6667

6. Yes, the company can sell the 54,000 transferred to finished goods plus 10/30 x 54,000 = 18,000 for a total of 72,000 by August 10.

   CGA-Adapted

Problem 4-27

Larado Company
Department 2
Cost of Production Report
For the Month of November 2001

	Physical Flow	Transferred In Costs	Materials	Conversion Costs
Beginning Inventory(1,0,.4)	2,000			
Received from Department 1	35,000			
	37,000			
Transferred to Department 3	32,000	32,000	32,000	32,000
Normal spoilage (5% 16,000)	1,000	1,000	0	900
Ending inventory (1,0,.7)	4,000	4,000	0	2,800
Equivalent units	37,000	37,000	32,000	35,700
Costs:	**Total**			
Beginning inventory	$ 11,800	$ 10,000	0	$ 1,800
Current	322,500	205,000	$12,500	105,000
	$334,300	$215,000	$12,500	$106,800
Cost per equivalent unit	$9.19304	$5.81081	$0.39063	$2.99160
Cost accounted for:				
Transferred to department 3 (32,000 x $9.19304)				$ 294,177.28
Normal spoilage (1,000 x $5.81081) +(900 x $2.9916)				8,503.25
				$302,680.53
Abnormal spoilage				0
Ending inventory, WIP (4,000 x $5.81081)+(2,800 x $2.9916)				$ 31,619.72
Total (rounded)				$334,300
Transferred in				$334,300.00

2. Under the weighted-average method, units in the beginning work in process inventory are treated as if they were started and completed during the current period. The FIFO method distinguishes between units in the beginning work-in-process and those started during the current period. Therefore, the equivalent units under FIFO represents only work completed during the current period.

3. If spoilage were reduced to zero, Larado should save $8,503 based on November's results. This saving should be beneficial because of the reduction in waste, and the reduction in effort expended. However, workers could be laid-off so some costs might exist. Competitively, however, Larado should be better off thus helping employment.

CGA-Adapted

Problem 4-29

Milliners Flour Limited
Cost of Production Report
For the Month of June 2001

	Physical Flow	Materials	Conversion Costs
Beginning Inventory	0		
Started during June	5,676		
	5,676		
Transferred to Finished goods	5,000	5,000	0,000
Normal spoilage (**)	516	516	258
Abnormal spoilage	0	0	0
Ending inventory	160	160	120
Equivalent units	5,676	5,676	5,378
Costs:	**Total**		
Beginning inventory	$ 0	$ 0	$ 0
Current	109,580	56,760	52,820
	$109,580	$30,000	$19,000
Cost per equivalent unit	$19.821	$10.00	$9.821
Cost accounted for:			
Transferred to finished goods before spoilage	$ 99,105		
Normal spoilage (5,000/5,160) x $7,694	7,455		
Transferred to finished goods	(a) $106,560		
Ending WIP before spoilage	2,779	160 x $10	120 x $9.821
Normal spoilage (160/5,160) x $7,694	239		
Ending WIP inventory	(b) $3,018		
Total costs accounted for	(a+b) $109,578		

**Normal spoilage = .1 of good units passing inspection

Good units + .1(good units) = 5,676

1.1 good units	=	5,676	Units begun	5,676	
good units	=	5,160	Finished	5,000	
Normal spoilage	=	516		676	
			Normal spoilage	516	
			Ending WIP	160	

Chapter 5
Cost Behaviour: Analysis and Use

Exercise 5-1 (20 minutes)

1.

	Guest-Days	Custodial Supplies Expense
High activity level (July)	12,000	$13,500
Low activity level (March)	4,000	7,500
Change...	8,000	$ 6,000

Variable cost element:

$$\frac{\text{Change in expense}}{\text{Change in activity}} = \frac{\$6,000}{8,000} = \$0.75/\,\text{guest-day}$$

Fixed cost element:

Custodial supplies expense at high activity level	$13,500
Less variable cost element: 12,000 x $0.75.............	9,000
Total fixed cost..	$ 4,500

The cost formula is $4,500 per month plus $0.75 per guest-day or
Y = $4,500 + $0.75 X.

2. Custodial supplies expense at an occupancy of 11,000 guest-days:

Variable cost: 11,000 × $0.75................................	$8,250
Fixed cost	4,500
Total cost	$12,750

Exercise 5-3 (30 minutes)

1.

	Units Shipped	Shipping Expense
High activity level (June).......	8	$2,700
Low activity level (July).........	2	1,200
Change...........................	6	$1,500

Variable cost element:

$$\frac{\text{Change in expense}}{\text{Change in activity}} = \frac{\$1,500}{6} = \$250/\text{unit.}$$

Fixed cost element:

Shipping expense at high activity level	$2,700
Less variable cost element ($250 × 8 units)............	2,000
Total fixed cost..	$ 700

The cost formula is $700 per month plus $250 per unit shipped or
$$Y = \$700 + \$250X.$$

2. a. See the graph on the following page.

   b. Note: Students' answers will vary, depending on their visual fit of the regression line to the data.

Total cost at 5 units shipped per month [a point falling on the regression line in (a)]	$2,000
Less fixed cost element (intersection of the Y axis) ...	1,000
Variable cost element	$1,000

$1,000 ÷ 5 units = $200 per unit.

The cost formula is $1,000 per month plus $200 per unit shipped or
$$Y = \$1,000 + \$200X.$$

Exercise 5-3 (continued)

2. a. The scattergraph would be:

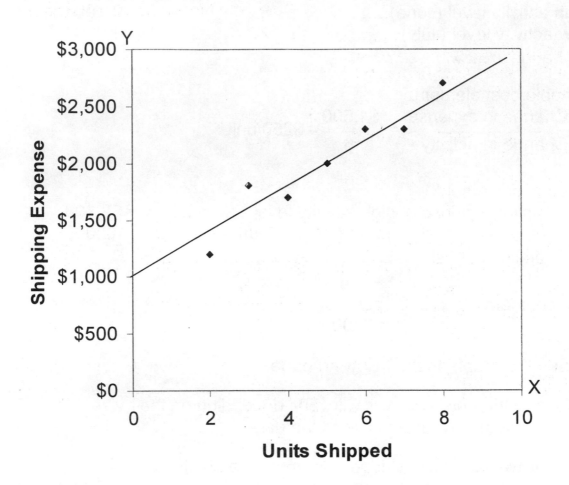

3. The cost of shipping units is likely to depend on the weight and volume of the units and the distance traveled as well as on the number of units shipped.

Exercise 5-5 (20 minutes)

1. a. Difference in cost:

Monthly operating costs at 80% occupancy:	
450 rooms × 80% = 360 rooms;	
360 rooms × $32 × 30 days..................................	$345,600
Monthly operating costs at 60% occupancy (given)...	326,700
Difference in cost	$ 18,900

Difference in activity:	
80% occupancy (450 rooms × 80% x 30 days).......	10,800
60% occupancy (450 rooms × 60% x 30 days).......	8,100
Difference in activity...	2,700

$$\frac{\text{Change in cost}}{\text{Change in activity}} = \frac{\$18,900}{2,700} = \$7 \text{ per room per day.}$$

b.

Monthly operating costs at 80% occupancy (above) ..	$345,600
Less variable costs:	
360 rooms x 30 days x $7	75,600
Fixed operating costs per month	270,000

2. 450 rooms x 70% = 315 rooms occupied.

Fixed costs	$270,000
Variable costs: 315 rooms x 30 days x $7.....................	66,150
Total expected costs	$336,150

Exercise 5-7 (20 minutes)

1. See the scattergraph on the following page.

2. Students' answers will vary, depending on their placement of the regression line.

   The approximate monthly fixed cost is $30,000—the point where the regression line intersects the cost axis. The variable cost per unit processed is:

Total cost at an 8,000-unit level of activity (a point falling on the regression line).....................	$46,000
Less fixed cost...	30,000
Variable cost at an 8,000-unit level of activity	$16,000

   $16,000 ÷ 8,000 units = $2 per unit.

   Therefore, the cost formula is $30,000 per month plus $2 per unit processed.

   (Observe from the scattergraph that if the company used the high-low method to determine the slope of the regression line, the line would be too steep, causing estimated fixed costs to be lower than they should be, and the variable cost per unit to be too high.)

Exercise 5-7 (continued)

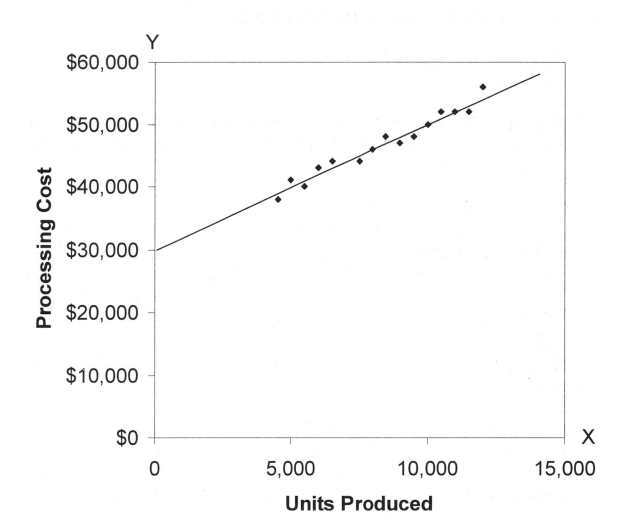

Exercise 5-9 (20 minutes)

1. The company's variable cost per unit would be:

$$\frac{\$180,000}{30,000 \text{ units}} = \$6 \text{ per unit.}$$

In accordance with the behaviour of variable and fixed costs, the completed schedule would be:

	Units produced and sold		
	30,000	**40,000**	**50,000**
Total costs:			
Variable costs	$180,000	$240,000	$300,000
Fixed costs	300,000	300,000	300,000
Total costs.............................	$480,000	$540,000	$600,000
Cost per unit:			
Variable cost...........................	$6.00	$6.00	$6.00
Fixed cost	10.00	7.50	6.00
Total cost per unit..................	$16.00	$13.50	$12.00

2. The company's income statement in the contribution format would be:

Sales (45,000 units × $16)..	$720,000
Less variable expenses (45,000 units × $6)..............	270,000
Contribution margin	450,000
Less fixed expense..	300,000
Net income	$150,000

Problem 5-11 (30 minutes)

1. Cost of goods sold .... Variable
    Advertising expense .... Fixed
    Shipping expense .... Mixed
    Salaries and commissions .... Mixed
    Insurance expense .... Fixed
    Depreciation expense .... Fixed

2. Analysis of the mixed expenses:

	Units	Shipping Expense	Salaries and Comm. Expense
High level of activity	5,000	A$38,000	A$90,000
Low level of activity	4,000	34,000	78,000
Change	1,000	A$ 4,000	A$12,000

Variable cost element:

$$\text{Variable rate} = \frac{\text{Change in cost}}{\text{Change in activity}}$$

Shipping expense: $\dfrac{\text{A\$4,000}}{\text{1,000 units}} = $ A$4 per unit.

Salaries and Comm. Expense: $\dfrac{\text{A\$12,000}}{\text{1,000 units}} = $ A$12 per unit.

Fixed cost element:

	Shipping Expense	Salaries and Comm. Expense
Cost at high level of activity	A$38,000	A$90,000
Less variable cost element:		
5,000 units × A$4	20,000	
5,000 units × A$12		60,000
Fixed cost element	A$18,000	A$30,000

The cost formulas are:

Shipping expense: A$18,000 per month plus A$4 per unit or
$$Y = \text{A\$18,000} + \text{A\$4X}.$$

Salaries and Comm. expense: A$30,000 per month plus A$12 per unit   or
$$Y = \text{A\$30,000} + \text{A\$12X}.$$

Problem 5-11 (continued)

3.

Morrisey & Brown, Ltd.
Income Statement
For the Month Ended September 30

Sales in units		5,000
Sales revenue (@ A$100).............................		A$500,000
Less variable expenses:		
Cost of goods sold (@ A$60)......................	A$300,000	
Shipping expense (@ A$4)........................	20,000	
Salaries and commissions expense		
(@ A$12)	60,000	380,000
Contribution margin		120,000
Less fixed expenses:		
Advertising expense...................................	21,000	
Shipping expense	18,000	
Salaries and commissions expense............	30,000	
Insurance expense	6,000	
Depreciation expense	15,000	90,000
Net income		A$ 30,000

Problem 5-13 (40 minutes)

1.   MARWICK'S PIANOS, INC.
                          Income Statement
                        For the Month of August

Sales (40 × $3,125)		$125,000
Less cost of goods sold (40 × $2,450)		98,000
Gross margin		27,000
Less operating expenses:		
Selling expenses:		
Advertising	$ 700	
Sales salaries and commissions		
[$950 + (8% x $125,000)]	10,950	
Delivery of pianos (40 x $30)	1,200	
Utilities	350	
Depreciation of sales facilities	800	
Total	14,000	
Administrative expenses:		
Executive salaries	2,500	
Insurance	400	
Clerical [$1,000 + (40 × $20)]	1,800	
Depreciation of office equipment	300	
Total	5,000	
Total operating expenses		19,000
Net income		$ 8,000

Problem 5-13 (continued)

2.
MARWICK's PIANOS, INC.
Income Statement
For the Month of August

	Total	Per Unit
Sales (40 × $3,125)	$125,000	$3,125
Less variable expenses:		
Cost of goods sold (40 × $2,450)	98,000	2,450
Sales commissions (8% × $125,000)	10,000	250
Delivery of pianos (40 × $30)	1,200	30
Clerical (40 × $20)	800	20
Total variable expenses	110,000	2,750
Contribution margin	15,000	$ 375
Less fixed expenses:		
Advertising	700	
Sales salaries	950	
Utilities	350	
Depreciation of sales facilities	800	
Executive salaries	2,500	
Insurance	400	
Clerical	1,000	
Depreciation of office equipment	300	
Total fixed expenses	7,000	
Net income	$ 8,000	

3. By definition, fixed costs remain constant in total but vary on a per unit basis inversely with changes in the activity level. As the activity level increases, for example, the fixed costs will decrease on a per unit basis. Showing fixed costs on a per unit basis on the income statement might mislead management into thinking that the fixed costs behave in the same way as the variable costs. That is, management might be misled into thinking that the per unit fixed costs would be the same regardless of how many pianos were sold during the month. For this reason, fixed costs generally are shown only in totals on a contribution format income statement.

Problem 5-15 (35 minutes)

1. Maintenance cost at the 90,000 machine-hour level of activity can be isolated as follows:

	Level of Activity	
	60,000 MH	**90,000 MH**
Total factory overhead cost.................	$174,000	$246,000
Deduct:		
Utilities cost @ $0.80/MH*...............	(48,000)	(72,000)
Supervisory salaries	(21,000)	(21,000)
Maintenance cost	$105,000	$153,000

*$48,000 ÷ 60,000 MH = $0.80/MH

2. High-low analysis of maintenance cost:

	Machine-Hours	Machine Cost
High activity level.........................	90,000	$153,000
Low activity level..........................	60,000	105,000
Change.....................................	30,000	$ 48,000

Variable rate:

$$\frac{\text{Change in cost}}{\text{Change in activity}} = \frac{\$48,000}{30,000 \text{ MH}} = \$1.60/\text{MH}.$$

Total fixed cost:

Total maintenance cost at the high activity level	$153,000
Less variable cost element (90,000 MH × $1.60).............	144,000
Fixed cost element	$ 9,000

Therefore, the cost formula for maintenance is: $9,000 per month plus $1.60 per machine-hour or

$$Y = \$9,000 + \$1.60X.$$

Problem 5-15 (continued)

3.

	Variable Rate per Machine-Hour	Fixed Cost
Maintenance cost	$1.60	$ 9,000
Utilities cost	0.80	
Supervisory salaries cost..............		21,000
Totals	$2.40	$30,000

Thus, the cost formula would be: Y = $30,000 + $2.40X.

4. Total overhead cost at an activity level of 75,000 machine-hours:

Fixed costs	$ 30,000
Variable costs:	
$2.40 × 75,000 MH	180,000
Total overhead costs..	$210,000

Problem 5-17 (40 minutes)

1.

	March—Low 6,000 Units	June—High 9,000 Units
Direct materials cost @ $6..............	$ 36,000	$ 54,000
Direct labour cost @ $10	60,000	90,000
Manufacturing overhead cost..........	78,000*	102,000*
Total manufacturing costs	174,000	246,000
Add: Work in process, beginning	9,000	32,000
	183,000	278,000
Deduct: Work in process, ending	15,000	21,000
Cost of goods manufactured...........	$168,000	$257,000

*Computed by working upwards through the statements.

2.

	Units Produced	Cost Observed
June—High level of activity...................	9,000	$102,000
March—Low level of activity	6,000	78,000
Change...	3,000	$ 24,000

$$\frac{\text{Change in cost}}{\text{Change in activity}} = \frac{\$24,000}{3,000 \text{ units}} = \$8 \text{ per unit}$$

Total cost at the high level of activity......................	$102,000
Less variable cost element ($8 × 9,000 units)........	72,000
Fixed cost element	$ 30,000

Therefore, the cost formula is: $30,000 per month, plus $8 per unit produced or

$$Y = \$30,000 + \$8.00X.$$

Problem 5-17 (continued)

3. The cost of goods manufactured if 7,000 units are produced:

Direct materials cost ($6 × 7,000)		$ 42,000
Direct labour cost ($10 × 7,000)		70,000
Manufacturing overhead cost:		
Fixed portion	$30,000	
Variable portion ($8 × 7,000)	56,000	86,000
Total manufacturing costs		198,000
Add: Work in process, beginning		—
		198,000
Deduct: Work in process, ending		—
Cost of goods manufactured		$198,000

Problem 5-19 (35 minutes)

1. Least-squares regression analysis:

Month	Miles Driven (000)(X)	Total Cost (Y)	XY	X^2
January	4	$ 3,000	$ 12,000	16
February	8	3,700	29,600	64
March	7	3,300	23,100	49
April	12	4,000	48,000	144
May	6	3,300	19,800	36
June	11	3,900	42,900	121
July	14	4,200	58,800	196
August	10	3,600	36,000	100
September	13	4,100	53,300	169
October	15	4,400	66,000	225
	100	$37,500	$389,500	1,120

$$b = \frac{n(\Sigma XY) - (\Sigma X)(\Sigma Y)}{n(\Sigma X^2) - (\Sigma X)^2}$$

$$= \frac{10(\$389,500) - (100)(\$37,500)}{10(1,120) - (100)^2}$$

$$= \$120.83 \text{ (rounded)}$$

$$a = \frac{(\Sigma Y) - b(\Sigma X)}{n}$$

$$= \frac{(\$37,500) - \$120.83(100)}{10}$$

$$= \$2,542 \text{ (rounded)}$$

(Note: The adjusted R^2 is 95.5%.)

Therefore, the cost of operating the fleet of autos is: $2,542 per month plus $120.83 per thousand miles driven or $0.121 per mile (rounded).

2. Y = $2,542 + $0.121X (where X = miles driven).

Problem 5-21 (30 minutes)

1. The least-squares regression method:

Month	Number of Scans (X)	Utilities Cost (Y)	XY	X^2
January	60	$ 2,200	$ 132,000	3,600
February	70	2,600	182,000	4,900
March	90	2,900	261,000	8,100
April	120	3,300	396,000	14,400
May	100	3,000	300,000	10,000
June	130	3,600	468,000	16,900
July	150	4,000	600,000	22,500
August	140	3,600	504,000	19,600
September	110	3,100	341,000	12,100
October	80	2,500	200,000	6,400
Total	1,050	$30,800	$3,384,000	118,500

$$b = \frac{n(\Sigma XY) - (\Sigma X)(\Sigma Y)}{n(\Sigma X^2) - (\Sigma X)^2}$$

$$= \frac{10(\$3,384,000) - (1,050)(\$30,800)}{10(118,500) - (1,050)^2}$$

$$= \$18.18 \text{ (rounded)}$$

$$a = \frac{(\Sigma Y) - b(\Sigma X)}{n}$$

$$= \frac{(\$30,800) - \$18.18(1,050)}{10}$$

$$= \$1,171 \text{ (rounded)}$$

(Note: The adjusted R2 is 96.5%.)
Therefore, the cost formula is: Y = $1,171 + $18.18X.

2. As shown in the graph in part (2) of problem 5-20, the high and low points in this case fall in such a way they are not representative of all points of cost data. A regression line drawn through these two points would be too steep and thus result in an inaccurate cost formula. This is the major defect in the high-low method; although it is simple to apply, the manager must be careful in its use or misleading information may result.

Chapter 6
Cost-Volume-Profit Relationships

Exercise 6-1 (20 minutes)

1. Sales = Variable expenses + Fixed expenses + Profits
   $30Q = $12Q + $216,000 + $0
   $18Q = $216,000
       Q = $216,000 ÷ $18
       Q = 12,000 units, or at $30 per unit, $360,000

   Alternative solution:

$$\text{Break-even point} = \frac{\text{Fixed expenses}}{\text{Unit contribution margin}}$$

$$\frac{\$216,000}{\$18} = 12,000 \text{ units,}$$

$$\text{or at } \$30 \text{ per unit, } \$360,000$$

2. The contribution margin is $216,000 since the contribution margin is equal to the fixed expenses at the break-even point.

3. Target sales $= \dfrac{\text{Fixed expenses} + \text{Target profit}}{\text{Unit contribution margin}}$

$$\frac{\$216,000 + \$90,000}{\$18} = 17,000 \text{ units}$$

	Total	Unit
Sales (17,000 units × $30)................................	$510,000	$30
Less variable expenses (17,000 units × $12).....	204,000	12
Contribution margin	306,000	$18
Less fixed expenses..	216,000	
Net income	$ 90,000	

Exercise 6-1 (continued)

4. Margin of safety in dollar terms:

   Margin of safety = Total sales – Break-even sales
   $450,000 – $360,000 = $90,000

   Margin of safety in percentage terms:

   $$\frac{\text{Margin of safety in dollars}}{\text{Total sales}} = \frac{\$90,000}{\$450,000} = 20\%$$

5. The CM ratio is 60%.

Expected total contribution margin: ($500,000 × 60%)...	$300,000
Present total contribution margin: ($450,000 × 60%)	270,000
Increased contribution margin...	$ 30,000

   Alternative solution: $50,000 incremental sales x 60% = $30,000.

   Since in this case the company's fixed expenses will not change, quarterly net income will also increase by $30,000.

Exercise 6-3 (25 minutes)

1. The contribution margin per person would be:

Price per ticket..		$35
Less variable expenses:		
Dinner...	$18	
Favours and program	2	20
Contribution margin per person		$15

The fixed expenses of the dinner-dance total $6,000. The break-even point would be:

Sales = Variable expenses + Fixed expenses + Profits

$35Q = $20Q + $6,000 + $0
$15Q = $6,000
$\qquad$ Q = $6,000 ÷ $15
$\qquad$ Q = 400 persons; or, at $35 per person, $14,000

Alternate solution:

$$\frac{\text{Fixed expenses,} \quad \$6,000}{\text{Unit contribution margin,} \quad \$15} = 400 \text{ persons}$$

or, at $35 per person, $14,000.

2.

Variable cost per person ($18 + $2).......................	$20
Fixed cost per person ($6,000 ÷ 300)	20
Ticket price per person to break even.................	$40

Exercise 6-3 (continued)

3. Cost-volume-profit graph:

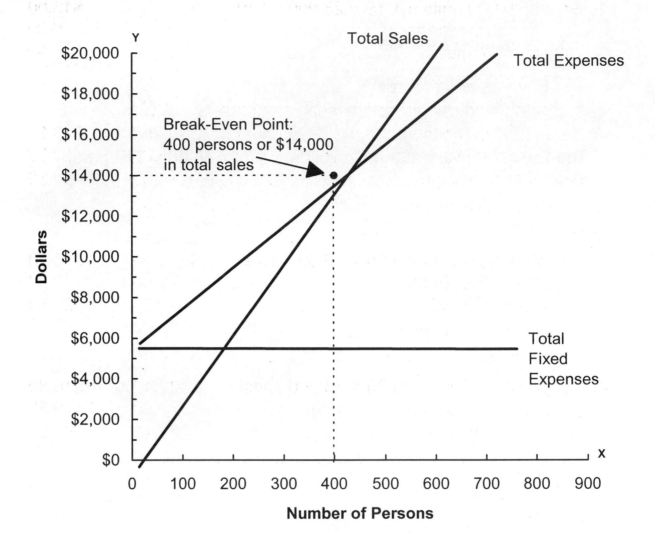

Exercise 6-5 (20 minutes)

	Total	Per Unit
1. Sales (20,000 units × 1.15 = 23,000 units)....	$345,000	$15.00
Less variable expenses	207,000	9.00
Contribution margin	138,000	$ 6.00
Less fixed expenses	70,000	
Net income	$ 68,000	
2. Sales (20,000 units × 1.25 = 25,000 units)....	$337,500	$13.50
Less variable expenses	225,000	9.00
Contribution margin	112,500	$4.50
Less fixed expenses	70,000	
Net income	$ 42,500	
3. Sales (20,000 units × 0.95 = 19,000 units)....	$313,500	$16.50
Less variable expenses	171,000	9.00
Contribution margin	142,500	$7.50
Less fixed expenses	90,000	
Net income	$ 52,500	
4. Sales (20,000 units × 0.90 = 18,000 units)....	$302,400	$16.80
Less variable expenses	172,800	9.60
Contribution margin	129,600	$7.20
Less fixed expenses	70,000	
Net income	$ 59,600	

Exercise 6-7 (25 minutes)

1.

	Flight Dynamic		Sure Shot		Total Company	
	Amount	Percent	Amount	Percent	Amount	Percent
Sales	P150,000	100	P250,000	100	P400,000	100.0
Less variable expenses....	30,000	20	160,000	64	190,000	47.5
Contribution margin	P120,000	80	P 90,000	36	210,000	52.5*
Less fixed expenses....					183,750	
Net income ...					P 26,250	

*P210,000 ÷ P400,000 = 52.5%.

2. The break-even point for the company as a whole would be:

$$\frac{\text{Fixed expenses}}{\text{Overall CM ratio}} = \frac{\text{P183,750}}{0.525} = \text{P350,000.}$$

3. Incremental contribution margin:

   P100,000 x 52.5% CM ratio P52,500

Assuming that there is no change in fixed expenses, all of the incremental contribution margin of P52,500 should drop to the bottom line as increased net income.

This answer assumes no change in selling prices, variable costs per unit, fixed expense, or sales mix.

Problem 6-9 (60 minutes)

1. Sales = Variable expenses + Fixed expenses + Profits
   $30Q = $18Q + $150,000 + $0
   $12Q = $150,000
       Q = $150,000 ÷ $12
       Q = 12,500 pairs of shoes

12,500 pairs of shoes x $30 = $375,000 in sales.

   Alternatively:

$$\frac{\text{Fixed expenses}}{\text{CM per unit}} = \frac{\$150,000}{\$12} = 12,500 \text{ pairs of shoes}$$

$$\frac{\text{Fixed expenses}}{\text{CM ratio}} = \frac{\$150,000}{0.40} = \$375,000 \text{ in sales}$$

2. See the graph on the following page.

3. The simplest approach is:

Break-even sales...........................	12,500 pairs of shoes
Actual sales...................................	12,000 pairs of shoes
Sales short of break-even..............	500 pairs of shoes

   500 pairs of shoes x $12 contribution margin = <u>$6,000 loss</u>

   Alternative solution:

Sales (12,000 pairs @ $30)................................	$360,000
Less variable expenses (12,000 pairs @ $18)......	216,000
Contribution margin	144,000
Less fixed expenses...	150,000
Net loss	$ (6,000)

Problem 6-9 (continued)

2. Cost-volume-profit graph:

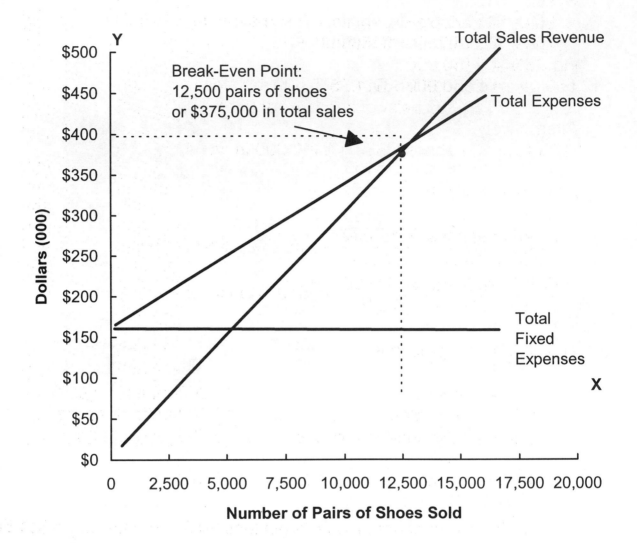

Problem 6-9 (continued)

4. The variable expenses will now be $18.75 per pair of shoes, and the contribution margin will be $11.25 per pair.

$$\text{Sales} = \text{Variable expenses} + \text{Fixed expenses} + \text{Profits}$$
$$\$30Q = \$18.75Q + \$150,000 + \$0$$
$$\$11.25Q = \$150,000$$
$$Q = \$150,000 \div \$11.25$$
$$Q = 13,333 \text{ pairs of shoes (rounded)}$$

13,333 pairs of shoes x $30 = $400,000 in sales.

Alternative solution:

$$\frac{\text{Fixed expenses,}\ \$150,000}{\text{CM per unit,}\ \ \ \$11.25} = 13,333 \text{ pairs of shoes}$$

$$\frac{\text{Fixed expenses,}\ \$150,000}{\text{CM ratio,}\ \ \ \ 0.375} = \$400,000 \text{ in sales}$$

5. The simplest approach is:

Actual sales....................................	15,000 pairs of shoes
Break-even sales..........................	12,500 pairs of shoes
Excess over break-even sales.......	2,500 pairs of shoes

2,500 pairs of shoes x $11.50* = $28,750 profit

*$12 present contribution margin less $0.50 commission = $11.50

Alternative solution:

Sales (15,000 pairs @ $30)................................	$450,000
Less variable expenses (12,500 pairs @ $18; 2,500 pairs @$18.50).....................................	271,250
Contribution margin	178,750
Less fixed expenses...	150,000
Net income	$ 28,750

Problem 6-9 (continued)

6. The new variable expense will be $13.50 per pair of shoes.

    Sales = Variable expenses + Fixed expenses + Profits
    $30.00Q = $13.50Q + $181,500 + $0
    $16.50Q = $181,500
    Q = $181,500 ÷ $16.50
    Q = 11,000 pairs of shoes

11,000 pairs of shoes x $30 = $330,000 in sales.

Although the change will lower the break-even point from 12,500 pairs to 11,000 pairs, the company must consider whether this reduction in the break-even point is more than offset by the possible loss in sales arising from having the sales staff on a salaried basis. Under a salary arrangement, the sales staff may have far less incentive to sell than under the present commission arrangement, resulting in a loss of sales and a reduction of profits. Although it generally is desirable to lower the break-even point, management must consider the other effects of a change in the cost structure. The break-even point could be reduced dramatically by doubling the selling price but it does not necessarily follow that this would improve the company's overall well-being.

Problem 6-11 (35 minutes)

1.

	White		Product Fragrant		Loonzain		Total	
Percentage of total sales............	40%		24%		36%		100%	
Sales..............	B300,000	100%	B180,000	100%	B270,000	100%	B750,000	100%
Less variable expenses	216,000	72	36,000	20	108,000	40	360,000	48
Contribution margin.........	B 84,000	28%	B144,000	80%	B162,000	60%	390,000	52%*
Less fixed expenses........							449,280	
Net income (loss)............							B (59,280)	

*B390,000 ÷ B750,000 = 52%.

2. Break-even sales would be:

$$\frac{\text{Fixed expenses, B449,280}}{\text{CM ratio,} \quad 0.52} = \text{B864,000}$$

Problem 6-11 (continued)

3. Memo to the president:

Although the company met its sales budget of B750,000 for the month, the mix of products sold changed substantially from that budgeted. This is the reason the budgeted net income was not met, and the reason the break-even sales were greater than budgeted. The company's sales mix was planned at 20% White, 52% Fragrant, and 28% Loonzain. The actual sales mix was 40% White, 24% Fragrant, and 36% Loonzain.

As shown by these data, sales shifted away from Fragrant Rice, which provides our greatest contribution per dollar of sales, and shifted strongly toward White Rice, which provides our least contribution per dollar of sales. Although the company met its budgeted level of sales, these sales provided considerably less contribution margin than we had planned, with a resulting decrease in net income. Notice from the attached statements that the company's overall CM ratio was only 52%, as compared to a planned CM ratio of 64%. This also explains why the break-even point was higher than planned. With less average contribution margin per dollar of sales, a greater level of sales had to be achieved to provide sufficient contribution margin to cover fixed costs.

Problem 6-13 (30 minutes)

1. The contribution margin per sweat shirt would be:

Selling price		$13.50
Less variable expenses:		
Purchase cost of the sweat shirts.................	$8.00	
Commission to the student salespersons	1.50	9.50
Contribution margin..		$ 4.00

Since there are no fixed costs, the number of unit sales needed to yield the desired $1,200 in profits can be obtained by dividing the target $1,200 profit by the unit contribution margin:

$$\frac{\text{Target profit,} \quad \$1{,}200}{\text{Unit contribution margin,} \quad \$4} = 300 \text{ sweat shirts}$$

300 sweat shirts × $13.50 = $4,050 in total sales.

2. Since an order has been placed, there is now a "fixed" cost associated with the purchase price of the sweat shirts (i.e., the sweat shirts can't be returned). For example, an order of 75 sweat shirts requires a "fixed" cost (investment) of $600 (75 shirts × $8 = $600). The variable costs drop to only $1.50 per shirt, and the new contribution margin per shirt becomes:

Selling price...	$13.50
Less variable expenses (commissions only).....	1.50
Contribution margin	$12.00

Since the "fixed" cost of $600 must be recovered before Mr. Hooper shows any profit, the break-even computation would be:

$$\frac{\text{Fixed expenses (Investment),} \quad \$600}{\text{Unit contribution margin,} \quad \$12} = 50 \text{ sweat shirts}$$

50 sweat shirts × $13.50 = $675 in total sales.

If a quantity other than 75 sweat shirts were ordered, the answer would change accordingly.

Problem 6-15 (45 minutes)

1. a.

	Caper Fantasy		Island Joy		Total	
	Amount	%	Amount	%	Amount	%
Sales	$300,000	100	500,000	100	$800,000	100
Less variable expenses...............	180,000	60	100,000	20	280,000	35
Contribution margin ..	$120,000	40	$400,000	80	520,000	65
Less fixed expenses .					475,800	
Net income					$ 44,200	

b.

$$\frac{\text{Fixed expenses, } \$475,800}{\text{CM ratio, } \qquad 0.65} = \$732,000 \text{ in sales}$$

Margin of safety:

Margin of safety = Actual sales – Break-even sales

$800,000 – $732,000 = $68,000

$$\text{Margin of safety in percentage} = \frac{\text{Margin of safety in dollars}}{\text{Actual sales}}$$

$$\frac{\$68,000}{\$800,000} = 8.5\%$$

Problem 6-15 (continued)

2. a.

	Hawaiian Fantasy		Tahitian Joy		Samoan Delight		Total	
	Amount	%	Amount	%	Amount	%	Amount	%
Sales............................	$300,000	100	$500,000	100	$450,000	100	$1,250,000	100.0
Less variable expenses ..	180,000	60	100,000	20	360,000	80	640,000	51.2
Contribution margin.........	$120,000	40	$400,000	80	$ 90,000	20	610,000	48.8
Less fixed expenses							475,800	
Net income.....................							$134,200	

Problem 6-15 (continued)

b.

$$\frac{\text{Fixed expenses, } \$475,800}{\text{CM ratio, } \quad 0.488} = \$975,000$$

Margin of safety:

Margin of safety = Actual sales – Break-even sales

$1,250,000 – $975,000 = $275,000

$$\text{Margin of safety in percentage} = \frac{\text{Margin of safety in dollars}}{\text{Actual sales}}$$

$$\frac{\$275,000}{\$1,250,000} = 22\%$$

3. The reason for the increase in the break-even point can be traced to the decrease in the company's overall contribution margin ratio when the third product is added. Note from the income statements above that this ratio drops from 65% to only 48.8% with the addition of the third product. This product (the Samoan Delight) has a CM ratio of only 20%, which causes the mix of the company's products to shift downward in terms of average contribution margin per dollar of sales.

This problem shows the somewhat tenuous nature of break-even analysis when more than one product is involved. The manager must be very careful of his or her assumptions regarding sales mix, including the addition (or deletion) of new products.

It should be pointed out to the president that even though the break-even point is higher with the addition of the third product, the company's margin of safety is also greater. Notice that the margin of safety increases from $68,000 to $275,000 or from 8.5% to 22%. Thus, the addition of the new product shifts the company much further from its break-even point, even though the break-even point is higher.

Problem 6-17 (50 minutes)

1. Sales = Variable expenses + Fixed expenses + Profits
   $40Q = $16Q + $60,000 + $0
   $24Q = $60,000
       Q = $60,000 ÷ $24
       Q = 2,500 pairs

    2,500 pairs × $40 = $100,000 in sales

    Alternative solution:

$$\frac{\text{Fixed expenses}}{\text{CM per unit}} = \frac{\$60,000}{\$24} = 2,500 \text{ pairs}$$

$$\frac{\text{Fixed expenses}}{\text{CM ratio}} = \frac{\$60,000}{0.60} = \$100,000 \text{ in sales}$$

2. See the graph at the end of this solution.

3. Sales = Variable expenses + Fixed expenses + Profits
   $40Q = $16Q + $60,000 + $18,000
   $24Q = $78,000
       Q = $78,000 ÷ $24
       Q = 3,250 pairs

    Alternative solution:

$$\frac{\text{Fixed expenses + Target profit, } \$60,000 + \$18,000}{\text{CM per unit, } \$24} = 3,250 \text{ pairs}$$

4. Incremental contribution margin:

$25,000 increased sales × 60% CM ratio.............	$15,000
Incremental fixed salary cost	8,000
Increased net income	$ 7,000

    Yes, the position should be converted to a full-time basis.

Problem 6-17 (continued)

5. a.

$$\frac{\text{Contribution margin, } \$72{,}000}{\text{Net income, } \qquad \$12{,}000} = 6 \text{ (Degree of operating leverage)}$$

b. 6 × 50% sales increase = 300% *increase* in net income. Thus, net income next year would be: $12,000 + ($12,000 x 300%) = $48,000. Note that the operating leverage focuses on the *increase* in income resulting from the increase in sales.

Problem 6-17 (continued)

2. Cost-volume-profit graph:

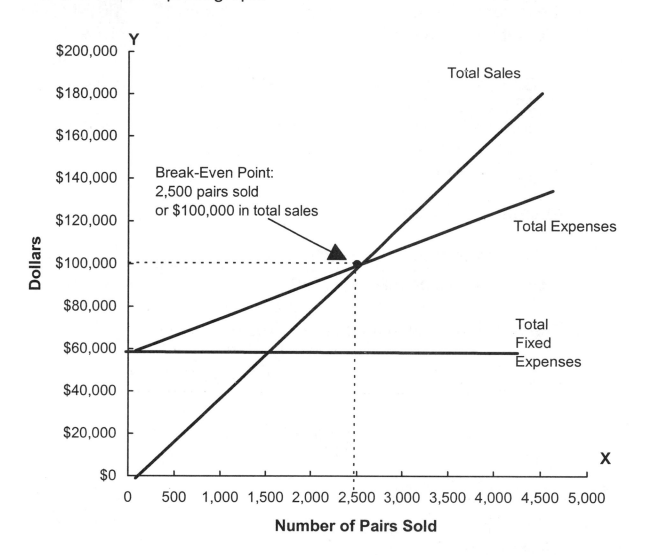

Problem 6-19 (60 minutes)

1. a. Selling price... $25   100%
       Less variable expenses 15   60
       Contribution margin $10   40%

   Sales = Variable expenses + Fixed expenses + Profits
   $25Q = $15Q + $210,000 + $0
   $10Q = $210,000
      Q = $210,000 ÷ $10
      Q = 21,000 balls

   Alternative solution:

   $$\frac{\text{Fixed expenses,} \quad \$210,000}{\text{Unit contribution margin,} \quad \$10} = 21,000 \text{ balls}$$

   b. The degree of operating leverage would be:

   $$\text{Degree of operating leverage} = \frac{\text{Contribution margin}}{\text{Net income}}$$

   $$\frac{\$300,000}{\$90,000} = 3.33 \text{ (rounded)}$$

2. The new CM ratio will be:

   Selling price... $25   100%
   Less variable expenses 18   72
   Contribution margin .... $ 7   28%

Problem 6-19 (continued)

The new break-even point will be:

Sales = Variable expenses + Fixed expenses + Profits

$25Q = $18Q + $210,000 + $0

$7Q = $210,000

Q = $210,000 ÷ $7

Q = 30,000 balls

Alternative solution:

$$\frac{\text{Fixed expenses,} \quad \$210{,}000}{\text{Unit contribution margin,} \quad \$7} = 30{,}000 \text{ balls}$$

3.　　Sales = Variable expenses + Fixed expenses + Profits

$25Q = $18Q + $210,000 + $90,000

$7Q = $300,000

Q = $300,000 ÷ $7

Q = 42,857 balls (rounded)

Alternative solution:

$$\text{Target sales} = \frac{\text{Fixed expenses} + \text{Target profit}}{\text{Unit contribution margin}}$$

$$\frac{\$210{,}000 + \$90{,}000}{\$7} = 42{,}857 \text{ balls}$$

Thus, sales will have to increase by 12,857 balls (42,857 balls, less 30,000 balls currently being sold) to earn the same amount of net income as last year. The computations above and in part (2) show quite clearly the dramatic effect that increases in variable costs can have on an organization. The effects on Northwood Company are summarized below:

	Present	Expected
Combination margin ratio............................	40%	28%
Break-even point (in balls)...........................	21,000	30,000
Sales (in balls) needed to earn a $90,000 profit	30,000	42,857

Note particularly that if variable costs do increase next year, then the company will just break even if it sells the same number of balls (30,000) as it did last year.

Problem 6-19 (continued)

4. The contribution margin ratio last year was 40%. If we let P equal the new selling price, then:

$$P = \$18 + 0.40P$$
$$0.60P = \$18$$
$$P = \$18 \div 0.60$$
$$P = \$30$$

To verify:

Selling price	$30	100%
Less variable expenses.................	18	60
Contribution margin.......................	$12	40%

Therefore, to maintain a 40% CM ratio, a $3 increase in variable costs would require a $5 increase in the selling price.

5. The new CM ratio would be:

Selling price............................	$25	100%
Less variable expenses..........	9*	36
Contribution margin	$16	64%

$$*\$15 - (\$15 \times 40\%) = \$9$$

The new break-even point would be:

$$\text{Sales} = \text{Variable expenses} + \text{Fixed expenses} + \text{Profits}$$
$$\$25Q = \$9Q + \$420{,}000 + \$0$$
$$\$16Q = \$420{,}000$$
$$Q = \$420{,}000 \div \$16$$
$$Q = 26{,}250 \text{ balls}$$

Alternative solution:

$$\frac{\text{Fixed expenses,} \quad \$420{,}000}{\text{Unit contribution margin,} \quad \$16} = 26{,}250 \text{ balls}$$

Although this break-even figure is greater than the company's present break-even figure of 21,000 balls [see Part (1) above], it is less than the break-even point will be if the company does not automate and variable labour costs rise next year [see Part (2) above].

Problem 6-19 (continued)

6. a. Sales = Variable expenses + Fixed expenses + Profits
    $25Q = $9Q + $420,000 + $90,000
    $16Q = $510,000
        Q = $510,000 ÷ $16
        Q = 31,875 balls

Alternative solution:

$$\text{Target sales} = \frac{\text{Fixed expenses} + \text{Target profit}}{\text{Unit contribution margin}}$$

$$\frac{\$420,000 + \$90,000}{\$16} = 31,875 \text{ balls}$$

Thus, the company will have to sell 1,875 more balls (31,875 – 30,000 = 1,875) than now being sold to earn a profit of $90,000 per year. However, this is still far less than the 42,857 balls that would have to be sold to earn a $90,000 profit if the plant is not automated and variable labour costs rise next year [see Part (3) above].

b. The contribution income statement would be:

Sales (30,000 balls × $25)	$750,000
Less variable expenses (30,000 balls x $9)	270,000
Contribution margin	480,000
Less fixed expenses	420,000
Net income	$ 60,000

The degree of operating leverage would be:

$$\frac{\text{Contribution margin, } \$480,000}{\text{Net income,} \qquad \$60,000} = 8$$

Problem 6-19 (continued)

c. This problem shows the difficulty faced by many firms today. Variable costs for labour are rising, yet because of competitive pressures it is often difficult to pass these cost increases along in the form of a higher price for products. Thus, firms are forced to automate (to some degree) resulting in higher operating leverage, often a higher break-even point, and greater risk for the company.

There is no clear answer as to whether one should have voted in favor of constructing the new plant. However, this question provides an opportunity to bring out points such as in the preceding paragraph and it forces students to think about the issues involved.

Problem 6-21 (60 minutes)

1. The income statements would be:

	Present			Proposed		
	Amount	Per Unit	%	Amount	Per Unit	%
Sales	$450,000	$30	100%	$450,000	$30	100%
Less variable expenses	315,000	21	70	180,000	12*	40
Contribution margin	135,000	$ 9	30%	270,000	$18	60%
Less fixed expenses	90,000			225,000		
Net income	$ 45,000			$ 45,000		

*$21 – $9 = $12.

2. a.

	Present	Proposed
Degree of operating leverage.........................	$\dfrac{\$135,000}{\$45,000} = 3$	$\dfrac{\$270,000}{\$45,000} = 6$

b.

	Present	Proposed
Break-even point in dollars	$\dfrac{\$90,000}{0.30} = \$300,000$	$\dfrac{\$225,000}{0.60} = \$375,000$

c.
Margin of safety = Total
sales less Break-even
sales:

	Present	Proposed
$450,000 – $300,000	$150,000	
$450,000 – $375,000		$75,000

Margin of safety
percentage = Margin of
safety divided by Total
sales:

	Present	Proposed
$150,000 ÷ $450,000	33 1/3%	
$75,000 ÷ $450,000		16 2/3%

Problem 6-21 (continued)

3. The major factor would be the sensitivity of the company's operations to cyclical movements in the economy. In years of strong economic activity, the company will be better off with the new equipment. The reason is that the new equipment will increase the CM ratio, thereby permitting profits to rise more rapidly in years that sales are strong. However, in periods of economic recession, the company will be worse off with the new equipment. The greater fixed costs created by the new equipment will cause losses to be deeper and sustained more quickly than at present. Thus, management must decide whether the potential for greater profits in good years is worth the risk of deeper losses in bad years.

4. Notice that no information is given on either the new variable expenses or the new contribution margin ratio. Both of these items must be determined before the new break-even point can be computed. The computations are:

New variable expenses:

$$\text{Sales} = \text{Variable expenses} + \text{Fixed expenses} + \text{Profits}$$
$$\$540,000^* = \text{Variable expenses} + \$48,000 + \$60,000^{**}$$
$$\$432,000 = \text{Variable expenses}$$

*New level of sales: $\$450,000 \times 1.20 = \$540,000$
**New level of net income: $\$45,000 \times 1\frac{1}{3} = \$60,000$

New CM ratio:

Sales	$540,000	100%
Less variable expenses	432,000	80
Contribution margin	$108,000	20%

With the above data, the new break-even point can be computed:

$$\frac{\text{New level of fixed costs, } \$48,000}{\text{New CM ratio, } \quad 0.20} = \$240,000$$

Problem 6-23 (20 minutes)

1. The break-even point in number of units:

   Selling Price $25 ($800,000/32,000 units)
   Variable cost   15 ($480,000/32,000 units)
   CM per unit $10

   BEP = Fixed Cost $150,000 = 15,000 units
         CM per unit $10

2. The number of units to be sold in order to earn a targeted after tax income:

   Targeted net income before taxes is equal to the net income after taxes divided by (1-tax rate) which is (1- .45) = .55. The pretax income is then added to fixed costs and then divided by the UCM to find the necessary number of units to earn the targeted amount.

   $99,000/.55 = $180,000 net income before taxes

   $150,000 FC + $180,000 net income = 33,000 units
               $10 UCM

3. The break-even point in units given increases in FC and VC:

   The UCM would decrease to $8 ($25 sales price - $17 new unit variable cost), and FC would increase by $3,000, next year's portion of amortization (18,000/6 years). New FC would be $153,000.

   BEP = $153,000 = 19,125 units
          $8 UCM

4. The number of units necessary to earn the same amount after taxes as last year with increases in fixed and variable costs:

Problem 6-23 (continued)

To earn the same net income after taxes as last year would require earning the same net income before taxes (i.e., $170,000). As computed in requirement 3, fixed costs have increased to $153,000, and the CM has declined to $8.00 per unit.

$$BEP = \frac{\$153,000 \ FC + \$170,000}{\$8.00 \ UCM} = 40,375 \text{ units}$$

5. The selling price to maintain the came CM ratio given increases in FC and VC

This year's contribution margin ratio was 40% ($10 CM/$25 SP), which gives a variable cost ratio of 60% ($15 VC/$25 SP). Variable costs are to be increased to $17 per unit. Thus, to hold the CM ratio steady, a selling price of $28.33 is necessary ($17/.60).

CGA -adapted

Problem 6-25 (20 minutes)

IF win

Proposals	Costs	Profits	Net	Tax 40%	After Tax
A	$80,000	$250,000	$170,000	$68,000	$102,000
B	30,000	250,000	220,000	88,000	132,000

IF Lose

A	80,000	0	(80,000)	32,000	(48,000)
B	30,000	0	(30,000)	12,000	(18,000)

Decision Tree   Win $102,000   ×   .60 $ 61,200

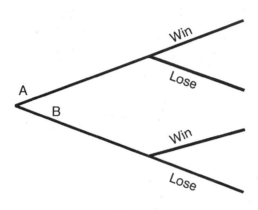

Lose   (48,000) ×   .40   (19,200)
                                      $42,000

Win   132,000 ×   .30 $ 39,600

Lose   (18,000) ×   .70   (12,600)
                                                         $ 27,000

Decision analysis:

The firm may be indifferent between either alternative. However proposal B may have more risk than proposal A. The actual recommendation will depend on the risk preferences of the decision maker.

(SMAC Adapted)

Problem 6-27 (15 minutes)

(a)   Decision Tree

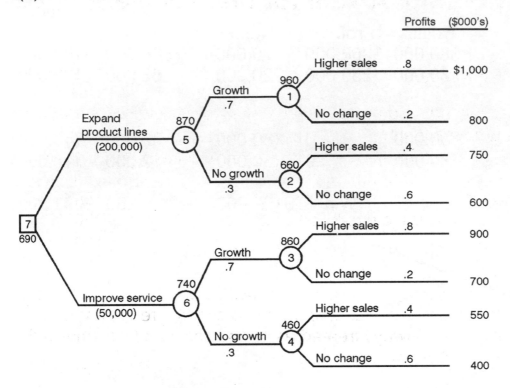

(b)   Node 1:   .8 (1,000)   +   .2 (800)   =   960
      Node 2:   .4 (750   +   .6 (600)   =   660
      Node 3:   .8 (900)   +   .2 (700)   =   860
      Node 4:   .4 (550)   +   .6 (400)   =   460
      Node 5:   .7 (960)   +   .3 (660)   =   870
      Node 6:   .7 (860)   +   .3 (460)   =   740

Expand Product Lines: 870 − 200 = 670
Improve Service: 740 − 50 = 690 (Node 7)

Therefore, Acme should improve service on the existing product lines to maximize expected net profit.
(CGAC Solution Adapted)

Chapter 7
Variable Costing: A Tool for Management

Exercise 7-1 (20 minutes)

1. Under variable costing, only the variable manufacturing costs are included in product costs.

Direct materials	$ 50
Direct labour	80
Variable manufacturing overhead	20
Unit product cost	$150

Note that selling and administrative expenses are not treated as product costs; that is, they are not included in the costs that are inventoried. These expenses are always treated as period costs and are charged against the current period's revenue.

2. The variable costing income statement appears below:

Sales		$3,990,000
Less variable expenses:		
Variable cost of goods sold:		
Beginning inventory	$ 0	
Add variable manufacturing costs		
(20,000 units × $150)	3,000,000	
Goods available for sale	3,000,000	
Less ending inventory		
(1,000 units × $150)	150,000	
Variable cost of goods sold*	2,850,000	
Variable selling and administrative		
expenses (19,000 units × $10)	190,000	3,040,000
Contribution margin		950,000
Less fixed expenses:		
Fixed manufacturing overhead	700,000	
Fixed selling and administrative		
expenses	285,000	985,000
Net loss		$ (35,000)

© 2001 McGraw-Hill Ryerson Limited

Exercise 7-1 (continued)

* The variable cost of goods sold could be computed more simply as: 19,000 units sold × $150 = $2,850,000.

3. The break-even point in units sold can be computed using the contribution margin per unit as follows:

Selling price per unit	$210
Variable cost per unit	160
Contribution margin per unit	$ 50

$$\text{Break-even unit sales} = \frac{\text{Fixed expenses,} \quad \$985,000}{\text{Unit contribution margin,} \quad \$50} = 19,700 \text{ units}$$

Exercise 7-3 (10 minutes)

(Note: All currency values are in thousands of rupiah.)

1. Under absorption costing, all manufacturing costs (variable and fixed) are included in product costs.

Direct materials	Rp100
Direct labour	320
Variable manufacturing overhead	40
Fixed manufacturing overhead (Rp60,000 ÷ 250 units)	240
Unit product cost	Rp700

2. Under variable costing, only the variable manufacturing costs are included in product costs.

Direct materials	Rp100
Direct labour	320
Variable manufacturing overhead	40
Unit product cost	Rp460

Note that selling and administrative expenses are not treated as product costs under either absorption or variable costing; that is, they are not included in the costs that are inventoried. These expenses are always treated as period costs and are charged against the current period's revenue.

Exercise 7-5 (10 minutes)

1. The company is using variable costing. The computations are:

	Variable Costing	Absorption Costing
Direct materials	$ 9	$ 9
Direct labour..............................	10	10
Variable manufacturing overhead	5	5
Fixed manufacturing overhead ($150,000 ÷ 25,000 units)........	—	6
Unit product cost	$24	$30
Total cost, 3,000 units................	$72,000	$90,000

2. a. No, the $72,000 figure is not the correct figure to use, since variable costing is not generally accepted for external reporting purposes or for tax purposes.

b. The Finished Goods inventory account should be stated at $90,000, which represents the absorption cost to manufacture the 3,000 unsold units.

Exercise 7-7 (20 minutes)

1.

Sales (35,000 units at $25).........................		$875,000
Less variable expenses:		
Variable cost of goods sold (35,000 units at $12*)	$420,000	
Variable selling and administrative expenses (35,000 units at $2)...............	70,000	490,000
Contribution margin		385,000
Less fixed expenses:		
Fixed manufacturing overhead	160,000	
Fixed selling and administrative expenses	210,000	370,000
Net income		$ 15,000

*Direct materials	$ 5
Direct labour......................................	6
Variable manufacturing overhead......	1
Total variable manufacturing cost ...	$12

2. The difference in net income can be explained by the $20,000 in fixed manufacturing overhead deferred in inventory under the absorption costing method:

Variable costing net income	$15,000
Add: Fixed manufacturing overhead cost deferred in inventory under absorption costing: 5,000 units × $4 in fixed manufacturing cost per unit........................	20,000
Absorption costing net income	$35,000

Problem 7-9 (25 minutes)

1. The unit product cost under the variable costing method would be computed as follows:

Direct materials	$ 4
Direct labour	7
Variable manufacturing overhead	1
Unit product cost	$12

With this figure, the variable costing income statements can be prepared:

	Year 1	Year 2
Sales	$1,000,000	$1,250,000
Less variable expenses:		
Variable cost of goods sold (@ $12)	480,000	600,000
Variable selling and administrative expenses (@ $2)	80,000	100,000
Total variable expenses	560,000	700,000
Contribution margin	440,000	550,000
Less fixed expenses:		
Fixed manufacturing overhead	270,000	270,000
Fixed selling and administrative expenses	130,000	130,000
Total fixed expenses	400,000	400,000
Net income	$ 40,000	$ 150,000

	Year 1	Year 2
2. Variable costing net income	$40,000	$150,000
Add: Fixed manufacturing overhead deferred in inventory under absorption costing (5,000 units × $6 per unit)	30,000	—
Deduct: Fixed manufacturing overhead released from inventory under absorption costing (5,000 units × $6 per unit)	—	30,000
Absorption costing net income	$70,000	$120,000

Problem 7-11 (40 minutes)

1. a. and b.

	Absorption Costing	Variable Costing
Direct materials..	$48	$48
Variable manufacturing overhead	2	2
Fixed manufacturing overhead ($360,000 ÷ 12,000 units)...............................	30	—
Unit product cost...	$80	$50

2. Absorption costing income statement:

Sales (10,000 units x $150)		$1,500,000
Less cost of goods sold:		
Beginning inventory	$ 0	
Add cost of goods manufactured (12,000 units x $80).....................................	960,000	
Good available for sale	960,000	
Less ending inventory (2,000 units x $80).......	160,000	800,000
Gross margin..		700,000
Less selling and administrative expenses..........		650,000*
Net income		$ 50,000
*Variable (12% x $1,500,000)	$180,000	
Fixed..	470,000	
Total	$650,000	

Problem 7-11 (continued)

3.   Variable costing income statement:

Sales (10,000 units x $150)		$1,500,000
Less variable expenses:		
Variable cost of goods sold:		
Beginning inventory	$ 0	
Add variable manufacturing costs		
(12,000 units x $50)	600,000	
Goods available for sale	600,000	
Less ending inventory		
(2,000 units x $50)	100,000	
Variable cost of goods sold	500,000*	
Variable selling and administrative		
expenses	180,000	680,000
Contribution margin		820,000
Less fixed expenses:		
Fixed manufacturing overhead	360,000	
Fixed selling and administrative expenses.....	470,000	830,000
Net loss..		$ (10,000)

* This figure could be computed more simply as:
    10,000 units x $50 = $500,000.

4. Most managers would prefer to take the statement prepared under the absorption approach in part (2), since it shows a profit for the month. As long as inventory levels are rising, absorption costing will report higher profits than variable costing. Notice in the situation above that the company is operating below its theoretical break-even point, but yet reports a profit under the absorption approach.

5.
Variable costing net loss	$ (10,000)
Add: Fixed manufacturing overhead cost	
deferred in inventory under absorption	
costing (2,000 units × $30).............................	60,000
Absorption costing net income...........................	$ 50,000

Problem 7-13 (60 minutes)

1.

	Year 1	Year 2	Year 3
Sales	$800,000	$640,000	$800,000
Less variable expenses:			
Variable cost of goods sold @ $2	100,000	80,000	100,000
Selling and administrative expenses @ $1	50,000	40,000	50,000
Total variable expenses	150,000	120,000	150,000
Contribution margin	650,000	520,000	650,000
Less fixed expenses:			
Manufacturing overhead	480,000	480,000	480,000
Selling and administrative expenses	140,000	140,000	140,000
Total fixed expenses	620,000	620,000	620,000
Net income (loss)	$ 30,000	$(100,000)	$ 30,000

Problem 7-13 (continued)

2. a.

	Year 1	Year 2	Year 3
Variable manufacturing cost	$ 2.00	$ 2.00	$ 2.00
Fixed manufacturing cost:			
$480,000 ÷ 50,000 units	9.60		
$480,000 ÷ 60,000 units		8.00	
$480,000 ÷ 40,000 units			12.00
Unit product cost	$11.60	$10.00	$14.00

	Year 1	Year 2	Year 3
b. Variable costing net income (loss)	$30,000	$(100,000)	$ 30,000
Add (Deduct): Fixed manufacturing overhead cost deferred in inventory from Year 2 to Year 3 under absorption costing (20,000 units × $8.00)...........................		160,000	(160,000)
Add: Fixed manufacturing overhead cost deferred in inventory from Year 3 to the future under absorption costing (10,000 units × $12.00).....................................			120,000
Absorption costing net income (loss)	$30,000	$ 60,000	$ (10,000)

3. Production went up sharply in Year 2 thereby reducing the unit product cost, as shown in (2a) above. This reduction in cost per unit, combined with the large amount of fixed manufacturing overhead cost deferred in inventory for the year, more than offset the loss of revenue. The net result is that the company's net income increased.

Problem 7-13 (continued)

The fixed manufacturing overhead cost deferred in inventory from Year 2 was charged against Year 3 operations, as shown in the reconciliation in (2b). This added charge against Year 3 operations was offset somewhat by the fact that part of Year 3's fixed manufacturing overhead costs were deferred in inventory to future years [again see (2b)]. Overall, the added costs charged against Year 3 were greater than the costs deferred to future years, so the company reported less income for the year even though the same number of units was sold as in Year 1.

4. a. Several things would have been different if the company had been using JIT inventory methods. First, in each year production would have been geared to sales so that little or no inventory of finished goods would have been built up in either Year 2 or Year 3. Second, unit product costs probably would have been the same in all three years, since these costs would have been established on the basis of *expected* sales (50,000 units) for each year. Third, since only 40,000 units were sold in Year 2, the company would have produced only that number of units and therefore would have had some underapplied overhead cost for the year. (See the discussion on underapplied overhead in the following paragraph.)

   b. If JIT had been in use, the net income under absorption costing would have been the same as under variable costing in all three years. The reason is that with production geared to sales, there would have been no ending inventory on hand, and therefore there would have been no fixed manufacturing overhead costs deferred in inventory to other years. Assuming that the company *expected* to sell 50,000 units in each year and that unit product costs were set on the basis of that level of expected activity, the income statements under absorption costing would have appeared as follows:

Problem 7-13 (continued)

	Year 1	Year 2	Year 3
Sales	$ 800,000	$ 640,000	$ 800,000
Less cost of goods sold:			
Cost of goods manufactured (@ $11.60) ...	580,000	464,000*	580,000
Add underapplied overhead.............................		96,000**	
Cost of goods sold	580,000	560,000	580,000
Gross margin	220,000	80,000	220,000
Selling and administrative expenses	190,000	180,000	190,000
Net income (loss)....................	$ 30,000	$(100,000)	$ 30,000

* 40,000 units x $11.60 = $464,000.

** 10,000 units *not* produced x $9.60 fixed manufacturing overhead cost per unit = $96,000 fixed manufacturing overhead cost not applied to products.

Problem 7-15 (25 minutes)

1. Because of soft demand for the Brazilian Division's product, the inventory should be drawn down to the minimum level of 50 units on hand. Drawing inventory down to the minimum level would require production as follows during the last quarter:

Desired inventory, December 31	50 units
Expected sales, last quarter	600 units
Total needs...	650 units
Less inventory, September 30	400 units
Required production	250 units

Drawing inventory down to the minimum level would save inventory carrying costs such as storage (rent, insurance), interest, and obsolescence.

The number of units scheduled for production will not affect the reported net income or loss for the year if variable costing is in use. All fixed manufacturing overhead cost will be treated as an expense of the period regardless of the number of units produced. Thus, no fixed manufacturing overhead cost will be shifted between periods through the inventory account and income will be a function of the number of units sold, rather than a function of the number of units produced.

2. To maximize the Brazilian Division's operating income, Mr. Cavalas could produce as many units as storage facilities will allow. By building inventory to the maximum level, Mr. Cavalas will be able to defer a portion of the year's fixed manufacturing overhead costs to future years through the inventory account, rather than having all of these costs appear as deductions on the current year's income statement. Building inventory to the maximum level of 1,000 units would require production as follows during the last quarter:

Desired inventory, December 31	1,000 units
Expected sales, last quarter	600 units
Total needs...	1,600 units
Less inventory, September 30	400 units
Required production	1,200 units

Problem 7-15 (continued)

Thus, by producing enough units to build inventory to the maximum level that storage facilities will allow, Mr. Cavalas could relieve the current year of fixed manufacturing overhead cost and thereby maximize the current year's operating income.

3. Mr. Cavalas faces an ethical dilemma in that by setting a production schedule that will maximize his division's operating income—and maximize his own bonus—he will be acting against the best interests of the company as a whole. The extra units that will be added to inventory aren't needed and will be expensive to carry. Moreover, there is no indication that demand will be any better next year than it has been in the current year, so the company may be required to carry the extra units in inventory a long time before they are shipped to customers.

Mr. Cavalas faces a further ethical dilemma in that the company's bonus plan undoubtedly is intended to increase sales and to control expenses. If Mr. Cavalas sets a production schedule as shown in part (2) above, he will obtain his bonus as a result of *producing* rather than as a result of selling. Moreover, he will obtain it by creating *greater* expenses—rather than less expenses—for the company as a whole.

Problem 7-17

1. a)

Singh Enterprises
Income Statements
For the months ended
(Absorption Costing)

	January	February	March
Sales	$144,000	$168,000	$216,000
Costs of goods sold:			
Beginning inventory	16,000	40,000	72,000
Variable manufacturing Cost	75,000	90,000	65,000
Fixed manufacturing Cost	45,000	54,000	39,000
Cost of good manufactured	120,000	144,000	104,000
Goods available for sale	136,000	184,000	176,000
Less: ending inventory	40,000	72,000	32,000
	96,000	112,000	144,000
Under or (over) applied FOH	(3,000)	(12,000)	3,000
Adjusted Cost of goods sold	93,000	100,000	147,000
Gross margin	$ 51,000	$ 68,000	$ 69,000
Selling and admin expenses:			
Variable	24,000	28,000	36,000
Fixed	20,000	20,000	20,000
	44,000	48,000	56,000
Net income (loss)	$ 7,000	$ 20,000	$ 13,000
Net income (loss)	$ (2,000)	$ 8,000	$ 28,000

Problem 7-17 (continued)

	January	February
Sales	$144,000	$168,000
Costs of goods sold:		
Beginning inventory	16,000	40,000
Variable manufacturing Cost	75,000	90,000
Fixed manufacturing Cost	45,000	54,000
Cost of good manufactured	120,000	144,000
Goods available for sale	136,000	184,000
Less: ending inventory	40,000	72,000
	96,000	112,000
Under or (over) applied FOH	(3,000)	(12,000)
Adjusted Cost of goods sold	93,000	100,000
Gross margin	$ 51,000	$ 68,000
Selling and admin expenses:		
Variable	24,000	28,000
Fixed	20,000	20,000
	44,000	48,000
Net income (loss)	$ 7,000	$ 20,000

b)

Singh Enterprises
Income Statements
For the months ended
(Variable Costing)

	January	February	March
Sales	$144,000	$168,000	$216,000
Costs of goods sold:			
Beginning inventory	10,000	25,000	45,000
Variable manufacturing Cost	75,000	90,000	65,000
Goods available for sale	85,000	115,000	110,000
Less: ending inventory	25,000	45,000	20,000
Contribution margin	60,000	70,000	90,000
Fixed expenses:			
Manufacturing overhead	42,000	42,000	42,000
Selling and administration	20,000	20,000	20,000
	62,000	62,000	62,000
Net income (loss)	$ (2,000)	$ 8,000	$ 28,000

Problem 7-17 (continued)

2. As shown in the answer to part a) under the absorption costing income statements, February's net income was $20,000 when 14,000 units were sold but in March when 18,000 units were sold, net income was $13,000; $7,000 less when in fact, 4,000 more units were sold.

Under absorption costing, profits are affected by both sales and production. When production exceeds sales in a given month, a portion of the fixed overhead cost of these months is deferred to the future as opposed to being expensed as is done under variable costing. In absorption costing the fixed overhead is a product cost and is therefore not expensed until the product is sold. In variable costing, fixed overhead is treated as a period cost and is expensed in the period incurred.

January's net income under absorption costing was $7,000, but under variable costing there was a loss of $2,000. This $9,000 difference between these two net incomes is accounted for by the fact that in January 3,000 more units were produced than were sold. The fixed overhead cost per unit is $3.00. Under variable costing $9,000 more would have been expensed than under absorption costing since under absorption costing the fixed overhead "attaches" to the product and is not expensed until sold.

In February, the same happened as in January in that Singh produced 4,000 more units than sold, resulting in a difference of $12,000 (4,000 x $3) between the incomes reported.

In March, however, Singh sold 5,000 units more than were produced, resulting in the variable costing approach showing $15,000 more income than was reported under absorption costing. This is because the fixed overhead component of these 5,000 units have already been expensed in a previous month under variable costing.

Problem 7-17 (continued)

3. Advantages of using variable costing for internal reporting

i. Aids in forecasting and reporting income for decision-making purposes.
ii. Fixed costs are reported in total amount, thereby increasing the opportunity for more effective control of these units.
iii. Profits vary directly with sales volume and are not affected by changes in inventory levels.
iv. Analysis of cost-volume-profit relationships is faciliated and management is able to determine the break-even point and total profits for a given volume of production and sales.

Disadvantages of using variable costing;
i. Management may fail to consider properly the fixed cost elements and their effect in the decision-making process.
ii. The distinction between fixed and variable costs is arbitrary.

CGA -adapted

Chapter 8
Activity-Based Costing:
A Tool to Aid Decision Making

Exercise 8-1 (10 minutes)

	Activity	Activity Level
a.	Sales representatives' periodic visits to customers to keep them informed about the services provided by CD Express ..	Customer-level
b.	Ordering labels from the printer for a particular CD*	Product-level
c.	Setting up the CD duplicating machine to make copies from a particular master CD	Batch-level
d.	Loading the automatic labeling machine with labels for a particular CD*	Batch-level
e.	Visually inspecting CDs and placing them by hand into protective plastic cases prior to shipping	Unit-level
f.	Preparation of the shipping documents for the order	Product-level
g.	Periodic maintenance of equipment..........	Organization-sustaining
h.	Lighting and heating the company's production facility	Organization-sustaining
i.	Preparation of quarterly financial reports ..	Organization-sustaining

*The cost of the labels themselves would be part of direct materials.

Exercise 8-3 (15 minutes)

1. and 2.

	Activity	Level of Activity	Possible Activity Measures
a.	Machine settings are changed between batches of different products	Batch-level	Number of batches; time to change settings
b.	Parts inventories are maintained in the storeroom	Product-level	Number of part types maintained in inventory
c.	Products are milled on a milling machine	Unit-level	Machine-hours; labour hours
d.	New employees are hired by the personnel office	Organization-sustaining	Not applicable*
e.	New products are designed	Product-level	Hours of design time
f.	Periodic maintenance is performed on general-purpose production equipment	Organization-sustaining	Not applicable*
g.	A bill is sent to a customer who is late in making payments	Customer-level	Number of bills
h.	Yearly taxes are paid on the company's facilities	Organization-sustaining	Not applicable*
i.	Purchase orders are issued for materials to be used in production	Batch-level	Number of purchase orders

* Organization-sustaining costs should not be allocated to products or customers.

Note: Some of these classifications and activity measures are debatable.

Exercise 8-5 (20 minutes)

1. Computation of activity rates:

	Opening Accounts	Processing Deposits and Withdrawals	Processing Other Customer Transactions
Total activity	500 new accounts	100,000 deposits and withdrawals	5,000 other customer transactions
Teller wages	$16.00	$1.04	$ 6.40
Assistant branch manager salary	22.50	0.04	4.50
Branch manager salary	8.00	0.00	1.60
Total cost	$46.50	$1.08	$12.50

Example: $8,000 ÷ 500 new accounts = $16.00 per new account

Teller wages attributable to opening accounts from the first-stage allocation in Exercise E8-4.

Exercise 8-5 (continued)

2. The cost of opening an account at the Westfield branch is apparently much higher than at the lowest cost branch ($46.50 versus $26.75). On the other hand, the cost of processing deposits and withdrawals is lower than at the lowest cost branch ($1.08 versus $1.24). And the cost of processing other customer transactions is somewhat higher at the Westfield branch ($12.50 versus $11.86). This suggests that the other branches may have something to learn from Westfield concerning processing deposits and withdrawals and Westfield may benefit from learning about how some of the other branches open accounts and process other transactions. It may be particularly instructive to compare the details of the activity rates. For example, is the cost of opening accounts at Westfield apparently high because of the involvement of the assistant branch manager in this activity?

It should be mentioned that the apparent differences in the costs of the activities at the various branches could be due to inaccuracies in employees' reports of the amount of time they devote to the activities. The differences in costs may also reflect different strategies. For example, the Westfield branch may purposely spend more time with new customers in order to win their loyalty. The higher cost of opening new accounts at the Westfield branch may be justified by future benefits of having more satisfied customers. Nevertheless, comparative studies of the costs of activities may provide a useful starting point for identifying best practices within a company and where improvements can be made.

Exercise 8-7 (30 minutes)

1. The order requires 250 direct labour-hours (1,000 units @ 0.25 DLH per unit) and is run in two batches. Therefore, the overhead cost of the order according to the activity-based costing system would be computed as follows:

	Volume	Batch Processing	Order Processing	Customer Service	Total
Activity	250 DLHs	2 batches	1 order	Not applicable	
Production overhead:					
Indirect labour	$ 150.00	$120.00	$ 20.00	$0.00	$ 290.00
Factory equipment depreciation	1,000.00	34.00	0.00	0.00	1,034.00
Factory administration	25.00	14.00	25.00	0.00	64.00
General selling and administrative overhead:					
Wages and salaries	100.00	40.00	160.00	0.00	300.00
Depreciation	0.00	6.00	10.00	0.00	16.00
Marketing expenses	112.50	0.00	60.00	0.00	172.50
Total cost	$1,387.50	$214.00	$275.00	$0.00	$1,876.50

Example: 250 DLHs × $0.60 per DLH = $150.00

Exercise 8-7 (continued)

The product margin on the order can be computed as follows:

Sales (1,000 units @ $20 per unit)		$20,000.00
Costs:		
Direct materials (1,000 units @ $8.50 per unit)	$8,500.00	
Direct labour (1,000 units @ $6.00 per unit)	6,000.00	
Volume related overhead	1,387.50	
Batch processing-related overhead	214.00	
Order processing-related overhead	275.00	16,376.50
Product margin		$ 3,623.50

2. The customer margin for sales to Lyon Gate Trucking is computed as follows:

Product Margin (above)	$3,623.50
Less: Customer service overhead (1 customer @ $2,463 per customer)	2,463.00
Customer margin	$1,160.50

Exercise 8-9 (30 minutes)

An action analysis report for the customer can be prepared by including the customer service costs in the overhead analysis.

	Volume	Batch Processing	Order Processing	Customer Service	Total
Activity............	250 DLHs	2 batches	1 order	1 customer	
Production overhead:					
Indirect labour.........	$ 150.00	$120.00	$ 20.00	$0.00	$ 290.00
Factory equipment depreciation............	1,000.00	34.00	0.00	0.00	1,034.00
Factory administration	25.00	14.00	25.00	150.00	214.00
General selling and administrative overhead:					
Wages and salaries	100.00	40.00	160.00	1,600.00	1,900.00
Depreciation	0.00	6.00	10.00	38.00	54.00
Marketing expenses	112.50	0.00	60.00	675.00	847.50
Total cost.........	$1,387.50	$214.00	$275.00	$2,463.00	$4,339.50

Example: 250 DLHs × $0.60 per DLH = $150.00

Exercise 8-9 (continued)

The action analysis report for the order can be constructed using the row totals from the activity rate table, organized according to the ease of adjustment codes:

Sales (1,000 units @ $20 per unit)		$20,000.00
Green costs:		
Direct materials (1,000 units @ $8.50 per unit)	$8,500.00	8,500.00
Green margin		11,500.00
Yellow costs:		
Direct labour (1,000 units @ $6.00 per unit)	6,000.00	
Indirect labour	290.00	
Marketing expenses	847.50	7,137.50
Yellow margin		4,362.50
Red costs:		
Factory equipment depreciation	1,034.00	
Factory administration	214.00	
Selling and adminsitrative wages and salaries	1,900.00	
Selling and administrative depreciation	54.00	3,202.00
Red margin		$ 1,160.50

Exercise 8-11 (30 minutes)

1. The first step is to determine the activity rates:

	Serving a Party	Serving a Diner	Serving Drinks
Total cost (a)	$33,000	$138,000	$24,000
Total activity (b)	6,000 parties	15,000 diners	10,000 drinks
Cost per unit of activity (a)÷(b)	$5.50 per party	$9.20 per diner	$2.40 per drink

Exercise 8-11 (continued)

According to the activity-based costing system, the cost of serving each of the parties can be computed as follows:

	Serving a Party	Serving a Diner	Serving Drinks	Total
Cost per unit of activity	$5.50 per party	$9.20 per diner	$2.40 per drink	
a. Party of four diners who order three drinks	1 party	4 diners	3 drinks	
Cost	$5.50	$36.80	$7.20	$49.50
b. Party of two diners who order no drinks	1 party	2 diners	0 drinks	
Cost	$5.50	$18.40	$-0-	$23.90
c. Party of one diner who orders two drinks	1 party	1 diner	2 drinks	
Cost	$5.50	$9.20	$4.80	$19.50

Exercise 8-11 (continued)

2. The average cost per diner for each party can be computed by dividing the total cost of the party by the number of diners in the party as follows:

 a. $49.50 ÷ 4 diners = $12.375 per diner
 b. $23.90 ÷ 2 diners = $11.95 per diner
 c. $19.40 ÷ 1 diner = $19.40 per diner

3. The average cost per diner differs from party to party under the activity-based costing system for two reasons. First, the cost of serving a party ($5.50) does not depend upon the number of diners in the party. Therefore, the average cost per diner of this activity decreases as the number of diners in the party increases. With only one diner, the cost is $5.50. With two diners, the average cost per diner is cut in half to $2.75. With five diners, the average cost per diner would be only $1.10. And so on. Second, the average cost per diner differs also because of the differences in the number of drinks ordered by the diners. If a party does not order any drinks, as was the case with the party of two, no costs of serving drinks are assigned to the party.

The average cost per diner differs from the overall average cost of $16 per diner for several reasons. First, the average cost of $16 per diner includes organization-sustaining costs which are excluded from the computations in the activity-based costing system. Second, the $16 per diner figure does not recognize differences in the diners' demands on resources. It does not recognize that some diners order more drinks than others nor does it recognize that there are some economies of scale in serving larger parties. (The batch-level costs of serving a party can be spread over more diners if the party is larger.)

We should note that the activity-based costing system itself does not recognize all of the differences in diners' demands on resources. For example, there are undoubtedly differences in the costs of preparing the various meals on the menu. It may or may not be worth the effort to build a more detailed activity-based costing system that would take such nuances into account.

Problem 8-13 (45 minutes)

1. The detailed cost analysis of local commercials appears below:

	Animation Concept	Animation Production	Contract Administration	Total
Activity level	25 proposals	5 minutes	10 contracts	
Technical staff salaries	$100,000	$30,000	$16,000	$146,000
Animation equipment depreciation	9,000	5,625	0	14,625
Administrative wages and salaries	36,000	750	48,000	84,750
Supplies costs	3,000	1,500	1,600	6,100
Facility costs	3,000	750	2,400	6,150
Total cost	$151,000	$38,625	$68,000	$257,625

Example: 25 proposals × $4,000 per proposal = $100,000

The cost of technical staff salaries per proposal.

Problem 8-13 (continued)

2. The margin for local commercial work is negative, as shown below:

Sales......................................		$180,000
Costs:		
Animation concept...............	$151,000	
Animation production	38,625	
Contract administration	68,000	257,625
Margin............................		($77,625)

3. The action analysis report is constructed by using the row totals from the cost report in part (1) above:

Sales...		$180,000
Green costs:		
Supplies costs..	$ 6,100	6,100
Green margin		173,900
Yellow costs:		
Administrative wages and salaries	84,750	84,750
Yellow margin.......................................		89,150
Red costs:		
Technical staff salaries.........................	146,000	
Animation equipment depreciation	14,625	
Facility costs	6,150	166,775
Red margin		($ 77,625)

Problem 8-13 (continued)

4.   At first glance, it appears that the company is losing money on local commercials. However, the action analysis report indicates that if this market segment were dropped, most of the costs are likely to continue being incurred. The nature of the technical staff salaries is clearly critical since it makes up the bulk of the costs. Management has suggested that the technical staff are the company's most valuable asset and that they would be the last to go in case of financial difficulties. Nevertheless, there are at least two situations in which these costs would be relevant. First, dropping the local commercial market segment may reduce future hiring of new technical staff. This would have the effect of reducing future spending and therefore would reduce the company's costs. Second, if technical staff time is a constraint, dropping the local commercial market segment would allow managers to shift technical staff time to other, presumably more profitable, work. However, if this is the case, there are better ways to determine which projects should get technical staff attention. This subject will be covered in Chapter 13 in the section on utilization of a constrained resource.

Finally, the cost of the animation concept at the proposal stage is a major drag on the profitability of the local commercial market. The activity-based costing system, as currently designed, assumes that all project proposals require the same effort. This may not be the case. Proposals for local commercials may be far less elabourate than proposals for major special effects animation sequences for motion pictures. If management *has* been putting about the same amount of effort into every proposal, the above activity-based costing analysis suggests that this may be a mistake. Management may want to consider cutting back on the effort going into animation concepts for local commercials at the project proposal stage. Of course, this may lead to an even lower success rate on bids for local commercials.

Problem 8-15 (30 minutes)

1. The first-stage allocation of costs to activity cost pools for the CDG operation appears below. All figures are in French francs.

	Meal Preparation	Flight-Related	Customer Service	Other	Totals
Cooks and delivery personnel wages	18,000,000	4,800,000	0	1,200,000	24,000,000
Kitchen supplies	300,000	0	0	0	300,000
Chef salaries	540,000	360,000	720,000	180,000	1,800,000
Equipment depreciation	360,000	0	0	240,000	600,000
Administrative wages and salaries	0	300,000	900,000	300,000	1,500,000
Building costs	0	0	0	1,200,000	1,200,000
Total cost	19,200,000	5,460,000	1,620,000	3,120,000	29,400,000

According to the data in the problem, 75% of the cooks and delivery personnel wages is attributable to meal preparation activities.

75% of 24,000,000 FF = 18,000,000 FF

Other entries in the table are determined in a similar manner.

Problem 8-15 (continued)

2. The activity rates at the CDG operation are:

Activity at CDG	Meal Preparation		Flight-related		Customer Service	
	1,500,000		7,500		10	
	meals		flights		airlines	
Cooks and delivery personnel wages	12.00	FF	640	FF	0	FF
Kitchen supplies	0.20		0		0	
Chef salaries	0.36		48		72,000	
Equipment depreciation	0.24		0		0	
Administrative wages and salaries	0.00		40		90,000	
Building costs	0.00		0		0	
Total cost	12.80	FF	728	FF	162,000	FF

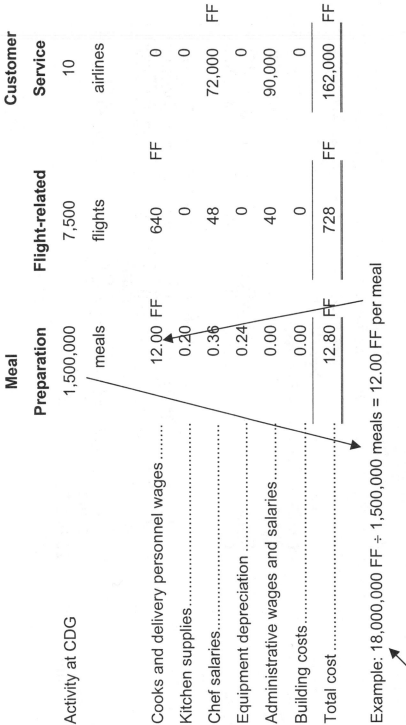

Example: 18,000,000 FF ÷ 1,500,000 meals = 12.00 FF per meal

Cooks and delivery personnel wages attributable to meal preparation from the first-stage allocation.

Problem 8-15 (continued)

3. Managers should be cautious when comparing operations using activity-based costing data—particularly when the activity-based costing data rely on interviews. Nevertheless, comparisons of the data can provide insights and may suggest where it would be fruitful to investigate further. In this case, side-by-side comparison of the Orly and CDG activity rates reveals that the cost per meal and cost per flight is less at CDG than at Orly, but the cost per airline for customer service activities is higher at CDG than at Orly. This suggests that Orly might have something to learn from CDG concerning meal preparation and flight-related activities, but CDG may be able to learn from Orly concerning customer service activities.

Overall, CDG seems to be more efficient than Orly by about 657,500 FF as shown in the table below.

	CDG	Orly	Difference	Activity at CDG	Difference x Activity at CDG
Meal preparation ..	12.80 FF per meal	12.86 FF per meal	(0.06) FF per meal	1,500,000 meals	(90,000) FF
Flight-related..........	728 FF per flight	857 FF per flight	(129) FF per flight	7,500 flights	(967,500) FF
Customer service ..	162,000 FF per airline	122,000 FF per airline	40,000 FF per airline	10 airlines	400,000 FF
Total.............					(657,500) FF

Problem 8-15 (continued)

Examination of the detailed listing of activity rates may reveal more insights. For example, the cost of chef salaries is much lower at Orly than at CDG for all three activities. Why is this? Are more senior, and higher-paid, chefs at CDG? Is the head chef for the entire company stationed at CDG and included in the CDG figures? Are there too many chefs at CDG? We would need more information to pin down the real reason, but the point is that comparisons of the detailed activity rates may lead to interesting questions for managers to pursue.

Problem 8-17 (75 minutes)

1. The first-stage allocation of costs to activity cost pools appears below:

	Cleaning Carpets	Travel to Jobs	Job Support	Other	Totals
Wages....................	$105,000	$30,000	$ 0	$15,000	$150,000
Cleaning supplies............	40,000	0	0	0	40,000
Cleaning equipment depreciation............	16,000	0	0	4,000	20,000
Vehicle expenses.........	0	48,000	0	32,000	80,000
Office expenses.........	0	0	27,000	33,000	60,000
President's compensation....	0	0	32,000	48,000	80,000
Total cost..............	$161,000	$78,000	$59,000	$132,000	$430,000

According to the data in the problem, 70% of the wages of $150,000 is attributable to activities associated with cleaning carpets.

70% of $150,000 = $105,000

Other entries in the table are determined in a similar manner.

Exercise 8-17 (continued)

2. The activity rates are computed as follows:

	Cleaning Carpets	Travel to jobs	Job Support
Total activity	20,000 hundred square metres	60,000 kilometres driven	2,000 jobs
Wages	$5.25	$0.50	$13.50
Cleaning supplies	2.00		
Cleaning equipment	0.80		
Vehicle expenses		0.80	
Office expenses			16.00
President's compensation			
Total cost	$8.05	$1.30	$29.50

Example: $105,000 ÷ 20,000 hundred square feet = $5.25 per hundred square feet

Wages attributable to cleaning carpets from the first-stage allocation above.

Exercise 8-17 (continued)

3. The cost for the Miller Dairy Farm job is computed as follows:

Activity for the Miller Dairy Farm job...	Cleaning Carpets 5 hundred square feet	Travel to Jobs 75 kilometres driven	Job Support 1 job	Total
Wages	$26.25	$37.50		$63.75
Cleaning supplies	10.00			10.00
Cleaning equipment depreciation	4.00			4.00
Vehicle expenses		60.00		60.00
Office expenses			$13.50	13.50
President's compensation			16.00	16.00
Total cost	$40.25	$97.50	$29.50	$167.25

Example: $5.25 × 5 hundred square feet = $26.25

Activity rate for wages and cleaning carpets.

Problem 8-17 (continued)

4. The product margin can be easily computed below from an activity view by using the costs along the bottom row of the cost table prepared in part (3) above.

Sales		$140.00
Costs:		
Cleaning carpets..........	$40.25	
Travel to jobs	97.50	
Job support..................	29.50	167.25
Product margin		($ 27.25)

5. The product margin can also be easily computed for the activity analysis. In this case, the costs along the right-most column of the cost table prepared in part (3) above are used.

Sales...		$140.00
Green costs:		
Wages..	$63.75	
Cleaning supplies.................................	10.00	
Cleaning equipment depreciation	4.00	
Vehicle expenses	60.00	137.75
Green margin		2.25
Yellow costs:		
Office expenses	13.50	13.50
Yellow margin...		(11.25)
Red costs:		
President's compensation	16.00	16.00
Red margin		($ 27.25)

Problem 8-17 (continued)

4.   The product margin can be easily computed below from an
      activity view by using the costs along the bottom row of the cost
      table prepared in part (3) above.

Sales		$140.00
Costs:		
Cleaning carpets..........	$40.25	
Travel to jobs	97.50	
Job support..................	29.50	167.25
Product margin		($ 27.25)

5.   The product margin can also be easily computed for the activity
      analysis. In this case, the costs along the right-most column of
      the cost table prepared in part (3) above are used.

Sales..		$140.00
Green costs:		
Wages..	$63.75	
Cleaning supplies	10.00	
Cleaning equipment depreciation	4.00	
Vehicle expenses	60.00	137.75
Green margin		2.25
Yellow costs:		
Office expenses	13.50	13.50
Yellow margin...		(11.25)
Red costs:		
President's compensation	16.00	16.00
Red margin		($ 27.25)

Chapter 9
Profit Planning

Exercise 9-1 (20 minutes)

1.

	April	May	June	Total
February sales:				
$230,000 × 10%	$ 23,000			$ 23,000
March sales:				
$260,000 × 70%,				
10%	182,000	$ 26,000		208,000
April sales:				
$300,000 × 20%,				
70%, 10%	60,000	210,000	$ 30,000	300,000
May sales:				
$500,000 × 20%,				
70%		100,000	350,000	450,000
June sales:				
$200,000 × 20%			40,000	40,000
Total cash				
collections	$265,000	$336,000	$420,000	$1,021,000

Observe that even though sales peak in May, cash collections peak in June. This occurs because the bulk of the company's customers pay in the month following sale. The lag in collections which this creates is even more pronounced in some companies. Indeed, it is not unusual for a company to have the least cash available in the months when sales are greatest.

2. Accounts receivable at June 30:

From May sales: $500,000 × 10%................	$ 50,000
From June sales: $200,000 × (70% + 10%) .	160,000
Total accounts receivable..........................	$210,000

Exercise 9-3 (15 minutes)

	Year 2				Year 3
	First	Second	Third	Fourth	First Quarter
Required production in bottles	60,000	90,000	150,000	100,000	70,000
Number of grams per bottle	× 3	× 3	× 3	× 3	× 3
Total production needs—grams	180,000	270,000	450,000	300,000	210,000

	Year 2				
	First	Second	Third	Fourth	Year
Production needs—grams (above)	180,000	270,000	450,000	300,000	1,200,000
Add desired ending inventory—grams*	54,000	90,000	60,000	42,000	42,000
Total needs—grams.........	234,000	360,000	510,000	342,000	1,242,000
Less beginning inventory—grams.......	36,000	54,000	90,000	60,000	36,000
Raw materials to be purchased—grams......	198,000	306,000	420,000	282,000	1,206,000
Cost of raw materials to be purchased at 150 roubles per gram (thousands of roubles)	29,700	45,900	63,000	42,300	180,900

*20% of next quarters production needs, eg: .20 × 270,000 = 54,000 g.

Exercise 9-5 (20 minutes)

	Quarter (000 omitted)				
	1	**2**	**3**	**4**	**Year**
Cash balance, beginning	$ 6*	$ 5	$ 5	$ 5	$ 6
Add collections from customers	65	70	96*	92	323*
Total cash available	71*	75	101	97	329
Less disbursements:					
Purchase of inventory	35*	45*	48	35*	163
Operating expenses	28	30*	30*	25*	113*
Equipment purchases	8*	8*	10*	10	36*
Dividends	2*	2*	2*	2*	8
Total disbursements	73	85*	90	72	320
Excess (deficiency) of cash available over disbursements	(2)*	(10)	11*	25	9
Financing:					
Borrowing	7	15*	—	—	22
Repayments (including interest)	—	—	(6)	(17)*	(23)
Total financing	7	15	(6)	(17)	(1)
Cash balance, ending	$ 5	$ 5	$ 5	$ 8	$ 8

*Given.

Exercise 9-7 (15 minutes)

1. Average weekly usage...................... 50   units
   Lead time... × 4   weeks
   Reorder point..................................... 200   units

The company should reorder when inventory has been depleted to 200 units remaining.

2. a.

   Maximum weekly usage.................... 60   units
   Average weekly usage 50   units
      Difference...................................... 10   units
   Lead time .... × 4   weeks
   Safety stock 40   units

   b.

   Reorder point from part (1) above 200   units
   Add the safety stock from (2a) above. 40   units
   Reorder point 240   units

The company should reorder when the inventory has been depleted to 240 units remaining.

Exercise 9-9 (5 minutes)

1.	b.	3.	a.	5.	b.	7.	b.	9.	a.
2.	a.	4.	a.	6.	b.	8.	a.	10.	b.

Problem 9-11 (40 minutes)

1. Production budget:

	July	August	September	October
Budgeted sales (units).................	35,000	40,000	50,000	30,000
Add desired ending inventory......................................	11,000	13,000	9,000	7,000
Total needs..............................	46,000	53,000	59,000	37,000
Less beginning inventory.............	10,000	11,000	13,000	9,000
Required production....................	36,000	42,000	46,000	28,000

2. During July and August the company is building inventories in anticipation of peak sales in September. Therefore, production exceeds sales during these months. In September and October inventories are being reduced in anticipation of a decrease in sales during the last months of the year. Therefore, production is less than sales during these months to cut back on inventory levels.

3. Raw materials purchases budget:

	July	August	September	Third Quarter
Required production (units)	36,000	42,000	46,000	124,000
Material A production needs per unit	× 3 cc	× 3 cc	× 3 cc	× 3 cc
Production needs (cc)	108,000	126,000	138,000	372,000
Add desired ending inventory (cc)...................	63,000	69,000	42,000 *	42,000
Total material A needs	171,000	195,000	180,000	414,000
Less beginning inventory (cc)....................	54,000	63,000	69,000	54,000
Material A purchases (cc)	117,000	132,000	111,000	360,000

* 28,000 units (October production) × 3 cc = 84,000 cc;
   84,000 cc × 1/2 = 42,000 cc.

As shown in part (1), production is greatest in September; however, as shown in the raw material purchases budget, purchases of materials are greatest a month earlier—in August. The reason for the large purchases of materials in August is that the materials must be on hand to support the heavy production scheduled for September.

Problem 9-13 (40 minutes)

1. a. The reasons that Marge Atkins and Pete Granger use budgetary slack include the following:

    - These employees are hedging against the unexpected (reducing uncertainty/risk).
    - The use of budgetary slack allows employees to exceed expectations and/or show consistent performance. This is particularly important when performance is evaluated on the basis of actual results versus budget.
    - Employees are able to blend personal and organizational goals through the use of budgetary slack as good performance generally leads to higher salaries, promotions, and bonuses.

    b. The use of budgetary slack can adversely affect Atkins and Granger by

    - limiting the usefulness of the budget to motivate their employees to top performance.
    - affecting their ability to identify trouble spots and take appropriate corrective action.
    - reducing their credibility in the eyes of management.

    Also, the use of budgetary slack may affect management decision-making as the budgets will show lower contribution margins (lower sales, higher expenses). Decisions regarding the profitability of product lines, staffing levels, incentives, etc., could have an adverse effect on Atkins' and Granger's departments.

Problem 9-13 (continued)

2.   The use of budgetary slack, particularly if it has a detrimental effect on the company, may be unethical. In assessing the situation, the specific standards that should be considered are listed below.

Competence
Clear reports using relevant and reliable information should be prepared.

Confidentiality
The standards of confidentiality do not apply in this situation.

Integrity
- Any activity that subverts the legitimate goals of the company should be avoided.
- Favourable as well as unfavourable information should be communicated.

Objectivity
- Information should be fairly and objectively communicated.
- All relevant information should be disclosed.

(Unofficial CMA Solution)

Problem 9-15 (60 minutes)

1. The sales budget for the third quarter:

| | Month | | | |
	July	August	September	Quarter
Budgeted sales in units	30,000	70,000	50,000	150,000
Selling price per unit...............	× $12	× $12	× $12	× $12
Budgeted sales...................	$360,000	$840,000	$600,000	$1,800,000

The schedule of expected cash collections from sales:

	July	August	September	Quarter
Accounts receivable, June 30: $300,000 × 65%......................................	$195,000			$195,000
July sales: $360,000 × 30%, 65%............................	108,000	$234,000		342,000
August sales: $840,000 × 30%, 65%.........................		252,000	$546,000	798,000
September sales: $600,000 × 30%			180,000	180,000
Total cash collections	$303,000	$486,000	$726,000	$1,515,000

2. The production budget for July-October:

	July	August	September	October
Budgeted sales in units	30,000	70,000	50,000	20,000
Add desired ending inventory..............	10,500	7,500	3,000	1,500
Total needs......................................	40,500	77,500	53,000	21,500
Less beginning inventory....................	4,500	10,500	7,500	3,000
Required production............................	36,000	67,000	45,500	18,500

Problem 9-15 (continued)

3. The material purchases budget for the third quarter:

	July	August	September	Quarter
		Month		
Required production (above)	36,000	67,000	45,500	148,500
Raw material needs per unit	× 1 m	× 1 m	× 1 m	× 1 m
Production needs (m)	36,000	67,000	45,500	148,500
Add desired ending inventory (m)	33,500	22,750	9,250*	9,250*
Total needs (m)	69,500	89,750	54,750	157,750
Less beginning inventory (m)	18,000	33,500	22,750	18,000
Raw materials to be purchased (m)	51,500	56,250	32,000	139,750
Cost of raw materials to be purchased at $3.20 per m	$164,800	$180,000	$102,400	$447,200

*18,500 units (October) × 1 m. = 18,500 m.; 18,500 m. × 1/2 = 9,250 m.

The schedule of expected cash payments:

	July	August	September	Quarter
Accounts payable, June 30	$ 76,000			$ 76,000
July purchases: $164,800	82,400	$ 82,400		164,800
August purchases: $180,000		90,000	$90,000	180,000
September purchases: $102,400			51,200	51,200
Total cash payments	$158,400	$172,400	$141,200	$472,000

Problem 9-17 (60 minutes)

1. a. Schedule of expected cash collections:

	2000 Quarter				
	First	Second	Third	Fourth	Total
1999—Fourth quarter sales:					
$200,000 × 33%	$ 66,000				$ 66,000
2000—First quarter sales:					
$300,000 × 65%	195,000				195,000
300,000 × 33%		$ 99,000			99,000
2000—Second quarter sales:					
$400,000 × 65%		260,000			260,000
400,000 × 33%			$132,000		132,000
2000—Third quarter sales:					
$500,000 × 65%			325,000		325,000
500,000 × 33%				$165,000	165,000
2000—Fourth quarter sales:					
$200,000 × 65%				130,000	130,000
Total cash collections	$261,000	$359,000	$457,000	$295,000	$1,372,000

Problem 9-17 (continued)

b. Schedule of budgeted cash disbursements for merchandise purchases:

| | 2000 Quarter | | | | |
	First	Second	Third	Fourth	Total
1999—Fourth quarter purchases:					
$126,000 × 20%	$ 25,200				$ 25,200
2000—First quarter purchases:					
$186,000 × 80%	148,800				148,800
186,000 × 20%		$ 37,200			37,200
2000—Second quarter purchases:					
$246,000 × 80%		196,800			196,800
246,000 × 20%			$ 49,200		49,200
2000—Third quarter purchases:					
$305,000 × 80%			244,000		244,000
305,000 × 20%				$ 61,000	61,000
2000—Fourth quarter purchases:					
$126,000 × 80%				100,800	100,800
Total cash payments	$174,000	$234,000	$293,200	$161,800	$863,000

Problem 9-17 (continued)

2. Budgeted operating expenses for 2000:

	2000 Quarter				
	First	Second	Third	Fourth	Year
Budgeted sales	$300,000	$400,000	$500,000	$200,000	$1,400,000
Variable expense rate	× 15%	× 15%	× 15%	× 15%	× 15%
Variable expenses	45,000	60,000	75,000	30,000	210,000
Fixed expenses	50,000	50,000	50,000	50,000	200,000
Total expenses	95,000	110,000	125,000	80,000	410,000
Less depreciation	20,000	20,000	20,000	20,000	80,000
Net cash payments	$ 75,000	$ 90,000	$105,000	$ 60,000	$ 330,000

Problem 9-17 (continued)

3. Cash budget for 2000:

	2000 Quarter				
	First	**Second**	**Third**	**Fourth**	**Year**
Cash balance, beginning	$ 10,000	$ 12,000	$ 10,000	$ 10,800	$ 10,000
Add collections from sales	261,000	359,000	457,000	295,000	1,372,000
Total cash available	271,000	371,000	467,000	305,800	1,382,000
Less disbursements:					
Merchandise purchases	174,000	234,000	293,200	161,800	863,000
Operating expenses (above)	75,000	90,000	105,000	60,000	330,000
Dividends	10,000	10,000	10,000	10,000	40,000
Equipment	-0-	75,000	48,000	-0-	123,000
Total	259,000	409,000	456,200	231,800	1,356,000
Excess (deficiency) of receipts over disbursements	12,000	(38,000)	10,800	74,000	26,000
Financing:					
Borrowing	-0-	48,000	-0-	-0-	48,000
Repayments	-0-	-0-	-0-	(48,000)	(48,000)
Interest	-0-	-0-	-0-	(3,600)	(3,600)
Total	-0-	48,000	-0-	(51,600)*	(3,600)
Cash balance, ending	$ 12,000	$ 10,000	$ 10,800	$ 22,400	$ 22,400

*48,000 × 10% × 9/12 = $3,600.

Problem 9-19 (45 minutes)

1. Computation of the EOQ

	Gross Ordered				
	1	2	3	4	5
a. Average inventory in units	0.5	1.0	1.5	2.0	2.5
b. Number of purchase orders	36	18	12	9	7.2
c. Delivered cost per gross*	$NZ 500	$NZ 500	$NZ 500	$NZ 500	$NZ 500
d. Value of average inventory	$NZ 250	$NZ 500	$NZ 750	$NZ 1,000	$NZ 1,250
Delivered cost of inventory	$NZ18,000	$NZ18,000	$NZ18,000	$NZ18,000	$NZ18,000
Annual carrying cost at 20% of line d (above)	50	100	150	200	250
Annual storage cost at $NZ24 × line a (above)	12	24	36	48	60
Annual ordering cost at $NZ30 × line b (above)	1,080	540	360	270	216
Total annual cost	$NZ19,142	$NZ18,664	$NZ18,546	$NZ18,518	$NZ18,526

The EOQ would be 4 gross.

* Delivered cost = purchase cost plus cost of freight = $NZ800 × .6 + $NZ20 = $NZ500

Problem 9-19 (continued)

2. Average daily usage = $\dfrac{5{,}184 \text{ * annual usage}}{259 \text{ working days}}$ = 20 units per day

Normal lead time = 20 working days
Average lead-period usage: 20 x 20 =   400   units

Maximum daily usage............................	28	units per day
Less average daily usage......................	20	units per day
Excess above average	8	units per day
Times normal lead time	20	days
Safety stock required............................	160	units
Average lead-period usage (above).......	400	units
Safety stock required............................	160	units
Minimum stock reorder point	560	units

Note: The computed minimum stock requirements would increase the carrying and storage costs calculated in part 1. However, the increased costs would be equal for all lot sizes and, therefore, would not affect the EOQ of 4 gross.

*   36 gross × 144 = 5,184 units per year.

Problem 9-21 (120 minutes)

1. Schedule of expected cash collections:

	April		May	June	Quarter
Cash sales	$36,000	*	$43,200	$54,000	$133,200
Credit sales[1]	20,000	*	24,000	28,800	72,800
Total collections	$56,000	*	$67,200	$82,800	$206,000

[1]40% of the preceding month's sales.

*Given.

2. Inventory purchases budget:

	April	May	June	Quarter
Budgeted cost of goods sold[1]	$45,000*	$ 54,000*	$67,500	$166,500
Add desired ending inventory[2]	43,200*	54,000	28,800	28,800
Total needs	88,200*	108,000	96,300	195,300
Less beginning inventory.......	36,000*	43,200	54,000	36,000
Required purchases	$52,200*	$ 64,800	$42,300	$159,300

[1]For April sales: $60,000 sales × 75% cost ratio = $45,000.

[2]At April 30: $54,000 × 80% = $43,200.
 At June 30: July sales $48,000 × 75% cost ratio × 80% = $28,800.

*Given.

Schedule of Expected Cash Disbursements—Purchases

	April	May	June	Quarter
March purchases.................	$21,750*			$ 21,750*
April purchases....................	26,100*	$26,100*		52,200*
May purchases...................		32,400	$32,400	64,800
June purchases..................			21,150	21,150
Total disbursements	$47,850*	$58,500	$53,550	$159,900

*Given.

Problem 9-21 (continued)

3. Schedule of Expected Cash Disbursements—Operating Expenses

	April	May	June	Quarter
Salaries and wages	$ 7,200*	$ 8,640	$10,800	$26,640
Rent	2,500*	2,500	2,500	7,500
Other expenses	3,600*	4,320	5,400	13,320
Total disbursements	$13,300*	$15,460	$18,700	$47,460

*Given.

4. Cash budget:

	April	May	June	Quarter
Cash balance, beginning	$ 8,000*	$ 4,350	$ 4,590	$ 8,000
Add cash collections	56,000*	67,200	82,800	206,000
Total cash available	64,000*	71,550	87,390	214,000
Less disbursements:				
For inventory	47,850*	58,500	53,550	159,900
For expenses	13,300*	15,460	18,700	47,460
For equipment	1,500*	—	—	1,500
Total	62,650*	73,960	72,250	208,860
Excess (deficiency) of cash	1,350*	(2,410)	15,140	5,140
Financing:				
Borrowing	3,000	7,000	—	10,000
Repayments	—	—	(10,000)	(10,000)
Interest	—	—	(230)	(230)
Total financing	3,000	7,000	(10,230)	(230)
Cash balance, ending	$ 4,350	$ 4,590	$ 4,910	$ 4,910

[1]$3,000 x 12% x 3/12 = $ 90

7,000 x 12% x 2/12 =   140

Total interest $230

*Given.

Problem 9-21 (continued)

5.

SHILOW COMPANY
Income Statement
For the Quarter Ended June 30

Sales ($60,000 + $72,000 + $90,000)..........		$222,000
Less cost of goods sold:		
Beginning inventory (Given)	$ 36,000	
Add purchases (Part 2).............................	159,300	
Goods available for sale...........................	195,300	
Ending inventory (Part 2).........................	28,800	166,500*
Gross margin..		55,500
Less operating expenses:		
Salaries and wages (Part 3)	26,640	
Rent (Part 3)...	7,500	
Depreciation ($900 x 3)............................	2,700	
Other expenses (Part 3)...........................	13,320	50,160
Net operating income		5,340
Less interest expense (Part 4)		230
Net income		$ 5,110

*A simpler computation would be: $222,000 × 75% = $166,500.

Problem 9-21 (continued)

6.

SHILOW COMPANY
Balance Sheet
June 30

Assets

Current assets:		
Cash (Part 4)...		$ 4,910
Accounts receivable ($90,000 x 40%)		36,000
Inventory (Part 2)......................................		28,800
Total..		69,710
Fixed assets—net ($120,000 + $1,500 – $2,700)		118,800
Total assets		$188,510

Liabilities and Equity

Accounts payable (Part 2: $42,300 × 50%)..		$ 21,150
Shareholders' equity:		
Capital stock (Given)................................	$150,000	
Retained earnings	17,360*	167,360
Total liabilities and equity........................		$188,510
* Retained earnings, beginning.......................	$ 12,250	
Add net income	5,110	
Retained earnings, ending	$ 17,360	

Problem 9-23 (50 minutes)

1. Collection pattern:

		Percentage of Sales Uncollected at June 30*	Percentage to Be Collected in July
a.	March	1½%	1½%
b.	April	6%	(b) – (a) = 4½%
c.	May	20%	(c) – (b) = 14%
d.	June	100%	(d) – (c) = 80%

*Given.

Schedule of expected cash collections:

From March sales (1½% × $430,000)	$ 6,450
From April sales (4½% × $590,000)	26,550
From May sales (14% × $640,000)...............	89,600
From June sales (80% × $720,000)..............	576,000
Total...	698,600
Less cash discounts ($576,000 × 50% × 2½%)	7,200
Net cash collections	$691,400

2. a. Budgeted cash payments for raw materials purchases:

Accounts payable, June 30.......................	$172,000
July purchases: ½ ($342,000 + $18,000)..	180,000
Total cash payments.............................	$352,000

   b. Budgeted cash payments for overhead:

Indirect labour...		$36,000
Utilities..		1,900
Payroll benefits:		
Company pension plan ($7,000 - $800)..	$ 6,200	
Group insurance (6 x $900)	5,400	
Unemployment insurance	1,300	
Vacation pay...	14,100	27,000
Total cash payments.................................		$64,900

Problem 9-23 (continued)

3.

WALLACE PRODUCTS, LTD.
Cash Budget
July

Cash balance, beginning.............................		$ 78,000
Add collections from customers...................		691,400
Total cash available		769,400
Less disbursements:		
Raw material purchases (above)..............	$352,000	
Direct labour...	95,000	
Overhead (above)	64,900	
Advertising..	110,000	
Sales salaries	50,000	
Administrative salaries............................	35,000	
Shipping	2,100	
Equipment purchases..............................	45,000	754,000
Excess (deficiency) of cash........................		15,400
Financing:		
Borrowing..		60,000
Repayments		—
Interest		—
Total effects		60,000
Cash balance, ending.................................		$ 75,400

4. The statement is incorrect. Even though the cash budget shows that there is an overall excess of cash during the month, there is no assurance that shortages will not develop on a day-to-day basis *during* the month. For example, cash receipts may come later in the month than cash payments— resulting in temporary cash shortages. Unless cash receipts and payments occur uniformly over time, cash budgeting may need to be done on a weekly or daily basis. In addition, unexpected events can create a cash shortage.

Problem 9-25 (20 minutes)

State of Nature (demand)

Quantity Produced	20	22	24	26	28
20	20(2) = 40	40	40	40	40
22	20(2) − 2 = 38	22(2) = 44	44	44	44
24	20(2) − 4 = 36	22(2) − 2 = 42	24(2) = 48	48	48
26	20(2) − 6 = 34	22(2) − 4 = 40	24(2) − 2 = 46	26(2) = 52	52
28	20(2) − 8 = 32	22(2) − 6 = 38	24(2) − 4 = 44	26(2) − 2 = 50	28(2) = 56

EV(produce 20) = $40

EV(produce 22) = .1(38) + .9(44) = $43.40

EV(produce 26) = .1(36) + .2(42) + .7(48) = $45.60

EV(produce 26) = .1(34) + .2(40) + .3(46) + .4(52) = $46.00*

EV(produce 28) = .1(32) + .2(38) + .3(44) + .3(50) + .1(56) = $44.60

Bruno's Bakery should produce 26 dozen doughnuts each morning to maximize net income.

(SMAC Solution, adapted)

Chapter 10
Standard Costs and the Balanced Scorecard

Exercise 10-1 (20 minutes)

1. Cost per 60-litre container $115.00
   Less 2% cash discount 2.30
     Net cost 112.70
   Add freight cost per container
     ($130 ÷ 100) 1.30
   Total cost per 60-litre container .... $114.00 (a)
   Number of quarts per container .... 60 (b)
   Standard cost per quart purchased
     (a) ÷ (b)... $ 1.90

2. Content per bill of materials .... 7.6   lts.
   Add allowance for evaporation and
     spillage (7.6 lts. ÷ 0.95 = 8.0 lts.;
     8.0 qts. – 7.6 lts. = 0.4 lts.)........................... 0.4   lts.
       Total .... 8.0   lts.
   Add allowance for rejected units
     (8.0 lts. ÷ 40 bottles) .... 0.2   lts.
   Standard quantity per salable bottle
     of solvent .... 8.2   lts.

3.

Item	Standard Quantity	Standard Price	Standard Cost per Bottle
Echol	8.2 lts.	$1.90 per lt.	$15.58

Exercise 10-3 (15 minutes)

1.

Actual Quantity of Inputs, at Actual Price (AQ × AP)	Actual Quantity of Inputs, at Standard Price (AQ × SP)	Standard Quantity Allowed for Output, at Standard Price (SQ × SP)
20,000 kgs. × $2.35 per kg. = $47,000	20,000 kgs. × $2.50 per kg. = $50,000	18,400 kgs.* × $2.50 per kg. = $46,000

Price Variance, $3,000 F	Quantity Variance, $4,000 U
Total Variance, $1,000 U	

*4,000 units × 4.6 kgs. per unit = 18,400 kgs.

Alternatively:

Materials price variance = AQ (AP – SP)
20,000 kgs. ($2.35 per kg. – $2.50 per kg.) = $3,000 F

Materials quantity variance = SP (AQ – SQ)
$2.50 per kg. (20,000 kgs. – 18,400 kgs.) = $4,000 U

Exercise 10-3 (continued)

2.

Actual Hours of Input, at the Actual Rate (AH × AR)	Actual Hours of Input, at the Standard Rate (AH × SR)	Standard Hours Allowed for Output, at the Standard Rate (SH × SR)
$10,425	750 hrs. × $12.00 per hr. = $9,000	800 hrs.* × $12.00 per hr. = $9,600

Rate Variance, $1,425 U	Efficiency Variance, $600 F

Total Variance, $825 U

*4,000 units × 0.2 hrs. per unit = 800 hrs.

Alternatively:

Labour rate variance = AH (AR − SR)
750 hrs. ($13.90 per hr.* − $12.00 per hr.) = $1,425 U

*10,425 ÷ 750 hrs. = $13.90 per hr.

Labour efficiency variance = SR (AH − SH)
$12.00 per hr. (750 hrs. − 800 hrs.) = $600 F

Exercise 10-5 (20 minutes)

1. Number of units manufactured............................. 20,000
   Standard labour time per unit................................ × 0.3*
   Total standard hours of labour time allowed........... 6,000
   Standard direct labour rate per hour .... × $12
   Total standard direct labour cost........................... $72,000

   *18 minutes ÷ 60 minutes per hour = 0.3 hours

   Actual direct labour cost $73,600
   Standard direct labour cost.................................... 72,000
   Total variance—unfavourable .... $ 1,600

2. | Actual Hours of Input, at the Actual Rate | Actual Hours of Input, at the Standard Rate | Standard Hours Allowed for Output, at the Standard Rate |
   |---|---|---|

   Alternate Solution:

   Labour rate variance = AH (AR – SR)
   5,750 hrs. ($12.80 per hr.* – $12.00 per hr.) = $4,600 U

   *$73,600 ÷ 5,750 hrs. = $12.80 per hr.

   Labour efficiency variance = SR (AH – SH)
   $12.00 per hr. (5,750 hrs. – 6,000 hrs.) = $3,000 F

Exercise 10-5 (continued)

3.

Actual Hours of Input, at the Actual Rate (AH × AR)	Actual Hours of Input, at the Standard Rate (AH × SR)	Standard Hours Allowed for Output, at the Standard Rate (SH × SR)
$21,850	5,750 hrs. × $4.00 per hr. = $23,000	6,000 hrs. × $4.00 per hr. = $24,000

Spending Variance, $1,150 F	Efficiency Variance, $1,000 F
Total Variance, $2,150 F	

Alternate Solution:

Variable overhead spending variance = AH (AR − SR)
5,750 hrs. ($3.80 per hr.* − $4.00 per hr.) = $1,150 F

*$21,850 ÷ 5,750 hrs. = $3.80 per hr.

Variable overhead efficiency variance = SR (AH − SH)
$4.00 per hr. (5,750 hrs. − 6,000 hrs.) = $1,000 F

Exercise 10-7 (20 minutes)

1. If the total variance is $93 unfavourable, and the rate variance is $87 favourable, then the efficiency variance must be $180 unfavourable, since the rate and efficiency variances taken together always equal the total variance. Knowing that the efficiency variance is $180 unfavourable, one approach to the solution would be:

> Efficiency variance = SR (AH − SH)
> $9.00 per hr. (AH − 125 hrs.*) = $180 U
> $9.00 per hr. x AH − $1,125 = $180**
> $9.00 per hr. x AH = $1,305
>   AH = 145 hrs.

> *50 jobs × 2.5 hrs. per job = 125 hrs.
> **When used with the formula, unfavourable variances are positive and favourable variances are negative.

2. Rate variance = AH (AR − SR)
   145 hrs. (AR − $9.00 per hr.) = $87 F
   145 hrs. x AR − $1,305 = −$87*
   145 hrs. x AR = $1,218
               AR = $8.40

 * When used with the formula, unfavourable variances are positive and favourable variances are negative.

Exercise 10-7 (continued)

An alternative approach to each solution would be to work from known to unknown data in the columnar model for variance analysis:

Actual Hours of Input, at the Actual Rate (AH × AR)	Actual Hours of Input, at the Standard Rate (AH × SR)	Standard Hours Allowed for Output, at the Standard Rate (SH × SR)
145 hrs. × $8.40 per hr. = $1,218	145 hrs. × $9.00 per hr.* = $1,305	125 hrs.[1] × $9.00 per hr.* = $1,125

Rate Variance, $87 F*	Efficiency Variance, $180 U

Total Variance, $93 U*

[1]50 tune-ups* × 2.5 hrs. per tune-up* = 125 hrs.
*Given

Exercise 10-9 (30 minutes)

1. a.

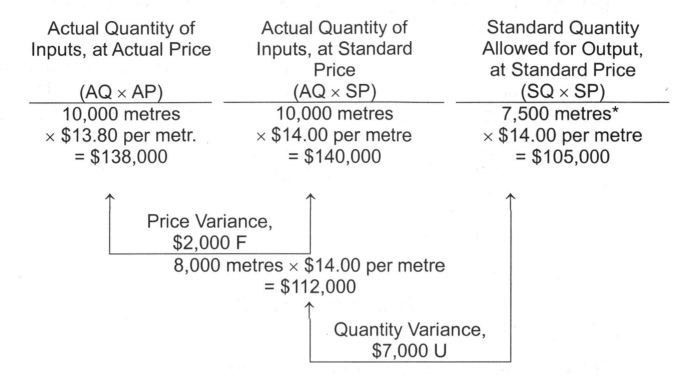

Actual Quantity of Inputs, at Actual Price	Actual Quantity of Inputs, at Standard Price	Standard Quantity Allowed for Output, at Standard Price
(AQ × AP)	(AQ × SP)	(SQ × SP)
10,000 metres × $13.80 per metr. = $138,000	10,000 metres × $14.00 per metre = $140,000	7,500 metres* × $14.00 per metre = $105,000

Price Variance,
$2,000 F

8,000 metres × $14.00 per metre
= $112,000

Quantity Variance,
$7,000 U

*3,000 units × 2.5 metres per unit = 7,500 metres.

Alternatively:

Materials price variance = AQ (AP – SP)
10,000 metres ($13.80 per metre. – $14.00 per metre) = $2,000 F

Materials quantity variance = SP (AQ – SQ)
$14.00 per metre (8,000 metre. – 7,500 metres) = $7,000 U

Exercise 10-9 (continued)

  b. The journal entries would be:

Raw Materials (10,000 metres × $14.00 per metre)	140,000	
Materials Price Variance (10,000 metres × $0.20 per metre F)...		2,000
Accounts Payable (10,000 metres × $13.80 per metre)...		138,000
Work in Process (7,500 metres × $14.00 per metre)...........	105,000	
Materials Quantity Variance (500 metres U × $14.00 per metre)...	7,000	
Raw Materials (8,000 metres × $14.00 per metre)		112,000

2. a.

Actual Hours of Input, at the Actual Rate (AH × AR)	Actual Hours of Input, at the Standard Rate (AH × SR)	Standard Hours Allowed for Output, at the Standard Rate (SH × SR)
$43,000	5,000 hrs. × $8.00 per hr. = $40,000	4,800 hrs.* × $8.00 per hr. = $38,400

Rate Variance, $3,000 U	Efficiency Variance, $1,600 U
Total Variance, $4,600 U	

*3,000 units × 1.6 hrs. per unit = 4,800 hrs.

Alternate Solution:

  Labour rate variance = AH (AR − SR)
  5,000 hrs. ($8.60 per hr.* − $8.00 per hr.) = $3,000 U

    *$43,000 ÷ 5,000 hrs. = $8.60 per hr.

  Labour efficiency variance = SR (AH − SH)
  $8.00 per hr. (5,000 hrs. − 4,800 hrs.) = $1,600 U

Exercise 10-9 (continued)

b. The journal entry would be:

Work in Process (4,800 hrs. × $8.00 per hr.)................ 38,400
Labour Rate Variance (5,000 hrs. × $0.60 per hr. U).... 3,000
Labour Efficiency Variance (200 hrs. U × $8.00 per   1,600
hr.)...
    Wages Payable (5,000 hrs. × $8.60 per hr.)..............   43,000

3. The entries are: entry (a), purchase of materials; entry (b), issue of materials to production; and entry (c), incurrence of direct labour cost.

	Raw Materials					Accounts Payable		
(a)	140,000	112,000	(b)				138,000	(a)
Bal.	28,000*							

	Materials Price Variance					Wages Payable		
		2,000	(a)				43,000	(c)

	Materials Quantity Variance			Labour Rate Variance		
(b)	7,000		(c)	3,000		

	Work in Process—Product A			Labour Efficiency Variance		
Materials				(c)	1,600	
Used (b)	105,000					
Labour						
Cost (c)	38,400					

*2,000 metres. of material at a standard cost of $14.00 per metre.

Problem 10-11 (45 minutes)

1. a. In the solution below, the materials price variance is computed on the entire amount of materials purchased whereas the materials quantity variance is computed only on the amount of materials used in production:

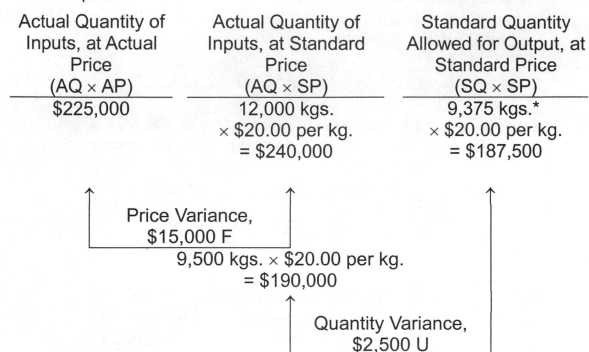

Actual Quantity of Inputs, at Actual Price (AQ × AP)	Actual Quantity of Inputs, at Standard Price (AQ × SP)	Standard Quantity Allowed for Output, at Standard Price (SQ × SP)
$225,000	12,000 kgs. × $20.00 per kg. = $240,000	9,375 kgs.* × $20.00 per kg. = $187,500

Price Variance, $15,000 F

9,500 kgs. × $20.00 per kg. = $190,000

Quantity Variance, $2,500 U

*3,750 units × 2.5 kgs. per unit = 9,375 kgs.

Alternatively:

Materials price variance = AQ (AP – SP)
12,000 kgs. ($18.75 per kg.* – $20.00 per kg.) = $15,000 F

  *$225,000 ÷ 12,000 kgs. = $18.75 per kg.

Materials quantity variance = SP (AQ – SQ)
$20.00 per kg. (9,500 kgs. – 9,375 kgs.) = $2,500 U

b. Yes, the contract probably should be signed. The new price of $18.75 per ounce is substantially lower than the old price of $20.00 per ounce, resulting in a favourable price variance of $15,000 for the month. Moreover, the material from the new supplier appears to cause little or no problem in production as shown by the small materials quantity variance for the month.

Problem 10-11 (continued)

2. a.

Actual Hours of Input, at the Actual Rate (AH × AR)	Actual Hours of Input, at the Standard Rate (AH × SR)	Standard Hours Allowed for Output, at the Standard Rate (SH × SR)
5,600 hrs.* × $12.00 per hr. = $67,200	5,600 hrs. × $12.50 per hr. = $70,000	5,250 hrs.** × $12.50 per hr. = $65,625

Rate Variance, $2,800 F	Efficiency Variance, $4,375 U

Total Variance, $1,575 U

*35 technicians × 160 hrs. per technician = 5,600 hrs.
**3,750 units × 1.4 hrs. per technician = 5,250 hrs.

Alternatively:

Labour rate variance = AH (AR − SR)
5,600 hrs. ($12.00 per hr. − $12.50 per hr.) = $2,800 F

Labour efficiency variance = SR (AH − SH)
$12.50 per hr. (5,600 hrs. − 5,250 hrs.) = $4,375 U

b. No, the new labour mix probably should not be continued.
Although it decreases the average hourly labour cost from $12.50
to $12.00, thereby causing a $2,800 favourable labour rate
variance, this savings is more than offset by a large unfavourable
labour efficiency variance for the month. Thus, the new labour mix
increases overall labour costs.

Problem 10-11 (continued)

3.

Actual Hours of Input, at the Actual Rate (AH × AR)	Actual Hours of Input, at the Standard Rate (AH × SR)	Standard Hours Allowed for Output, at the Standard Rate (SH × SR)
$18,200	5,600 hrs.* × $3.50 per hr. = $19,600	5,250 hrs.** × $3.50 per hr. = $18,375

Spending Variance, $1,400 F	Efficiency Variance, $1,225 U
Total Variance, $175 F	

* Based on direct labour hours : 35 technicians x 160 hours per technician = 5,600 hrs.

** 3,750 units x 1.4 hrs. per unit = 5,250 hrs.

Alternatively:

Variable overhead spending variance = AH (AR – SR)
5,600 hrs. ($3.25 per hr.* – $3.50 per hr.) = $1,400 F

*$18,200 ÷ 5,600 hrs. = $3.25 per hr.

Variable overhead efficiency variance = SR (AH – SH)
$3.50 per hr. (5,600 hrs. – 5,250 hrs.) = $1,225 U

Both the labour efficiency variance and the variable overhead efficiency variance are computed by comparing actual labour-hours to standard labour-hours. Thus, if the labour efficiency variance is unfavourable, then the variable overhead efficiency variance will be unfavourable as well.

Problem 10-13 (50 minutes)

1. a.

Actual Quantity of Inputs, at Actual Price (AQ × AP)	Actual Quantity of Inputs, at Standard Price (AQ × SP)	Standard Quantity Allowed for Output, at Standard Price (SQ × SP)
10,000 m. × $15.36 per m. = $153,600	10,000 m. × $16.00 per m. = $160,000	9,120 m.* × $16.00 per m. = $145,920

Price Variance, $6,400 F	Quantity Variance, $14,080 U

Total Variance, $7,670 U

*10,000 ÷ 1.25 = 8,000, 8,000 footballs × 1.25 m. = 9,120 m.

Alternative Solution:

Materials price variance = AQ (AP − SP)
10,000 m. ($16 per m. − $15.36 per m.) = $6,400 F

Materials quantity variance = SP (AQ − SQ)
$16.00 per m. (10,000 m. − 9,120 m.) = $14,080 U

b. Raw materials (10,000 m. x $16.00 per m.)........... 160,000
    Materials price variance (10,000 m. x
      $0.64 per m. F).. 6,400
    Accounts payable (10,000 m. x $15.36 per m.)... 153,600

Work in process (9,120 m. x $16.00 per m.).......... 145,920
Materials quantity variance (880 m. U
    x $16.00 per m.) 14,080
    Raw materials (10,000 m. x $16.00 per m.)........ 160,000

Problem 10-13 (continued)

2. a.

Actual Hours of Input, at the Actual Rate (AH × AR)	Actual Hours of Input, at the Standard Rate (AH × SR)	Standard Hours Allowed for Output, at the Standard Rate (SH × SR)
6,400 hrs.* × $8.00 per hr. = $51,200	6,400 hrs. × $7.50 per hr. = $48,000	7,200 hrs.** × $7.50 per hr. = $54,000

Rate Variance, $3,200 U	Efficiency Variance, $6,000 F

Total Variance, $2,800 F

*8,000 footballs × 0.8 hrs. per football = 6,400 hrs.
**8,000 footballs × 0.9 hrs. per football = 7,200 hrs.

Alternate Solution:

Labour rate variance = AH (AR − SR)
6,400 hrs. ($8.00 per hr. − $7.50 per hr.) = $3,200 U

Labour efficiency variance = SR (AH − SH)
$7.50 per hr. (6,400 hrs. − 7,200 hrs.) = $6,000 F

b. Work in process (7,200 hrs. x $7.50 per hr.) 54,000
   Labour rate variance (6,400 hrs. x $0.50 per hr. U) ... 3,200
     Labour efficiency variance (800 hrs. F x $7.50
     per hr.) 6,000
     Wages payable (6,400 hrs. x $8.00 per hr.) 51,200

Problem 10-13 (continued)

3.

Actual Hours of Input, at the Actual Rate (AH × AR)	Actual Hours of Input, at the Standard Rate (AH × SR)	Standard Hours Allowed for Output, at the Standard Rate (SH × SR)
6,400 hrs. × $2.75 per hr. = $17,600	6,400 hrs. × $2.50 per hr. = $16,000	7,200 hrs. × $2.50 per hr. = $18,000

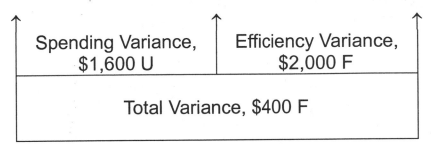

Spending Variance, $1,600 U	Efficiency Variance, $2,000 F

Total Variance, $400 F

Alternate Solution:

Variable overhead spending variance = AH (AR − SR)
6,400 hrs. ($2.75 per hr. − $2.50 per hr.) = $1,600 U

Variable overhead efficiency variance = SR (AH − SH)
$2.50 per hr. (6,400 hrs. − 7,200 hrs.) = $2,000 F

4. No. He is not correct in his statement. The company has a large, unfavourable materials quantity variance that should be investigated. Also, the overhead spending variance equals 10 percent of standard, which should also be investigated.

It appears that the company's strategy to increase output by giving raises was effective. Although the raises resulted in an unfavourable rate variance, this variance was more than offset by a large, favourable efficiency variance.

Problem 10-13 (continued)

5. There are many possible causes of the variances. Some of the more likely causes include the following:

Materials variances:

Favourable price variance: Fortunate buy, outdated standards, inferior quality materials, unusual discount due to quantity purchased, drop in market price, less costly method of freight.

Unfavourable quantity variance: Carelessness, poorly adjusted machines, unskilled workers, inferior quality materials, outdated standards.

Labour variances:

Unfavourable rate variance: Use of highly skilled workers, change in pay scale, outdated standards, overtime.

Favourable efficiency variance: Use of highly skilled workers, high quality materials, new equipment, outdated or inaccurate standards.

Variable overhead variances:

Unfavourable spending variance: Increase in costs, outdated standards, waste, theft, spillage, purchases in uneconomical lots.

Favourable efficiency variance: Same as for labour efficiency variance.

Problem 10-15 (30 minutes)

1. Salex quantity standard:

Required per 10-liter batch (9.6 liters ÷ 0.8)	12.0	litres
Loss from rejected batches (1/5 × 12 litres)	2.4	litres
Total quantity per good batch	14.4	litres

Nyclyn quantity standard:

Required per 10-litre batch (12 kgs. ÷ 0.8)	15.0	kgs.
Loss from rejected batches (1/5 × 15 kgs.)	3.0	kgs.
Total quantity per good batch	18.0	kgs.

Protet quantity standard:

Required per 10-litre batch	5.0	kgs.
Loss from rejected batches (1/5 × 5 kgs.)	1.0	kgs.
Total quantity per good batch	6.0	kgs.

2.

Total minutes per 8-hour day	480	min.
Less rest breaks and cleanup	60	min.
Productive time each day	420	min.

$$\frac{\text{Productive time each day,} \quad 420 \text{ min}}{\text{Time required per batch,} \quad 35 \text{ min.}} = \underline{\text{12 batches per day}}$$

Time required per batch	35	min.
Rest breaks and clean up time		
(60 min. ÷ 12 batches)	5	min.
Total	40	min.
Loss from rejected batches (1/5 × 40 min.)	8	min.
Total time per good batch	48	min.

3. Standard cost card:

	Standard Quantity or Time	Standard Price or Rate	Standard Cost
Salex	14.4 litres	$1.50/ltr.	$21.60
Nyclyn..........................	18.0 kgs.	2.80/kg.	50.40
Protet...........................	6.0 kgs.	3.00/kg.	18.00
Labour time	48 min., or 0.8 hrs.	9.00/hr.	7.20
Total standard cost.....			$97.20

Problem 10-17 (30 minutes)

1. a. Materials quantity variance = SP (AQ − SQ)

   $5.00 per m. (AQ − 9,600 m.*) = $4,500 U
   $5.00 per m. x AQ − $48,000 = $4,500**
   $5.00 per m. x AQ = $52,500
   AQ = 10,500 m.

   *$3,200 units x 3 m. per unit
   **When used with the formula, unfavourable variances are
     positive and favourable variances are negative.

   Therefore, $55,650 ÷ 10,500 m. = <u>$5.30 per m.</u>

   b. Materials price variance = AQ (AP − SP)

   10,500 m. ($5.30 per m. − $5.00 per m.) = <u>$3,150 U</u>

   The total variance for materials would be:

Materials price variance	$3,150	U
Materials quantity variance............	4,500	U
Total variance	$7,650	U

   Alternate approach to parts (a) and (b):

Actual Quantity of Inputs, at Actual Price (AQ × AP)	Actual Quantity of Inputs, at Standard Price (AQ × SP)	Standard Quantity Allowed for Output, at Standard Price (SQ × SP)
10,500 m.	10,500 m.	9,600 m.**
x $5.30 per m.	× $5.00 per m.*	× $5.00 per m.*
= $55,650*	= $52,500	= $48,000

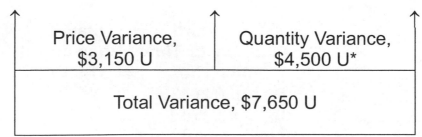

   * Given.
   **3,200 units x 3 m. per unit = 9,600 m.

Problem 10-17 (continued)

2. a. Labour rate variance = AH (AR − SR)

   4,900 hrs. ($7.50 per hr.* − SR) = $2,450 F**

   $36,750 − 4,900 hrs. x SR = −$2,450***

   4,900 hrs. x SR = $39,200

   SR = $8.00

   *$36,750 ÷ 4,900 hrs.
   **$1,650 F + $800 U.
   ***When used with the formula, unfavourable variances are
   positive and favourable variances are negative.

   b. Labour efficiency variance = SR (AH − SH)

   $8.00 per hr. (4,900 hrs. − SH) = $800 U

   $39,200 − $8 per hr. x SH = $800*

   $8.00 per hr. x SH = $38,400

   SH = 4,800 hrs.

   *When used with the formula, unfavourable variances are
   positive and favourable variances are negative.

   Alternate approach to parts (a) and (b):

Actual Hours of Input, at the Actual Rate (AH × AR)	Actual Hours of Input, at the Standard Rate (AH × SR)	Standard Hours Allowed for Output, at the Standard Rate (SH × SR)
$36,750*	4,900 hrs.* × $8.00 per hr. = $39,200	4,800 hrs. × $8.00 per hr. = $38,400

	Rate Variance, $2,450 F	Efficiency Variance, $800 U*
	Total Variance, $1,650 F*	

   *Given.

   c. The standard hours allowed per unit of product would be:

   4,800 hrs. ÷ 3,200 units = 1.5 hrs. per unit

Problem 10-19 (50 minutes)

1. a. Before the variances can be computed, we must first compute the standard and actual quantities of material per hockey stick. The computations are:

Direct materials added to work in process (a)............ $115,200
Standard direct materials cost per metre (b)............. $9.00
Standard quantity of direct materials—last year
  (a) ÷ (b).. 12,800 metres

Standard quantity of direct materials—last year (a) .. 12,800 metres
Number of sticks produced last year (b)   8,000
Standard quantity of direct materials per stick
  (a) ÷ (b)..   1.6 metres

Actual quantity of direct materials used per stick last year.

  1.6 metres + 0.06 metres = 1.66 metres.

With these figures, the variances can be computed as follows:

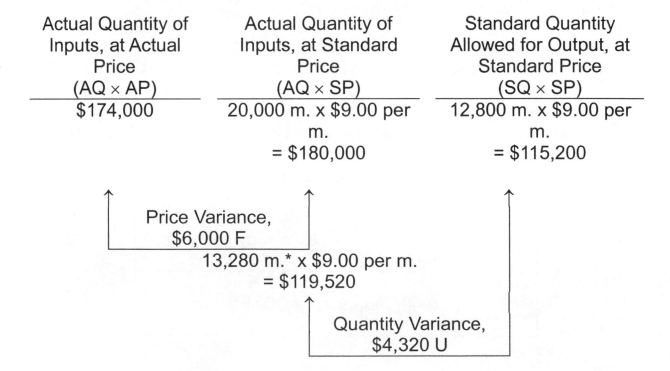

Actual Quantity of Inputs, at Actual Price (AQ × AP)	Actual Quantity of Inputs, at Standard Price (AQ × SP)	Standard Quantity Allowed for Output, at Standard Price (SQ × SP)
$174,000	20,000 m. x $9.00 per m. = $180,000	12,800 m. x $9.00 per m. = $115,200

Price Variance,
$6,000 F
13,280 m.* x $9.00 per m.
= $119,520

Quantity Variance,
$4,320 U

*8,000 units × 1.66 m. per unit = 13,280 m.

Problem 10-19 (continued)

Alternate Solution:

Materials price variance = AQ (AP − SP)
20,000 m. ($8.70 per m.* − $9.00 per m.) = $6,000 F

  *$174,000 ÷ 20,000 m. = $8.70 per m.

Materials quantity variance = SP (AQ − SQ)
$9.00 per m. (12,480 m. − 12,000 m.) = $4,320 U

b. Raw Materials (20,000 m. x $9.00 per m.).......... 180,000
   Materials price variance
     (20,000 m. x $0.30 per m. F)   6,000
     Accounts Payable (20,000 m. x $8.70 per m.)   174,000

   Work in Process (12,800 m. x $9.00)................. 115,200
   Materials quantity variance
     (480 m. U x $9.00 per m.)..............................   4,320
     Raw Materials (13,280 m. x $9.00 per m.)......   119,520

Problem 10-19 (continued)

2. a. Before the variances can be computed, we must first determine the actual direct labour hours worked for last year. This can be done through the variable overhead efficiency variance, as follows:

Variable overhead efficiency variance = SR (AH − SH)
$1.30 per hr. x (AH − 16,000 hrs.*) = $650 U
$1.30 per hr. x AH − $20,800 = $650**
$1.30 per hr. x AH = $21,450
　　　　　　AH = 16,500 hrs.

* 8,000 units x 2.0 hrs. per unit = 16,000 hrs.
**When used in the formula, an unfavourable variance is positive.

We must also compute the standard rate per direct labour hour. The computation is:

Labour rate variance = (AH x AR) − (AH x SR)
$79,200 − (16,500 hrs. x SR) = $3,300 F
$79,200 − 16,500 SR = −$3,300*
16,500 SR = $82,500
　　　SR = $5.00

* When used in the formula, a favourable variance is negative.

Problem 10-19 (continued)

Given these figures, the variances are:

Actual Hours of Input, at the Actual Rate (AH × AR)	Actual Hours of Input, at the Standard Rate (AH × SR)	Standard Hours Allowed for Output, at the Standard Rate (SH × SR)
$79,200	16,500 hrs. × $5.00 per hr. = $82,500	16,000 hrs. × $5.00 per hr. = $80,000

Rate Variance, $3,300 F	Efficiency Variance, $2,500 U

Total Variance, $800 F

Alternate Solution:

Labour rate variance = AH (AR – SR)
16,500 hrs. ($4.80 per hr.* – $5.00 per hr.) = $3,300 F

*79,200 ÷ 16,500 hrs. = $4.80 per hr.

Labour efficiency variance = SR (AH – SH)
$5.00 per hr. (16,500 hrs. – 16,000 hrs.) = $2,500 U

b. Work in process (16,000 hrs. x $5.00 per hr.) 80,000
   Labour efficiency variance (500 hrs. U x $5.00 per hr.).   2,500
      Labour rate variance (16,500 hrs. x $0.20 per hr. F)..   3,300
      Wages payable (16,500 hrs. x $4.80 per hr.)   79,200

Problem 10-19 (continued)

3.

Actual Hours of Input, at the Actual Rate (AH × AR)	Actual Hours of Input, at the Standard Rate (AH × SR)	Standard Hours Allowed for Output, at the Standard Rate (SH × SR)
$19,800	16,500 hrs. × $1.30 per hr. = $21,450	16,000 hrs. × $1.30 per hr. = $20,800

Spending Variance, $1,650 F	Efficiency Variance, $650 U

Total Variance, $1,000 F

Alternate Solution:

Variable overhead spending variance = AH (AR − SR)
16,500 hrs. ($1.20 per hr.* − $1.30 per hr.) = $1,650 F

*$19,800 ÷ 16,500 hrs. = $1.20 per hr.

Variable overhead efficiency variance = SR (AH − SH)
$1.30 per hr. (16,500 hrs. − 16,000 hrs.) = $650 U

Problem 10-19 (continued)

4. *For materials:*

Favourable price variance: Decrease in outside purchase price; fortunate buy; inferior quality materials; unusual discounts due to quantity purchased; less costly method of freight; inaccurate standards.

Unfavourable quantity variance: Inferior quality materials; carelessness; poorly adjusted machines; unskilled workers; inaccurate standards.

For labour:

Favourable rate variance: Unskilled workers (paid lower rates); piecework; inaccurate standards.

Unfavourable efficiency variance: Poorly trained workers; poor quality materials; faulty equipment; work interruptions; fixed labour and insufficient demand to fill capacity; inaccurate standards.

For variable overhead:

Favourable spending variance: Decrease in supplier prices; inaccurate standards; less usage of lubricants or indirect materials than planned.

Unfavourable efficiency variance: See comments under direct labour efficiency variance above.

5.

	Standard Quantity or Hours	Standard Price or Rate	Standard Cost
Direct materials.............	1.6 metres	$9.00 per metre	$14.40
Direct labour	2.0 hours	$5.00 per hour	10.00
Variable overhead.........	2.0 hours	$1.30 per hour	2.60
Total standard cost.....			$27.00

Problem 10-21 (30 minutes)

1. a., b., and c.

	Month			
	1	**2**	**3**	**4**
Throughput time—days:				
Process time (x)...............................	2.1	2.0	1.9	1.8
Inspection time	0.8	0.7	0.7	0.7
Move time...	0.3	0.4	0.4	0.5
Queue time during production..........	2.8	4.4	6.0	7.0
Total throughput time (y)	6.0	7.5	9.0	10.0
Manufacturing cycle efficiency (MCE):				
Process time (x) ÷ Throughput				
time (y)	35.0%	26.7%	21.1%	18.0%
Delivery cycle time—days:				
Wait time from order to start of				
production......................................	9.0	11.5	12.0	14.0
Throughput time	6.0	7.5	9.0	10.0
Total delivery cycle time...............	15.0	19.0	21.0	24.0

2. a. Areas where the company is improving:

Quality control. The number of defects has decreased by over 50% in the last four months. Moreover, both warranty claims and customer complaints are down sharply. In short, overall quality appears to have improved greatly with the new automated system.

Material control. The purchase order lead time is only half of what it was four months ago, which indicates that purchases are arriving in less time. This trend may be a result of the company's move toward JIT purchasing.

Delivery performance. The process time has decreased from 2.1 days to just 1.8 days over the last four months. This decrease in the process time probably is the result of the company's move toward automation of the production line.

Problem 10-21 (continued)

b. Areas of deterioration:

Material control. The scrap as a percentage of total cost has tripled over the last four months.

Machine performance. Machine downtime has doubled over the last four months. This may be a result of the greater setup time, or it may just reflect efforts to get the new equipment operating properly. Management certainly should direct attention toward reducing the setup time. Also note that use of the machines as a percentage of availability is declining rapidly.

Delivery performance. All delivery performance measures are moving in the wrong direction. Throughput time and delivery cycle time are both increasing, and the manufacturing cycle efficiency is decreasing. Overall, the company is giving poorer service to its customers.

3. a. and b.

	Month	
	5	**6**
Throughput time—days:		
Process time (x)...	1.8	1.8
Inspection time	0.7	—
Move time..	0.5	0.5
Queue time during production......................	—	—
Total throughput time (y)	3.0	2.3

Manufacturing cycle efficiency (MCE):
  Process time (x) ÷ Throughput time (y)......... 60.0%   78.3%

As a company reduces non-value-added activities, the manufacturing cycle efficiency increases rapidly. The goal, of course, is to have an efficiency of 100%. This is achieved when all non-value-added activities have been eliminated and process time is equal to throughput time.

Problem 10-23 (30 minutes)

1. Standard cost per ten-bottle batch of raspberry sherbet.

Direct material:

Raspberries (7.5 litres* x $0.80 per L.)	$6.00	
Other ingredients (10 bottles. x $0.45)............	4.50	$10.50

Direct labour:

Sorting $\left[\dfrac{(3\,\text{min.\,per\,litre.}\times 6\,\text{litres})}{60\,\text{min.\,per\,hr.}}\times \$9.00\,\text{per\,hr.}\right]$ 2.70

Blending (12 min. ÷ 60) x $9.00 per hr.	1.80	4.50
Packing (40 litres.** × $0.38 per litre.).............		15.20
Standard cost per ten-gallon batch		$30.20

*6 litres x (5 ÷ 4) = 7.5 litres required to obtain 6 acceptable litres.
**4 litres per bottle x 10 bottles = 40 litres.

2. a. In general, the purchasing manager is held responsible for unfavourable material price variances. Causes of these variances include the following:

- Incorrect standards.

- Failure to correctly forecast price increases.

- Purchasing in nonstandard or uneconomical lots.

- Failure to take purchase discounts available.

- Failure to control transportation costs.

- Purchasing from suppliers other than those offering the most favourable terms.

However, failure to meet price standards may be caused by a rush of orders or changes in production schedules. In this case, the responsibility for unfavourable material price variances should rest with the sales manager or the manager of production planning. There may also be times when variances are caused by external events and are therefore uncontrollable, e.g., a strike at a supplier's plant.

Problem 10-23 (continued)

b. In general, the production manager or foreman is held responsible for unfavourable labour efficiency variances. Causes of these variances include the following:

- Incorrect standards.
- Poorly trained labour.
- Substandard or inefficient equipment.
- Inadequate supervision.
- Machine breakdowns from poor maintenance.
- Poorly motivated employees/absenteeism.
- Fixed labour force with demand less than capacity.

Failure to meet labour efficiency standards may also be caused by the use of inferior materials or poor production planning. In these cases, responsibility should rest with the purchasing manager or the manager of production planning. There may also be times when variances are caused by external events and are therefore uncontrollable, e.g., lack of skilled workers caused by low unemployment.

(Unofficial CMA Solution, Adapted)

Problem 10-25

Material Variances
Equivalent units

To complete beginning WIP (15,000 units × 0%)	0
Started and completed (37,000 – 15,000	22,000
Ending WIP (15,000 × 100%)	15,000
Total units	37,000

Standard Cost of Materials Issued:

A 750,000 ×	.90	$ 675,000		Mix Variance
B 180,000 ×	2.50	450,000		
930,000		1,125,000		$ 5,400 U
				15,000 F
Actual material used as standard mix				$ 9,600 F

A $\frac{20}{25}$ 744,000 × .90 $ 669,600

B $\frac{5}{25}$ $\frac{186,000}{930,000}$ × 2.50 $\frac{465,000}{\$1,134,600}$ Yield Variance

Standard materials for actual production

		$3,600 U
A (37,000 × 20) × .90 $ 666,000		2,500 U
		$6,100 U

B (37,000 × 5) × 2.50 $\frac{462,500}{\$1,128,500}$

Labour Variances
  Equivalent units

To complete beginning WIP (15,000 × .80)	12,000
Started and completed (37,000 – 15,000)	22,000
Ending WIP (14,000 × .75).	10,500
Total units	44,500

Actual labour costs $3,248,250

Problem 10-25 (continued)

		$53,250 U
		Rate Variance
Standard of actual hours		
213,000 × $15	3,195,000	
		$46,875 U
		Efficiency
Cost of actual production		Variance
44,500 × 4.75 × $15	3,241,875	

Chapter 11
Flexible Budgets and Overhead Analysis

Exercise 11-1 (10 minutes)

Note: All numbers below are in Swiss francs, with the exception of the number of cars.

LAVAGE RAPIDE
Flexible Budget
For the Month Ended August 31

Overhead Costs	Cost Formula (per car)	Activity (cars) 8,000	9,000	10,000
Variable overhead costs:				
Cleaning supplies	0.80	6,400	7,200	8,000
Electricity	0.30	2,400	2,700	3,000
Maintenance	0.20	1,600	1,800	2,000
Total variable overhead costs	1.30	10,400	11,700	13,000
Fixed overhead costs:				
Operator wages		9,000	9,000	9,000
Depreciation		6,000	6,000	6,000
Rent		8,000	8,000	8,000
Total fixed overhead costs		23,000	23,000	23,000
Total overhead costs		33,400	34,700	36,000

Exercise 11-3 (10 minutes)

Note: All numbers below are in Swiss francs, with the exception of the number of cars.

LAVAGE RAPIDE
Flexible Budget Performance Report
For the Month Ended August 31

Budgeted number of cars 8,800
Actual number of cars 8,900

Overhead Costs	Cost Formula (per car)	Actual Costs Incurred for 8,900 Cars	Budget Based on 8,900 Cars	Variance
Variable overhead costs:				
Cleaning supplies	0.80	7,080	7,120	40 F
Electricity	0.30	2,460	2,670	210 F
Maintenance	0.20	1,550	1,780	230 F
Total variable overhead costs	1.30	11,090	11,570	480 F
Fixed overhead costs:				
Operator wages		9,100	9,000	100 U
Depreciation		7,000	6,000	1,000 U
Rent		8,000	8,000	-0-
Total fixed overhead costs		24,100	23,000	1,100 U
Total overhead costs		35,190	34,570	620 U

Some may wonder why there are variances for operator wages and for depreciation. Fixed costs can change; they just don't vary with the level of activity. Operator wages can differ from what was budgeted for a variety of reasons including an unanticipated increase in the wage rate; changes in the mix of workers between those earning lower and higher wages; changes in the number of operators on duty; and overtime. Depreciation may have increased because of the acquisition of new equipment or because of a loss on equipment that must be scrapped—perhaps due to poor maintenance. (This assumes that the loss flows through the depreciation account on the performance report.)

Exercise 11-5 (20 minutes)

1.
MURRAY COMPANY
Variable Overhead Performance Report

Budgeted machine-hours.. 12,000
Actual machine-hours worked............................... 11,500

	Actual 11,500 hours	Budget 11,500 hours	Spending Variance
Variable overhead costs:			
Supplies.......................	$ 2,400	$ 2,300	$ 100 U
Maintenance................	8,000	9,200	1,200 F
Utilities.........................	1,100	1,150	50 F
Rework time.................	5,300	4,600	700 U
Total costs.................	$16,800	$17,250	$ 450 F

2. Favourable variances can be as much a matter of managerial concern
as unfavourable variances. The favourable maintenance variance undoubtedly would require investigation. Efforts should be made to determine if scheduled maintenance is not being carried out. In terms of percentage deviation from budgeted allowances, the rework time variance is even more significant (equal to 15% of the budget allowance). It may be that this unfavourable variance in rework time is a result of poor maintenance of machines. Some may say that if the two variances are related, then the trade-off is a good one, since the savings in maintenance cost is greater than the added cost of rework time. But this is shortsighted reasoning. Poor maintenance can reduce the life of equipment, as well as decrease overall output, thereby costing far more in the long run than any short-run savings.

Exercise 11-7 (10 minutes)

1. Predetermined overhead rate:

$$\frac{\text{Total overhead from the flexible budget at the denominator activity,}}{\text{Denominator activity,}} \quad \frac{\$225{,}000}{30{,}000 \text{ DLH}} = \$7.50 \text{ per DLH}$$

Variable element: $57,000 ÷ 30,000 DLH = $1.90 per DLH

Fixed element: $168,000 ÷ 30,000 DLH = $5.60 per DLH

2.
Direct materials, 2.5 metres @ $8.60......................	$21.50
Direct labour, 3 hours* @ $6.00.............................	18.00
Variable overhead, 3 hours @ $1.90......................	5.70
Fixed overhead, 3 hours @ $5.60..........................	16.80
Total standard cost per unit.................................	$62.00

*30,000 hours ÷ 10,000 units = 3 hours per unit.

Exercise 11-9 (10 minutes)

Company A: A favourable volume variance, since the standard hours allowed for the actual production are greater than the denominator hours.

Company B: An unfavourable volume variance, since the standard hours allowed for the actual production are less than the denominator hours.

Company C: No volume variance, since the standard hours allowed for the actual production and the denominator hours are the same.

Exercise 11-11 (15 minutes)

1. 14,000 units produced x 3 hrs. per unit = 42,000 standard hours.

2. Actual fixed overhead costs $267,000
    Add: Favourable budget variance 3,000
    Flexible budget fixed overhead cost...................... $270,000

$$\frac{\text{Flexible budget fixed overhead cost, } \$270,000}{\text{Denominator hours, } 45,000} = \$6 \text{ per MH}$$

3. $\text{Volume variance} = \text{Fixed portion of the predetermined overhead rate} \left(\text{Denominator hours} - \text{Standard hours allowed} \right)$

$6 per hr. (45,000 hrs. − 42,000 hrs.) = $18,000 U

Alternate solution to parts 1-3:

Actual Fixed Overhead Cost	Flexible Budget Fixed Overhead Cost	Fixed Overhead Cost Applied to Work in Process
$267,000*	$270,000[1]	42,000 hrs.[2] × $6 per hr.[3] = $252,000

Budget Variance, $3,000 F*   Volume Variance, $18,000 U

[1] $267,000 + $3,000 = $270,000.

[2] 14,000 units × 3 hrs. per unit = 42,000 hrs.

[3] $270,000 ÷ 45,000 denominator hours = $6 per DLH.

*Given.

Exercise 11-13 (30 minutes)

1. The cost formulas in the flexible budget report below were obtained by dividing the costs on the static budget in the problem statement by the budgeted level of activity (500 liters). The fixed costs are carried over from the static budget.

ST. LUCIA BLOOD BANK
Flexible Budget Performance Report
For the Month Ended September 30

Budgeted activity (in liters) 500
Actual activity (in liters).................. 620

Costs	Cost Formula (per liter)	Actual Costs Incurred for 620 Liters	Budget Based on 620 Liters	Variance	
Variable costs:					
Medical supplies.................	$15.00	$ 9,350	$ 9,300	$ 50	U
Lab tests	12.00	6,180	7,440	1,260	F
Refreshments for donors....	2.00	1,340	1,240	100	U
Administrative supplies.......	0.50	400	310	90	U
Total variable costs	$29.50	17,270	18,290	1,020	F
Fixed costs:					
Staff salaries		10,000	10,000	-	
Equipment depreciation......		2,800	2,500	300	U
Rent		1,000	1,000	-	
Utilities		570	500	70	U
Total fixed costs		14,370	14,000	370	U
Total costs...........................		$31,640	$32,290	$ 650	F

Exercise 11-13 (continued)

2.   The overall variance is favourable and none of the unfavourable variances is particularly large. Nevertheless, the large favourable variance for lab tests is worrisome. Perhaps the blood bank has not been doing all of the lab tests for HIV, hepatitis, and other blood-transmittable diseases that it should be doing. This is well worth investigating and points out that favourable variances may warrant attention as much as unfavourable variances.

Some may wonder why there is a variance for depreciation. Fixed costs can change; they just don't vary with the level of activity. Depreciation may have increased because of the acquisition of new equipment or because of a loss on equipment that must be scrapped. (This assumes that the loss flows through the depreciation account on the performance report.)

Problem 11-15 (45 minutes)

1. Total rate: $\dfrac{PZ297,500}{35,000\ LH} = PZ8.50$ per LH

   Variable rate: $\dfrac{PZ87,500}{35,000\ LH} = PZ2.50$ per LH

   Fixed rate: $\dfrac{PZ210,000}{35,000\ LH} = PZ6.00$ per LH

2. 32,000 standard hours × PZ8.50 per LH = PZ272,000.

3. Variable overhead variances:

Actual Hours of Input, at the Actual Rate (AH × AR)	Actual Hours of Input, at the Standard Rate (AH × SR)	Standard Hours Allowed for Output, at the Standard Rate (SH × SR)
PZ78,000	30,000 hrs. × PZ2.50 per hr. = PZ75,000	32,000 hrs. × PZ2.50 per hr. = PZ80,000

Spending Variance, PZ3,000 U	Efficiency Variance, PZ5,000 F

Alternate solution:

Variable overhead spending variance = (AH × AR) − (AH × SR)
(PZ78,000) − (30,000 hrs. × PZ2.50 per hr.) = PZ3,000 U

Variable overhead efficiency variance = SR (AH − SH)
PZ2.50 per hr. (30,000 hrs. − 32,000 hrs.) = PZ5,000 F

Problem 11-15 (continued)

Fixed overhead variances:

Actual Fixed Overhead Cost	Flexible Budget Fixed Overhead Cost	Fixed Overhead Cost Applied to Work in Process
PZ209,400	PZ210,000	32,000 hrs. × PZ6 per hr. = PZ192,000

Budget Variance, PZ600 F | Volume Variance, PZ18,000 U

Alternate solution:

Budget variance:

$$\text{Budget variance} = \text{Actual fixed overhead cost} - \text{Flexible budget fixed overhead cost}$$

$$= PZ209,400 - PZ210,000 = PZ600 \text{ F}$$

Volume variance:

$$\text{Volume variance} = \text{Fixed portion of the predetermined overhead rate} \left(\text{Denominator hours} - \text{Standard hours allowed} \right)$$

PZ6 per hr. (35,000 hrs. − 32,000 hrs.) = PZ18,000 U

Verification:
Variable overhead:	
Spending variance	PZ 3,000U
Efficiency variance	5,000F
Fixed overhead:	
Budget variance	600F
Volume variance	18,000U
Underapplied overhead	PZ15,400

Problem 11-15 (continued)

4. Variable overhead

Spending variance: This variance includes both price and quantity elements. The overhead spending variance reflects differences between actual and standard prices for variable overhead items. It also reflects differences between the amounts of variable overhead inputs that were actually used and the amounts that should have been used for the actual output of the period. Since the variable overhead spending variance is unfavourable, either too much was paid for variable overhead items or too many of them were used.

Efficiency variance: The term "variable overhead efficiency variance" is a misnomer, since the variance does not measure efficiency in the use of overhead items. It measures the indirect effect on variable overhead of the efficiency or inefficiency with which the activity base is utilized. In this company, labour-hours is the activity base. If variable overhead is really proportional to labour-hours, then more effective use of labour-hours has the indirect effect of reducing variable overhead. Since 2,000 fewer labour-hours were required than indicated by the labour standards, the indirect effect was presumably to reduce variable overhead spending by about PZ 5,000 (PZ 2.50 per hour × 2,000 hours).

Fixed overhead

Budget variance: This variance is simply the difference between the budgeted fixed cost and the actual fixed cost. In this case, the variance is favourable which indicates that actual fixed costs were lower than anticipated in the budget.

Volume variance: This variance occurs as a result of actual activity being different from the denominator activity in the predetermined overhead rate. In this case, the variance is unfavourable, so actual activity was less than the denominator activity. It is difficult to place much of a meaningful economic interpretation on this variance. It tends to be large, so it often swamps the other, more meaningful variances if they are simply netted against each other.

Problem 11-17 (35 minutes)

1.

FAB COMPANY
Flexible Budget
For the Month Ended March 31

Overhead Costs	Cost Formula (per MH)	Machine-Hours		
		20,000	25,000	30,000
Variable costs:				
Utilities	$0.90	$ 18,000	$ 22,500	$ 27,000
Maintenance....................	1.60	32,000	40,000	48,000
Machine setup.................	0.30	6,000	7,500	9,000
Indirect labour	0.70	14,000	17,500	21,000
Total variable costs.......	$3.50	70,000	87,500	105,000
Fixed costs:				
Maintenance....................		40,000	40,000	40,000
Indirect labour		130,000	130,000	130,000
Depreciation....................		70,000	70,000	70,000
Total fixed costs............		240,000	240,000	240,000
Total overhead costs		$310,000	$327,500	$345,000

Problem 11-17 (continued)

2.

FAB COMPANY
Overhead Performance Report
For the Month Ended March 31

Budgeted machine-hours...................................... 30,000
Actual machine-hours 26,000

Overhead Costs	Cost Formula (per MH)	Actual 26,000 Hours	Budget 26,000 Hours	Spending or Budget Variance
Variable costs:				
Utilities	$0.90	$ 24,200	$ 23,400	$ 800U
Maintenance................	1.60	38,100*	41,600	3,500F
Machine setup.............	0.30	8,400	7,800	600U
Indirect labour	0.70	19,600	18,200	1,400U
Total variable costs...	$3.50	90,300	91,000	700F
Fixed costs:				
Maintenance................		40,000	40,000	—
Indirect labour		130,000	130,000	—
Depreciation................		71,500	70,000	1,500U
Total fixed costs........		241,500	240,000	1,500U
Total overhead costs		$331,800	$331,000	$ 800U

*$78,100 total maintenance cost, less $40,000 fixed maintenance cost, equals $38,100 variable maintenance cost. The variable element of other costs is computed in the same way.

3. In order to compute an overhead efficiency variance, it would be necessary to know the standard hours allowed for the 15,000 units produced during March.

Problem 11-19 (20 minutes)

Budgeted machine-hours................................ 11,250
Actual machine-hours................................... 9,250
Standard machine-hours allowed................. 9,000

Overhead Item	Cost Formula	Actual Costs Incurred (1)	Budget based on 9,250 hrs. (2)	Budget based on 9,000 hrs. (3)	Total Variance (1) – (3)	Breakdown of the Total Variance	
						Spending Variance (1) – (2)	Efficiency Variance (2) – (3)
Power........................	$0.30	$2,405	$2,775	$2,700	$ 295 F	$ 370 F	$ 75 U
Setup time	0.20	2,035	1,850	1,800	235 U	185 U	50 U
Polishing wheels......	0.16	1,110	1,480	1,440	330 F	370 F	40 U
Maintenance............	0.18	925	1,665	1,620	695 F	740 F	45 U
Total variable costs	$0.84	$6,475	$7,770	$7,560	$1,085 F	$1,295 F	$210 U

Problem 11-21 (45 minutes)

1. Total rate: $\dfrac{\$432{,}000}{40{,}000 \text{ DLH}} = \$10.80$ per DLH

   Variable rate: $\dfrac{\$72{,}000}{40{,}000 \text{ DLH}} = \$1.80$ per DLH

   Fixed rate: $\dfrac{\$360{,}000}{40{,}000 \text{ DLH}} = \$9$ per DLH

2.
Direct materials: 8 yds. at $4.50	$36.00
Direct labour: 2.5 hours at $6.00	15.00
Variable overhead: 2.5 hours at $1.80	4.50
Fixed overhead: 2.5 hours at $9	22.50
Standard cost per unit	$78.00

3. See the graph at the end of this solution.

4. a. Fixed overhead variances:

Actual Fixed Overhead Cost	Flexible Budget Fixed Overhead Cost	Fixed Overhead Cost Applied to Work in Process
$361,800	$360,000	35,000 hrs.* × $9 per hr. = $315,000

	Budget Variance, $1,800 U	Volume Variance, $45,000 U	

*14,000 units × 2.5 hrs. per unit = 35,000 hrs.

Problem 11-21 (continued)

Alternate approach:

Budget variance:

$$\text{Budget variance} = \text{Actual fixed overhead cost} - \text{Flexible budget fixed overhead cost}$$

$$= \$361,800 - \$360,000 = \$1,800 \text{ U}$$

Volume variance:

$$\text{Volume variance} = \text{Fixed portion of the predetermined overhead rate} \left(\text{Denominator hours} - \text{Standard hours allowed} \right)$$

$$\$9 \text{ per hr. } (40,000 \text{ hrs.} - 35,000 \text{ hrs.}) = \$45,000 \text{ U}$$

b. See the graph at the end of this solution.

5. a. The fixed overhead budget variance will not change. The fixed overhead volume variance will be:

Actual Fixed Overhead Cost $361,800	Flexible Budget Fixed Overhead Cost $360,000	Fixed Overhead Cost Applied to Work in Process 50,000 hrs.* × $9 per hr. = $450,000

	Budget Variance, $1,800 U	Volume Variance, $90,000 F

*20,000 units × 2.5 hrs. per unit = 50,000 hrs.

Problem 11-21 (continued)

Alternate solution to the volume variance:

$$\text{Volume variance} = \begin{pmatrix} \text{Fixed portion of the predetermined overhead rate} \end{pmatrix} \begin{pmatrix} \text{Denominator hours} - \text{Standard hours allowed} \end{pmatrix}$$

$9 per hr. (40,000 hrs. − 50,000 hrs.) = $90,000 F

b. See the graph on the following page.

Problem 11-21 (continued)

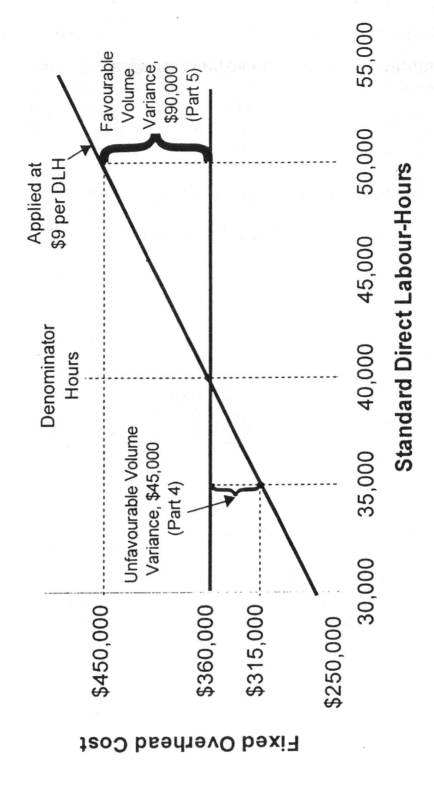

Problem 11-23 (45 minutes)

1. The overall readability of a flexible budget is enhanced if the variable and fixed costs are shown separately, as illustrated in the text, and if individual cost formulas are given. Fixed and variable costs can be separated (and cost formulas determined) by the high-low method. Incorporating these ideas, the revised flexible budget format would be:

GANT PRODUCTS, INC.
Flexible Budget

Overhead Costs	Cost Formula	Percentage of Capacity		
		80%	90%	100%
Machine-hours		4,800	5,400	6,000
Variable costs:				
Maintenance......................	$0.10/MH	$ 480	$ 540	$ 600
Supplies	0.40/MH	1,920	2,160	2,400
Utilities	0.30/MH	1,440	1,620	1,800
Machine setup..................	0.20/MH	960	1,080	1,200
Total variable costs.........	$1.00/MH	4,800	5,400	6,000
Fixed costs:				
Maintenance......................		1,000	1,000	1,000
Utilities		500	500	500
Supervision		3,000	3,000	3,000
Total fixed costs.............		4,500	4,500	4,500
Total overhead costs		$9,300	$9,900	$10,500

2. The cost formula for all overhead costs would be $4,500 plus $1.00 per machine-hour.

Problem 11-23 (continued)

3.

GANT PRODUCTS, INC.
Overhead Performance Report
For the Month of April

Budgeted machine-hours.......................................	6,000
Standard machine-hours	5,600
Actual machine-hours...	5,700*

Overhead Costs	Cost Formulas	Actual 5,700 MH	Budgeted 5,700 MH	Spending Variance
Variable overhead:				
Maintenance................	$0.10/MH	$ 1,083**	$ 570	$ 513 U
Supplies	0.40/MH	3,420	2,280	1,140 U
Utilities	0.30/MH	2,166**	1,710	456 U
Machine setup.............	0.20/MH	855	1,140	285 F
Total variable costs...	$1.00/MH	7,524	5,700	1,824 U
Fixed overhead:				
Maintenance................		1,000	1,000	—
Utilities		500	500	—
Supervision		3,000	3,000	—
Total fixed costs........		4,500	4,500	—
Total overhead costs		$12,024	$10,200	$1,824 U

*95% × 6,000 hrs. = 5,700 hrs.
**$2,083 less $1,000 fixed = $1,083.
  $2,666 less $500 fixed = $2,166.

4. a. Assuming that the variable overhead really should be proportional to actual machine-hours, the unfavourable spending variance in this situation would be a result of waste, rather than a result of price differentials. Unlike the price variance for materials and the rate variance for labour, the spending variance for variable overhead measures both price and waste elements. This is why the variance is called a "spending" variance. Total spending can be affected as much by waste as it can by greater (or lesser) prices paid for items.

Problem 11-23 (continued)

b. Efficiency variance = SR (AH – SH)
$1 per hr. (5,700 hrs. – 5,600 hrs.) = $100 U

The overhead efficiency variance is really misnamed, since it does not measure efficiency (waste) in use of variable overhead items. The variance arises solely because of the inefficiency in the *base* underlying the incurrence of variable overhead cost. If the incurrence of variable overhead costs is directly tied to the actual machine-hours worked, then the excessive number of machine-hours worked during April has caused the incurrence of an additional $100 in variable overhead costs.

Problem 11-25 (45 minutes)

1. and 2.

	Per Direct Labour-Hour		
	Variable	**Fixed**	**Total**
Denominator of 30,000 DLH:			
$135,000 ÷ 30,000 DLH........................	$4.50		$ 4.50
$270,000 ÷ 30,000 DLH........................		$9.00	9.00
Total predetermined rate			$13.50
Denominator of 40,000 DLH:			
$180,000 ÷ 40,000 DLH........................	$4.50		$ 4.50
$270,000 ÷ 40,000 DLH........................		$6.75	6.75
Total predetermined rate			$11.25

3.

Denominator Activity: 30,000 DLH		**Denominator Activity: 40,000 DLH**	
Direct materials, 4 ft. @ $8.75................	$35.00	Same	$35.00
Direct labour, 2 hrs. @ $5...................	10.00	Same	10.00
Variable overhead, 2 hrs. @ $4.50.............	9.00	Same	9.00
Fixed overhead, 2 hrs. @ $9.................	18.00	Fixed overhead, 2 hrs. @ $6.75.......	13.50
Standard cost per unit..........................	$72.00	Standard cost per unit....................	$67.50

4. a. 18,000 units × 2 hrs. per unit = 36,000 standard hours.

b.

Manufacturing Overhead		
Actual Costs 446,400	486,000*	Applied Costs
	39,600	Overapplied Overhead

*36,000 standard hours × $13.50 predetermined rate per hour = $486,000.

Problem 11-25 (continued)

c. Variable overhead variances:

Actual Hours of Input, at the Actual Rate (AH × AR)	Actual Hours of Input, at the Standard Rate (AH × SR)	Standard Hours Allowed for Output, at the Standard Rate (SH × SR)
$174,800	38,000 hrs. × $4.50 per hr. = $171,000	36,000 hrs. × $4.50 per hr. = $162,000

Spending Variance, $3,800 U   Efficiency Variance, $9,000 U

Alternate solution:

Variable overhead spending variance = (AH × AR) – (AH × SR)
($174,800) – (38,000 hrs. × $4.50 per hr.) = $3,800 U

Variable overhead efficiency variance = SR (AH – SH)
$4.50 per hr. (38,000 hrs. – 36,000 hrs.) = $9,000 U

Fixed overhead variances:

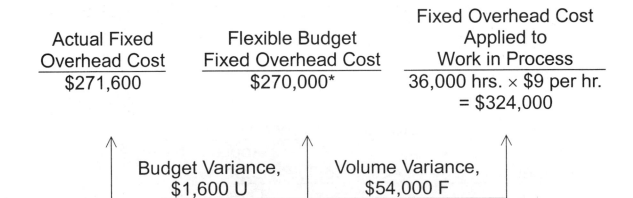

Actual Fixed Overhead Cost	Flexible Budget Fixed Overhead Cost	Fixed Overhead Cost Applied to Work in Process
$271,600	$270,000*	36,000 hrs. × $9 per hr. = $324,000

Budget Variance, $1,600 U   Volume Variance, $54,000 F

*Can be expressed as: 30,000 denominator hrs. × $9 per hr. = $270,000.

Problem 11-25 (continued)

Alternate solution:

Budget variance:

$$\text{Budget variance} = \text{Actual fixed overhead cost} - \text{Flexible budget fixed overhead cost}$$

$$= \$271,600 - \$270,000 = \$1,600 \text{ U}$$

Volume variance:

$$\text{Volume variance} = \text{Fixed portion of the predetermined overhead rate} \left(\text{Denominator hours} - \text{Standard hours allowed} \right)$$

$9.00 per hr. (30,000 hrs. − 36,000 hrs.) = $54,000 F

Summary of variances:

Variable overhead spending variance	$ 3,800 U
Variable overhead efficiency variance	9,000 U
Fixed overhead budget variance	1,600 U
Fixed overhead volume variance	54,000 F
Overapplied overhead	$39,600

Problem 11-25 (continued)

5. The major disadvantage is the large volume variance which is
    created as a result of using a denominator activity figure to
    compute the predetermined overhead rate which is far different
    from the activity level that is anticipated for the period. In the case
    at hand, the company has used a long-run normal activity figure of
    30,000 direct labour-hours to compute the predetermined
    overhead rate, whereas activity for the period was expected to be
    40,000 hours. This has resulted in a huge favourable volume
    variance that may be difficult for management to interpret. In
    addition, the large favourable volume variance in this case has
    masked the fact that the company did not achieve the budgeted
    level of activity for the period. The company had planned to work
    40,000 hours, but managed to work only 36,000 hours (at
    standard). This unfavourable result is concealed due to using a
    denominator figure that is out of step with current activity.

    On the other hand, by using long-run normal activity as a
    denominator, unit costs are stable from year to year. Thus,
    management's decisions are not clouded by unit costs that jump
    up and down as the activity level rises and falls.

Chapter 12
Decentralization
and Segment Reporting

Exercise 12-1 (15 minutes)

	Total		Weedban		Greengrow	
	Amount	%	Amount	%	Amount	%
Sales	$300,000	100	$90,000*	100	$210,000*	100
Less variable expenses	183,000	61	36,000	40	147,000	70
Contribution margin	117,000	39	54,000	60	63,000	30
Less traceable fixed expenses	66,000	22	45,000	50	21,000	10
Product line segment margin	51,000	17	$ 9,000	10	$ 42,000	20
Less common fixed expenses not traceable to products....................	33,000	11				
Net income	$ 18,000	6				

* Weedban: 15,000 units × $6 = $90,000; Greengrow: 28,000
    units × $7.50 = $210,000. Variable expenses are computed in the same
    way.

© 2001 McGraw-Hill Ryerson Limited

Exercise 12-3 (15 minutes)

1. The company should focus its campaign on the Dental market. The computations are:

	Medical	Dental
Increased sales	$40,000	$35,000
Market CM ratio	× 36%	× 48%
Incremental contribution margin	14,400	16,800
Less cost of the campaign	5,000	5,000
Increased segment margin and net income for the company as a whole	$ 9,400	$11,800

2. The $48,000 in traceable fixed expenses in Exercise 12-2 is now partly traceable and partly common. When we segment Winnipeg by market only $33,000 remains a traceable fixed expense. This amount represents costs such as advertising and salaries of individuals that can be identified with the markets on a nonarbitrary basis. The remaining $15,000 ($48,000 – $33,000) becomes a common cost when Winnipeg is segmented by market. This amount would include such costs as the salary of the manager of the Winnipeg office.

Exercise 12-5 (15 minutes)

A large number of costs are common to the sales departments and/or products of a grocery store. Building rent or depreciation would be a common cost, as would utilities, property taxes, insurance, and general management. In addition, the wages of inventory custodians and cashiers, depreciation on cash registers and check-out counters, advertising, and janitorial costs would all be common costs.

The existence of such costs complicates and limits the use of accounting data in decision making because the costs are often allocated on some arbitrary basis among departments and products. Such allocations can produce misleading results and distort the performance of a department or product line.

Exercise 12-7 (20 minutes)

1. ROI = Margin × Turnover

$$= \frac{\text{Net operating income}}{\text{Sales}} \times \frac{\text{Sales}}{\text{Average operating assets}}$$

Osaka Division:
$$= \frac{¥210,000}{¥3,000,000} \times \frac{¥3,000,000}{¥1,000,000}$$

$$= \quad 7\% \quad \times \quad 3 \quad = 21\%$$

Yokohama Division:
$$= \frac{¥720,000}{¥9,000,000} \times \frac{¥9,000,000}{¥4,000,000}$$

$$= \quad 8\% \quad \times \quad 2.25 \quad = 18\%$$

2.

	Osaka	Yokohama
Average operating assets (a)	¥1,000,000	¥4,000,000
Net operating income	¥ 210,000	¥ 720,000
Minimum required return on average operating assets—15% × (a)	150,000	600,000
Residual income....................................	¥ 60,000	¥ 120,000

3. No, the Yokohama Division is simply larger than the Osaka Division and for this reason one would expect that it would have a greater amount of residual income. As stated in the text, residual income can't be used to compare the performance of divisions of different sizes. Larger divisions will almost always look better, not necessarily because of better management but because of the larger amounts involved. In fact, in the case above, the Yokohama Division does not appear to be as well managed as the Osaka Division. Note from Part (1) that Yokohama has only an 18% ROI as compared to 21% for Osaka.

Exercise 12-9 (15 minutes)

	Company		
	A	**B**	**C**
Sales	$9,000,000*	$7,000,000*	$4,500,000*
Net operating income	540,000	280,000*	360,000
Average operating assets	3,000,000*	2,000,000	1,800,000*
Return on investment (ROI)	18%*	14%*	20%
Minimum required rate of return:			
Percentage	16%*	16%	15%*
Dollar amount	$ 480,000	$ 320,000*	$ 270,000
Residual income	60,000	(40,000)	90,000*

*Given.

$$ROI = Margin \times T/O$$

$$18\% = \frac{NOI}{9,000,000} \times \frac{9,00\cancel{0,000}^{\,3}}{3,000,000}$$

$$3\,NOI = 18\% \times 9000,000 =$$

$$NOI = 540,000$$

Exercise 12-11 (15 minutes)

1. Cost per customer class

	Small	Medium	Large	Total
Costs:				
Sales Expense............	$1,806	$ 6,505	$ 7,589	$15,900
Ordering Costs............	1,500	700	300	2,500
Coupons	800	1,200	2,000	4,000
Salaries......................	5,000	34,000	33,000	72,000
	$9,106	$42,405	$42,889	$94,400

2. Cost per unit sold $9.106 $11.779 $10.212

Exercise 12-13 (20 minutes)

1. The lowest acceptable transfer price from the perspective of the selling division is given by the following formula:

$$\text{Transfer price} \geq \frac{\text{Variable cost}}{\text{per unit}} + \frac{\text{Total contribution margin on lost sales}}{\text{Number of units transferred}}.$$

There is no idle capacity, so each of the 40,000 units transferred from Division X to Division Y reduces sales to outsiders by one unit. The contribution margin per unit on outside sales is $20 ($90 – $70).

$$\text{Transfer price} \geq (\$70 - \$3) + \frac{\$20 \times 40{,}000}{40{,}000} = \$67 + \$20 = \$87$$

The purchasing division, Division Y, can buy a similar unit from an outside supplier for $86. Therefore, Division Y would be unwilling to pay more than $86 per unit.

$$\text{Transfer price} \leq \text{Cost of buying from outside supplier} = \$86$$

The requirements of the two divisions are incompatible and no transfer will take place.

2. In this case, Division X has enough idle capacity to satisfy Division Y's demand. Therefore, there are no lost sales and the lowest acceptable price as far as the selling division is concerned is the variable cost of $60 per unit.

$$\text{Transfer price} \geq \$60 + \frac{\$0}{40{,}000} = \$60$$

The purchasing division, Division Y, can buy a similar unit from an outside supplier for $74. Therefore, Division Y would be unwilling to pay more than $74 per unit.

$$\text{Transfer price} \leq \text{Cost of buying from outside supplier} = \$74$$

In this case, the requirements of the two divisions are compatible and a transfer hopefully will take place at a transfer price within the range:

$$\$60 \leq \text{Transfer price} \leq \$74$$

Problem 12-15 (30 minutes)

1.

Sales Territory						
	Total Company		**Northern**		**Southern**	
Sales...	$750,000	100.0%	$300,000	100%	$450,000	100%
Less variable expenses....................	336,000	44.8	156,000	52	180,000	40
Contribution margin.........................	414,000	55.2	144,000	48	270,000	60
Less traceable fixed expenses.........	228,000	30.4	120,000	40	108,000	24
Territorial segment margin...............	186,000	24.8	$ 24,000	8%	$162,000	36%
Less common fixed expenses not traceable to sales territories........	150,000	20.0				
Net income.....................................	$ 36,000	4.8%				

Product Line						
	Northern Territory		**Paks**		**Tibs**	
Sales...	$300,000	100.0%	$50,000	100%	$250,000	100%
Less variable expenses....................	156,000	52.0	11,000	22	145,000	58
Contribution margin.........................	144,000	48.0	39,000	78	105,000	42
Less traceable fixed expenses.........	70,000	23.3	30,000	60	40,000	16
Product line segment margin............	74,000	24.7	$ 9,000	18%	$ 65,000	26%
Less common fixed expenses not traceable to product lines..........	50,000	16.7				
Territorial segment margin...............	$ 24,000	8.0%				

Problem 12-15 (continued)

2. Two points should be brought to the attention of management. First, the Northern territory has a low contribution margin ratio as compared to the Southern territory. Second, the Northern territory has high traceable fixed expenses. Overall, the Northern territory is very weak compared to the Southern territory.

3. Again, two points should be brought to the attention of management. First, the Northern territory has a poor sales mix. Note that the territory sells very little of the Paks product, which has a high contribution margin ratio. It is this poor sales mix that accounts for the low overall contribution margin ratio in the Northern territory mentioned in part 2 above. Second, the traceable fixed expenses of the Paks product seem very high in relation to sales. These high fixed expenses may simply mean that the Paks product is highly leveraged; if so, then an increase in sales of this product line would greatly enhance profits in the Northern territory and in the company as a whole.

Problem 12-17 (20 minutes)

1. Operating assets do not include investments in other companies or in undeveloped land.

	Ending Balances	Beginning Balances
Cash	$ 120,000	$ 140,000
Accounts receivable	530,000	450,000
Inventory	380,000	320,000
Plant and equipment (net)	620,000	680,000
Total operating assets	$1,650,000	$1,590,000

$$\text{Average operating assets} = \frac{\$1,650,000 + \$1,590,000}{2} = \$1,620,000$$

$$\text{Margin} = \frac{\text{Net operating income}}{\text{Sales}}$$

$$= \frac{\$405,000}{\$4,050,000} = 10\%$$

$$\text{Turnover} = \frac{\text{Sales}}{\text{Average operating assets}}$$

$$= \frac{\$4,050,000}{\$1,620,000} = 2.5$$

$$\text{ROI} = \text{Margin} \times \text{Turnover}$$
$$= 10\% \times 2.5 = 25\%$$

2.

Net operating income	$405,000
Minimum required return (15% × $1,620,000)	243,000
Residual income...	$162,000

Problem 12-19 (45 minutes)

1. The lowest acceptable transfer price from the perspective of the selling division is given by the following formula:

$$\text{Transfer price} \geq \frac{\text{Variable cost}}{\text{per unit}} + \frac{\text{Total contribution margin on lost sales}}{\text{Number of units transferred}}.$$

There is no idle capacity, so transfers from the Pulp Division to the Carton Division would cut directly into normal sales of pulp to outsiders. Since the costs are the same whether the pulp is transferred internally or sold to outsiders, the only relevant cost is the lost revenue of $70 per tonne from the pulp that could be sold to outsiders. This is confirmed in the following calculation:

$$\text{Transfer price} \geq \$42 + \frac{(\$70-\$42) \times 5,000}{5,000} = \$42 + (\$70-\$42) = \$70$$

Therefore, the Pulp Division will refuse to transfer at a price less than $70 a tonne.

The Carton Division can buy pulp from an outside supplier for $70 a tonne, less a 10% quantity discount of $7, or $63 a tonne. Therefore, the Division would be unwilling to pay more than $63 per tonne.

Transfer price $\leq$ Cost of buying from outside supplier = $63

The requirements of the two divisions are incompatible. The Carton Division won't pay more than $63 and the Pulp Division will not accept less than $70. Thus, there will be no mutually agreeable transfer price and no transfer will take place.

2. The price being paid to the outside supplier, net of the quantity discount, is only $63. If this price is met by the Pulp Division, then profits in the Pulp Division and in the company as a whole will drop by $35,000 per year:

Lost revenue per tonne	$70
Outside supplier's price...	63
Loss in contribution margin per tonne	7
Number of tonnes per year.......................................	× 5,000
Total loss in profits	$35,000

Profits in the Carton Division will remain unchanged, since it will be paying the same price internally as it is now paying externally.

Problem 12-19 (continued)

3. There is idle capacity, so transfers from the Pulp Division to the Carton Division do not cut into normal sales of pulp to outsiders. In this case, the minimum price as far as the Carton Division is concerned is the variable cost per tonne of $42. This is confirmed in the following calculation:

$$\text{Transfer price} \geq \$42 + \frac{\$0}{5{,}000} = \$42$$

The Carton Division can buy pulp from an outside supplier for $63 a tonne and would be unwilling to pay more than that for pulp in an internal transfer. If the managers understand their own businesses and are reasonably cooperative, they should agree to a transfer and should settle on a transfer price within the range:

$$\$42 \leq \text{Transfer price} \leq \$63$$

4. Yes, since the $59 figure represents a bona fide outside price. Even though $59 is less than the Pulp Division's $60 "full cost" per unit, it is within the range given in Part 3 and therefore will provide some contribution to the Pulp Division.

If the Pulp Division does not meet the $59 price, it will lose $85,000 in potential profits:

Price per tonne...	$59
Less variable costs	42
Contribution margin per tonne..........................	$17

5,000 tonnes × $17 = $85,000 potential increased profits

This $85,000 in potential profits applies to the Pulp Division and to the company as a whole.

5. No, the Carton Division should probably be free to go outside and get the best price it can. Even though this would result in suboptimization for the company as a whole, the purchasing division should probably not be forced to buy inside if better prices are available outside.

Problem 12-19 (continued)

6.   The Pulp Division will have an increase in profits:

Selling price	$70
Less variable costs	42
Contribution margin per tonne..........................	$28

5,000 tonnes × $28 = $140,000 increased profits

The Carton Division will have a decrease in profits:

Inside purchase price..	$70
Outside purchase price	59
Increased cost per tonne...................................	$11

5,000 tonnes × $11 = $55,000 decreased profits

The company as a whole will have an increase in profits:

Increased contribution margin in the Pulp Division	$28
Decreased contribution margin in the Carton Division ...	11
Increased contribution margin per ton..........................	$17

5,000 tonnes × $17 = $85,000 increased profits

So long as the selling division has idle capacity and the transfer price is greater than the selling division's variable costs, profits in the company as a whole will increase if internal transfers are made. However, there is a question of *fairness* as to how these profits should be split between the selling and buying divisions. The inflexibility of management in this situation causes damage to the profits of the Carton Division and greatly enhances the profits of the Pulp Division.

Problem 12-21

1.

	(a) Total Cost	(b) Total Activity		(a) ÷ (b) Rate
Sales support	$3,600,000	24,000	calls	$150/call
Order processing	1,720,000	8,600	orders	$200/order
Warehousing	940,000	39,000	square metres	$24.103/square metre
Packing and shipping	520,000	52,000	kilograms shipped	$10/kilogram shipped

Assignment of expenses to markets:

	Commercial Market		Home Market		School Market	
	Events or Transactions	Amount	Events or Transactions	Amount	Events or Transactions	Amount
Sales support, at $150/call	8,000	$1,200,000	5,000	$ 750,000	11,000	$1,650,000
Order processing, at $200/order	1,750	350,000	5,200	1,040,000	1,650	330,000
Warehousing, at $24.103/square metre	11,000	265,133	22,000	530,266	6,000	144,601*
Packing and shipping, at $10/kilogram	12,000	120,000	8,000	80,000	32,000	320,000

*Rounded

2. The segmented income statement follows:

	Total	%	Commercial	%	Home	%	School	%
					Market			
Sales	$20,000,000	100.0 %	$8,000,000	100.0 %	$5,000,000	100.0 %	$7,000,000	100.0 %
Less variable expenses:								
Cost of goods sold	9,500,000	47.5	3,900,000	48.7	2,400,000	48.0	3,200,000	45.7
Sales support	3,600,000	18.0	1,200,000	15.0	750,000	15.0	1,650,000	23.6
Order processing	1,720,000	8.6	350,000	4.4	1,040,000	20.8	330,000	4.7
Packing and shipping	520,000	2.6	120,000	1.5	80,000	1.6	320,000	4.6
Total variable Expenses	15,340,000	76.7	5,570,000	69.6	4,270,000	85.4	5,500,000	78.6
Contribution margin	4,660,000	23.3	2,430,000	30.4	730,000	14.6	1,500,000	21.4
Less traceable fixed expenses:								
Warehousing	940,000	4.7	265,133	3.3	530,266	10.6	144,601	2.1
Advertising	1,460,000	7.3	700,000	8.8	180,000	3.6	580,000	8.3
General mgmt—salaries	410,000	2.1	150,000	1.9	120,000	2.4	140,000	2.0
Total traceable fixed expenses	2,810,000	14.1	1,115,133	14.0	830,266	16.6	864,601	12.4
Market segment margin	1,850,000	9.3	$1,314,867	16.4 %	(100,266)	(2.0%)	635,399	9.1 %
Less common fixed expenses not traceable to markets:								
Advertising	230,000	1.2						
General management	900,000	4.5						
Total common fixed expenses	1,130,000	5.7						
Net income	$ 720,000	3.6 %						

Note: Percentage figures may not total down due to rounding.

Problem 12-21 (continued)

3. The following comments relate to the three markets:

Commercial market:

- Rather than being the weakest segment, the commercial market is the company's strongest segment. It is generating enough segment margin by itself to cover all of the company's common costs.

- The manager of the commercial market is doing an outstanding job of controlling expenses. Expenses as a percentage of sales are lower than the company average for every category except cost of sales and advertising, and these latter two costs do not seem out of line.

Home Market:

- The home market spends very little on advertising. A more generous advertising budget may yield a substantial increase in sales in this segment.

- Order processing expenses are extremely high in the home market. Note from the data in the problem that more orders are written in this market (5,200 orders) than in the other two markets combined. This large number of orders, combined with the low overall sales in the home market, means that the home market is taking many orders of a small dollar amount each.

- Warehousing expenses are also high in the home market. This is probably due to the need to carry large stocks of goods in order to fill thousands of small orders.

- The home market is not covering its own traceable costs. If sales can't be increased through a more generous advertising budget and through a concerted effort to make larger sales per order and other actions, then consideration should be given to eliminating this market segment.

Problem 12-21 (continued)

School Market:

- The school market has extremely high sales support expenses. This is because nearly as many sales calls are made to this market (11,000 calls) as are made to the other two markets combined. Can contacts be made by phone or by other means?

- Over 60% of the packing and shipping expenses are traceable to the school market. The company may want to investigate alternate methods of shipping in an effort to reduce shipping costs in this segment.

Problem 12-23 (60 minutes)

1. Segments defined as product lines:

	Glass Division		Flat Glass		Auto Glass		Specialty Glass	
		100%		100%		100%		100%
Sales...............	R600,000		R200,000		R300,000		R100,000	
Less variable expenses......	300,000	50	130,000	65	120,000	40	50,000	50
Contribution margin......	300,000	50	70,000	35	180,000	60	50,000	50
Less traceable fixed expenses:								
Advertising.........	120,000	20	30,000	15	42,000	14	48,000	48
Depreciation	48,000	8	10,000	5	24,000	8	14,000	14
Administration......	42,000	7	14,000	7	21,000	7	7,000	7
Total............	210,000	35	54,000	27	87,000	29	69,000	69
Product line segment margin.........	90,000	15	R 16,000	8%	R 93,000	31%	R (19,000)	(19%)
Less common fixed expenses not traceable to product lines:								
Administration......	60,000	10						
Divisional segment margin........	R 30,000	5%						

Problem 12-23 (continued)

2. Segments defined as markets for Specialty Glass:

	Specialty Glass		Sales Market Domestic		Foreign	
Sales	R100,000	100%	R60,000	100%	R 40,000	100%
Less variable expenses	50,000	50	30,000	50	20,000	50
Contribution margin	50,000	50	30,000	50	20,000	50
Less traceable fixed expenses:						
Advertising	48,000	48	18,000	30	30,000	75
Market segment margin	2,000	2	R12,000	20%	R(10,000)	(25%)
Less common fixed expenses not traceable to sales markets:						
Depreciation	14,000	14				
Administration	7,000	7				
Total	21,000	21				
Product line segment margin	R (19,000)	(19%)				

Problem 12-23 (continued)

3.

	Flat Glass	Auto Glass
Incremental contribution margin:		
35% × R40,000 increased sales	R14,000	
60% × R30,000 increased sales		R18,000
Less cost of the promotional campaign	8,000	8,000
Increased net income	R 6,000	R10,000

Based on these data, the campaign should be directed toward Auto Glass. Notice that the analysis uses the contribution margin ratio rather than the segment margin ratio.

Problem 12-25 (30 minutes)

1. To compute the ROI and residual income, it is necessary to first compute the average operating assets for the year. The computation is:

Ending balance	$12,960,000
Beginning balance ($12,960,000 ÷ 1.08).................	12,000,000
Total	$24,960,000
Average balance ($24,960,000 ÷ 2)	$12,480,000

a. ROI = Margin x Turnover

$$ROI = \frac{\text{Net operating income}}{\text{Sales}} \times \frac{\text{Sales}}{\text{Average operating assets}}$$

$$= \frac{\$1,872,000}{\$31,200,000} \times \frac{\$31,200,000}{\$12,480,000}$$

$$= \quad 6\% \quad \times \quad 2.5 \quad = 15\%$$

b.
Net operating income...........................		$1,872,000
Minimum required net operating income:		
Average operating assets..................	$12,480,000	
Minimum required return	× 11%	1,372,800
Residual income		$ 499,200

2. The management of Reigis Steel Division would have been more likely to accept the contemplated capital acquisition if residual income was used as the performance measure because the investment would have increased both the division's residual income and management bonuses. Using residual income, management would accept all investments with a return higher than 11% since these investments would increase the dollar amount of residual income. When using ROI as a performance measure, Reigis's management is likely to reject any investment that would lower the overall ROI (15% last year), even though the rate of return is higher than the required minimum for the company as a whole. The reason, of course, is that accepting such investments would adversely affect bonus awards.

3. Reigis must be free to control all items related to profit (revenues and expenses) and investment if it is to be evaluated fairly as an investment centre. This is true under both the ROI and residual income approaches.

Problem 12-27 (45 minutes)

1. The Quark Division will probably reject the $340 price. This is because the price is below the Quark Division's "variable costs" of $350 per set. Although these "variable" costs contain a $140 transfer price from the Cabinet Division, which in turn includes $30 per unit in fixed costs, from the perspective of the Quark Division the $140 purchase price from the Cabinet Division is a variable cost. Thus, it will reject the $340 price offered.

2. If both the Cabinet Division and the Quark Division have idle capacity, then from the perspective of the entire company the $340 offer should be accepted. By rejecting the $340 price, the company will lose $60 in potential contribution margin per set:

Price offered per set..		$340
Less variable costs per set:		
Cabinet Division...	$ 70	
Quark Division...	210	280
Potential contribution margin per set.........................		$ 60

3. If the Cabinet Division is operating at capacity, any cabinets transferred to the Quark Division to fill the overseas order will have to be diverted from outside customers. Whether a cabinet is sold to outside customers or is transferred to the Quark Division, its production cost is the same. However, if a set is diverted from outside sales, the Cabinet Division (and the entire company) loses the $140 in revenue. As a consequence, as shown below, there would be a net loss of $10 on each TV set sold for $340.

Price offered per set......................		$340
Less:		
Lost revenue from sales of		
cabinets to outsiders	$140	
Variable cost of Quark Division ..	210	350
Net loss per TV		$ (10)

Problem 12-27 (continued)

4. When the selling division has no idle capacity, as in part (3), market price works very well as a transfer price. The cost to the company of a transfer when there is no idle capacity is the lost revenue from sales to outsiders. If the market price is used as the transfer price, the purchasing division will view the market price of the transferred item as its cost—which is appropriate since that is the cost to the company. As a consequence, the manager of the purchasing division should be motivated to make decisions that are in the best interests of the company.

When the selling division has idle capacity, the cost to the company of the transfer is just the variable cost of producing the item. If the market price is used as the transfer price, the manager of the purchasing division will view that as his/her cost rather than the real cost to the company which is just variable cost. Hence, the manager will have the wrong cost information for making decisions as we observed in parts (1) and (2).

Problem 12-29 (90 minutes)

1.

	Total Company Amount	%	Product A Amount	%	Product B Amount	%	Product C Amount	%
Sales..........................	$1,500,000	100.0%	$600,000	100%	$400,000	100%	$500,000	100%
Less variable expenses:								
Production	336,000	22.4	108,000	18	128,000	32	100,000	20
Selling....................	142,000	9.5	60,000	10	32,000	8	50,000	10
Total variable expenses ..	478,000	31.9	168,000	28	160,000	40	150,000	30
Contribution margin.........	1,022,000	68.1	432,000	72	240,000	60	350,000	70
Less traceable fixed expenses:								
Production	376,000	25.1	180,000	30	36,000	9	160,000	32
Selling....................	282,000	18.8	102,000	17	80,000	20	100,000	20
Total traceable fixed expenses	658,000	43.9	282,000	47	116,000	29	260,000	52
Product segment margin......	364,000	24.3	$150,000	25%	$124,000	31%	$ 90,000	18%
Less common fixed expenses:								
Production	210,000	14.0						
Administrative...........	180,000	12.0						
Total common fixed expenses	390,000	26.0						
Net loss....................	$ (26,000)	(1.7%)						

Problem 12-29 (continued)

2. Product C should not be eliminated. As shown on the income statement in part 1, product C is covering all of its own traceable costs and it is generating a segment margin of $90,000 per month. If the product is eliminated, all of this segment margin will be lost to the company, thereby increasing the overall monthly losses.

3. No, the company should concentrate its remaining inventory of X7 chips on product A, not product B. The company should focus on the product that will provide the greatest amount of contribution margin. Under the conditions posed, product A will provide the greatest amount of contribution margin since (1) it has a CM ratio of 72% as compared to only 60% for product B; (2) the two products have the same selling price, and therefore, due to its higher CM ratio, product A will generate a greater amount of contribution margin per chip than product B; and (3) the two products require the same number of chips per unit.

4.a. An income statement showing product C segmented by markets follows:

Problem 12-29 (continued)

	Product C		Vending Market		Home Market	
	Amount	%	Amount	%	Amount	%
Sales	$500,000	100 %	$ 50,000	100%	$450,000	100.0%
Less variable expenses:						
Production	100,000	20	10,000	20	90,000	20.0
Selling	50,000	10	14,000	28	36,000	8.0
Total variable expenses	150,000	30	24,000	48	126,000	28.0
Contribution margin	350,000	70	26,000	52	324,000	72.0
Less traceable fixed expenses:						
Selling	75,000	15	45,000	90	30,000	6.7
Market segment margin	275,000	55	$ (19,000)	(38%)	$294,000	65.3%
Less common fixed expenses not traceable to market segments:						
Production	160,000	32				
Selling	25,000*	5				
Total common fixed expenses	185,000	37				
Product segment margin	$ 90,000	18%				

* Total fixed selling expenses $100,000
Less fixed selling expenses traceable to the markets ... 75,000
Fixed selling expenses common to the markets .... $ 25,000

Problem 12-29 (continued)

b. The following points should be brought to the attention of management:

1. Sales in the vending market are very low as compared to the home market.

2. Variable selling expenses are 28% of sales in the vending market as compared to only 8% in the home market. Is this just the nature of the markets, or are the high variable selling expenses in the vending market a result of poor cost control?

3. The traceable fixed selling expenses in the vending market are 50% higher than in the home market, even though the vending market has only a fraction of the sales of the home market. Why would these costs be so high in the vending market?

4. The vending market has a negative segment margin. If sales can't be increased enough in future months to permit the market to cover its own costs, then consideration should be given to eliminating the market. (Instructor's note: The question of elimination of product lines and other segments is covered in depth in Chapter 13.)

Problem 12-31 (75 minutes)

1. See the segmented statement on the following page. Supporting computations for the statement are given below:

Revenues:

Membership dues (20,000 × $100)	$2,000,000
Assigned to Magazine Subscriptions Division (20,000 × $20)	400,000
Assigned to Membership Division	$1,600,000
Non-member magazine subscriptions (2,500 × $30)	$ 75,000
Reports and texts (28,000 x $25)	$ 700,000
Continuing education courses:	
One-day (2,400 x $75)	$ 180,000
Two-day (1,760 x $125)	220,000
Total revenue	$ 400,000

Salary and personnel costs:

	Salaries	Personnel Costs (25% of Salaries)
Membership Division	$210,000	$ 52,500
Magazine Subscriptions Division	150,000	37,500
Books and Reports Division	300,000	75,000
Continuing Education Division	180,000	45,000
Total assigned to divisions	840,000	210,000
Corporate staff	80,000	20,000
Total	$920,000	$230,000

Problem 12-31 (continued)

Some may argue that, except for the $50,000 in rental cost directly attributed to the Books and Reports Division, occupancy costs are common costs that should not be allocated. The correct treatment of the occupancy costs depends upon whether they could be avoided in part by eliminating a division. In the solution below, we have assumed they could be avoided.

Occupancy costs ($230,000 allocated + $50,000 direct to the Books and
  Reports Division = $280,000):
  Allocated to:

Membership Division ($230,000 x 0.2)	$ 46,000
Magazine Subscriptions Division ($230,000 x 0.2) ..	46,000
Books and Reports Division ($230,000 x 0.3 + $50,000)	119,000
Continuing Education Division ($230,000 x 0.2)	46,000
Corporate staff ($230,000 x 0.1)	23,000
Total occupancy costs...	$280,000

Printing and paper costs		$320,000
Assigned to:		
Magazine Subscriptions Division (22,500 x $7)	$157,500	
Books and Reports Division (28,000 x $4)............	112,000	269,500
Remainder—Continuing Education Division		$ 50,500
Postage and shipping costs..		$176,000
Assigned to:		
Magazine Subscriptions Division (22,500 x $4)	$ 90,000	
Books and Reports Division (28,000 x $2)............	56,000	146,000
Remainder—corporate staff.................................		$ 30,000

Problem 12-31 (continued)

	Association Total	Division Membership	Magazine Subscriptions	Books & Reports	Continuing Education
Revenues:					
Membership dues	$2,000,000	$1,600,000	$400,000		
Non-member magazine subscriptions	75,000		75,000		
Advertising	100,000		100,000		
Reports and texts	700,000			$700,000	
Continuing education courses	400,000				$400,000
Total revenues	3,275,000	1,600,000	575,000	700,000	400,000
Expenses traceable to segments:					
Salaries	840,000	210,000	150,000	300,000	180,000
Personnel costs	210,000	52,500	37,500	75,000	45,000
Occupancy costs	257,000	46,000	46,000	119,000	46,000
Reimbursement of member costs to local chapters	600,000	600,000			
Other membership services	500,000	500,000			
Printing and paper	320,000		157,500	112,000	50,500
Postage and shipping	146,000		90,000	56,000	
Instructors' fees	80,000				80,000
Total traceable expenses	2,953,000	1,408,500	481,000	662,000	401,500
Division segment margin	322,000	$ 191,500	$ 94,000	$ 38,000	$ (1,500)
Less common expenses not traceable to divisions:					
Salaries—corporate staff	80,000				
Personnel costs	20,000				
Occupancy costs	23,000				
Postage and shipping	30,000				
General and administrative	38,000				
Total common expenses	191,000				
Excess of revenues over expenses	$ 131,000				

Problem 12-31 (continued)

2. Arguments for allocation of all costs:

- The profit centre managers need to be aware of the fact that common costs exist that must be covered by revenues generated by the profit centres.
- The amount of common cost may not be material and would therefore not affect segment results.

Arguments against allocation of all costs:

- Allocation bases will need to be chosen arbitrarily.
- Allocated common costs may create a bias for or against some segment.
- Top management may be led to unwisely eliminate a profitable segment.
- Profit centre (and investment centre) managers should not be held accountable for costs over which they have no control.
- Profit centre (and investment centre) managers may resent such allocations and ignore the entire performance report as arbitrary and unfair.

Problem 12-33 (50 minutes)

(Customer Profitability)

Profits by Customer Class

Class	$10,000 or More		$1,000 to $9,999		$0 to $999	
Number of Customers		50		350		1,600 (active)
Sales		$900,000		$1,225,000	†	$408,000
Variable Costs	70%	630,000	60%	735,000	55%	224,400
Contribution Margin	30%	270,000	40%	490,000	45%	183,600
Sales Dept. Costs						
Sales personnel (number of Calls)	250	7,750	1,500	46,500	5,200	161,200
Office staff ($2.40 × Number of Orders)	700	1,680	1,800	4,320	5,000	12,000
		9,430		50,820		173,200
		$260,570		$ 439,180		$ 10,400

Analysis of Sales Staff Costs			Rounded
Sales Salaries and Benefits	$280,000	per call (250 + 1,500 + 9,000) =	$26
Travel	$ 45,000	per call (250 + 1,500 + 9,000) =	4
Entertainment	$ 12,000	per call (250 + 1,500 + 9,000) =	1
Samples........................	$ 7,000	— not related to calls	—
			$31*

---

*Some alternatives are possible here.
†Given

Problem 12-33 (continued)

Contribution by Customer

Large	$260,570	
Medium	439,180	
Small	10,400	
Total		$710,150

Costs:

Calls for no sale 3,800 × $31			117,800
Office Costs not Allocated			
Supervision		48,000	
Clerical		18,000	
Samples		7,000	
Rent		6,900	
Other		3,800	
		83,700	
Less: Allocated (at $2.40 per order)	$ 1,680		
	4,320		
	12,000	18,000	65,700
			183,500
Net			$526,650

Analysis:

Each of the customer classes is profitable based on the analysis yet the small customers are just so. The $0 to $999 class of customer is charged a higher markup than the other classes. Such a markup, however, just covers the extensive selling costs and office cost. Consideration should be given to other ways of selling to this class given the current method costs $161,000 per year. Maybe these customers could use a 1-800 number or perhaps wholesalers or sales agents.

A related aspect is the $117,800 spent on calls for which no sale was received. If these calls were used to generate new customers then a benefit is possible. Alternatively, perhaps the 1,900 no sale customers could be contacted using direct mail or advertising rather than using salesperson calls.

Third, $65,700 of office costs were no allocated. It could prove fruitful to investigate these costs in terms of the value they add. As it stands, their value is not evident.

Problem 12-33 (continued)

Two potential economies concerning sales calls are worth investigating. Office time represents 20 percent of the sales time. A potential saving of .20 × ($280,000 + $45,000 + $12,000) or $67,400 is possible if sales people can reduce this time by using alternative technology or streamlining procedures. In addition, route analysis might be able to save 30 percent of call time by economizing travel time.

The above represents a few areas where investigations could prove useful in improving the focus and direction of sales activities.

Chapter 13
Relevant Costs for Decision Making

Exercise 13-1 (15 minutes)

	Case 1		Case 2	
Item	**Relevant**	**Not Relevant**	**Relevant**	**Not Relevant**
a. Sales revenue	X			X
b. Direct materials	X		X	
c. Direct labour.....................	X			X
d. Variable manufacturing overhead	X			X
e. Depreciation— Model B100 machine		X		X
f. Book value— Model B100 machine		X		X
g. Disposal value— Model B100 machine		X	X	
h. Market value—Model B300 machine (cost)	X		X	
i. Depreciation— Model B300 machine	X		X	
j. Fixed manufacturing overhead		X		X
k. Variable selling expense...	X			X
l. Fixed selling expense.......	X			X
m. General administrative overhead	X			X

Exercise 13-3 (20 minutes)

No, the bilge pump product line should not be discontinued. The computations are:

Contribution margin lost if the line is dropped		DR(460,000)
Fixed costs that can be avoided if the line is dropped:		
Advertising...	DR270,000	
Salary of the product line manager	32,000	
Insurance on inventories.........................	8,000	310,000
Net disadvantage of dropping the line.......		DR(150,000)

The same solution can be obtained by preparing comparative income statements:

	Keep Product Line	Drop Product Line	Difference Net Income Increase or (Decrease)
Sales...	DR850,000	DR -0-	DR(850,000)
Less variable expenses:			
Variable manufacturing expenses................................	330,000	-0-	330,000
Sales commissions	42,000	-0-	42,000
Shipping..................................	18,000	-0-	18,000
Total variable expenses........	390,000	-0-	390,000
Contribution margin....................	460,000	-0-	(460,000)
Less fixed expenses:			
Advertising	270,000	-0-	270,000
Depreciation of equipment	80,000	80,000	-0-
General factory overhead........	105,000	105,000	-0-
Salary of product line manager................................	32,000	-0-	32,000
Insurance on inventories	8,000	-0-	8,000
Purchasing department expenses................................	45,000	45,000	-0-
Total fixed expenses.............	540,000	230,000	310,000
Net loss.....................................	DR (80,000)	DR(230,000)	DR(150,000)

Exercise 13-5 (20 minutes)

1.

	A	B	C
(1) Contribution margin per unit.............................	$54	$108	$60
(2) Direct material cost per unit	$24	$ 72	$32
(3) Direct material cost per kilogram........................	$ 8	$ 8	$ 8
(4) Kilograms of material required per unit (2) ÷ (3)..	3 kgs.	9 kgs.	4 kgs.
(5) Contribution margin per kilogram (1) ÷ (4)	$18	$ 12	$15

2. The company should concentrate its available material on product A:

	A	B	C
Contribution margin per kilogram (above).................................	$ 18	$ 12	$ 15
Kilograms of material available..............	× 5,000	× 5,000	× 5,000
Total contribution margin.......................	$90,000	$60,000	$75,000

Although product A has the lowest contribution margin per unit and the second lowest contribution margin ratio, it is preferred over the other two products since it has the greatest amount of contribution margin per kilogram of material, and material is the company's constrained resource.

3. The price Barlow Company would be willing to pay per kilogram for additional raw materials depends upon how the materials would be used. If there are unfilled orders for all of the products, Barlow would presumably use the additional raw materials to make more of product A. Each kilogram of raw materials used in product A generates $18 of contribution margin over and above the usual cost of raw materials. Therefore, Barlow should be willing to pay up to $26 per kilogram ($8 usual price plus $18 contribution margin per kilogram) for the additional raw material, but would of course prefer to pay far less. The upper limit of $26 per kilogram to manufacture more product A signals to managers how valuable additional raw materials are to the company.

If all of the orders for product A have been filled, Barlow Company would then use additional raw materials to manufacture product C. The company would be willing to pay up to $23 per kilogram ($8 usual price plus $15 contribution margin per kilogram) for the additional raw materials to manufacture more product C, and up to $20 per kilogram ($8 usual price plus $12 contribution margin per kilogram) to manufacture more product B if all of the orders for product C have been filled as well.

Exercise 13-7 (10 minutes)

Cost savings if the high-speed wheel grinder is purchased:
    ($15,000 − $7,000 = $8,000; $8,000 ×

      5 years = $40,000) $40,000

Incremental cost:
  Cost of the high-speed wheel grinder $30,000
  Less salvage from the standard wheel grinder   9,000   21,000

Net advantage of purchasing the high-speed wheel
  grinder $19,000

Exercise 13-9 (10 minutes)

The costs that are relevant in a make or buy decision are those costs that can be avoided as a result of purchasing from the outside. The analysis for this exercise is:

	Per Unit Differential Costs		30,000 Units	
	Make	**Buy**	**Make**	**Buy**
Cost of purchasing		$21.00		$630,000
Cost of making:				
Direct materials	$ 3.60		$ 108,000	
Direct labour............................	10.00		300,000	
Variable overhead	2.40		72,000	
Fixed overhead	3.00*		90,000	
Total cost................................	$19.00	$21.00	$570,000	$630,000

  * The remaining $6 of fixed overhead cost would not be relevant, since it will continue regardless of whether the company makes or buys the parts.

The $80,000 rental value of the space being used to produce part S-6 represents an opportunity cost of continuing to produce the part internally. Thus, the completed analysis would be:

	Make	**Buy**
Total cost, as above	$570,000	$630,000
Rental value of the space (opportunity cost)	80,000	
Total cost, including opportunity cost......................	$650,000	$630,000
Net advantage in favour of buying..........................		$20,000

Problem 13-11 (25 minutes)

1. a. and b.

	Keep Old Machine	Buy New Machine	Difference
	5 Year Summary		
Sales ($200,000 × 5 years)	$1,000,000	$1,000,000	$ -0-
Selling and administrative expenses ($126,000 × 5 years)	630,000	630,000	-0-
Operating costs	210,000	70,000	140,000
Depreciation of the old machine, or loss write-off	50,000	50,000 *	-0-
Salvage value—old machine	—	(10,000) *	10,000
Depreciation—new machine		90,000	(90,000)
Total expenses	890,000	830,000	60,000
Net operating income	$ 110,000	$170,000	$ 60,000

* In a formal income statement, these two items should be shown
  as a single $40,000 "loss from disposal" figure.

The new machine should be purchased. The savings in operating
costs over the next five years will exceed the net investment by
$60,000.

2. Reduction in annual operating costs

($28,000 × 5 years)		$140,000
Investment in the new machine:		
Original cost	$90,000	
Less salvage value of the old machine	10,000	80,000
Net advantage of purchasing the new machine		$ 60,000

All other costs are either sunk or do not differ between the
alternatives.

Problem 13-13 (60 minutes)

1. Contribution margin lost if Department B is dropped:

Lost from Department B..	$600,000
Lost from Department A (10% × $2,100,000)	210,000
Total..	810,000
Less fixed costs that can be avoided ($800,000 − $340,000)	460,000
Decrease in profits for the company as a whole	$350,000

2. The target production level is 40,000 starters per period, as shown by the relationships between per-unit and total fixed costs.

	"Cost" Per Unit	Differential Costs Make	Buy	Explanation
Direct materials.......	$3.10	$3.10		Can be avoided by buying
Direct labour	2.70	2.70		Can be avoided by buying
Variable manufacturing overhead	0.60	0.60		Can be avoided by buying
Supervision.............	1.50	1.50		Can be avoided by buying
Depreciation	1.00	—		Sunk Cost
Rent........................	0.30	—		Allocated Cost
Outside purchase price....................		—	$8.40	
Total cost	$9.20	$7.90	$8.40	

The company should make the starters, rather than continuing to buy from the outside supplier. Making the starters will result in a $0.50 per starter cost savings, or a total savings of $20,000 per period:

$0.50 x 40,000 starters = $20,000

Problem 13-13 (continued)

3. Sales value if processed further (7,000 units x $12) ... $84,000
   Sales value at the split-off point (7,000 units x $9)...... <u>63,000</u>
      Incremental revenue.. 21,000
   Less cost of processing further..................................... <u>9,500</u>
   Net advantage of processing further........................... <u>$11,500</u>

4. The company should accept orders first for C, second for A, and third for B. The computations are:

		A	B	C
(1)	Direct materials required per unit	$24	$15	$9
(2)	Cost per kilogram..................................	$ 3	$ 3	$3
(3)	Kilograms required per unit (1) ÷ (2).....	8 kgs.	5 kgs.	3 kgs.
(4)	Contribution margin per unit.................	$32	$14	$21
(5)	Contribution margin per kilogram of materials used (4) ÷ (3).....................	$4/kg.	$2.80/kg.	$7/kg.

Since C uses the least amount of material per unit of the three products, and since it is the most profitable of the three in terms of its use of materials, some students will immediately assume that this is an infallible relationship. That is, they will assume that the way to spot the most profitable product is to find the one using the least amount of the constrained resource. The way to dispel this notion is to point out that product A uses more material (the constrained resource) than does product B, but yet it is preferred over product B. *The key factor is not how much of a constrained resource a product uses, but rather how much contribution margin the product generates per unit of the constrained resource.*

Problem 13-13 (continued)

5. Annual profits will be increased by $39,000:

	Per Unit	15,000 Units
Incremental sales	$14.00	$210,000
Incremental costs:		
Direct materials	5.10	76,500
Direct labour	3.80	57,000
Variable manufacturing overhead	1.00	15,000
Variable selling and administrative	1.50	22,500
Total	11.40	171,000
Incremental profits	$ 2.60	$ 39,000

The fixed costs are not relevant to the decision, since they will not change in total amount regardless of whether the special order is accepted or rejected.

6. The relevant cost figure is $1.50 (the variable selling and administrative expenses). All other variable costs are sunk, since the units have already been produced. The fixed costs would not be relevant, since they will not change in total regardless of the price charged for the left-over units.

Problem 13-15 (45 minutes)

1. The fl2.80 per drum general overhead cost is not relevant to the decision, since this cost will be the same regardless of whether the company decides to make or buy the drums. Also, the present depreciation figure of fl1.60 per drum is not a relevant cost, since it represents a sunk cost (in addition to the fact that the old equipment is worn out and must be replaced). The cost (depreciation) of the new equipment is a relevant cost, since the new equipment will not be purchased if the company decides to accept the outside supplier's offer. The cost of supervision is relevant to the decision, since this cost can be avoided by buying the drums.

	Differential Costs Per Drum		Total Differential Costs—60,000 Drums	
	Make	**Buy**	**Make**	**Buy**
Outside supplier's price		fl18.00		fl1,080,000
Direct materials....................	fl10.35		fl621,000	
Direct labour (fl6.00 × 70%) .	4.20		252,000	
Variable overhead (fl1.50 × 70%)	1.05		63,000	
Supervision.........................	0.75		45,000	
Depreciation	2.25*		135,000	
Total cost	fl18.60	fl18.00	fl1,116,000	fl1,080,000
Difference in favour of buying.................................		fl0.60		fl36,000

  *fl810,000 ÷ 6 years = fl135,000 per year;
   fl135,000 per year ÷ 60,000 drums = fl2.25 per drum.

Problem 13-15 (continued)

2. a. Notice that unit costs for both supervision and depreciation will change if the company needs 75,000 drums each year. The reason is that these fixed costs will be spread over a greater number of units, thereby reducing the cost per unit.

	Differential Costs Per Drum		Total Differential Costs—75,000 Drums	
	Make	**Buy**	**Make**	**Buy**
Outside supplier's price		fl18.00		fl1,350,000
Direct materials.....................	fl10.35		fl776,250	
Direct labour	4.20		315,000	
Variable overhead.................	1.05		78,750	
Supervision (fl45,000 ÷ 75,000 drums)	0.60		45,000	
Depreciation (fl135,000 ÷ 75,000 drums)	1.80		135,000	
Total cost	fl18.00	fl18.00	fl1,350,000	fl1,350,000
Difference	fl-0-		fl-0-	

The company would be indifferent between the two alternatives if 75,000 drums were needed each year.

Problem 13-15 (continued)

b. Again, notice that the unit costs for both supervision and depreciation decrease with the greater volume of units.

	Differential Costs Per Drum		Total Differential Costs—90,000 Drums	
	Make	Buy	Make	Buy
Outside supplier's price		fl18.00		fl1,620,000
Direct materials....................	fl10.35		fl931,500	
Direct labour	4.20		378,000	
Variable overhead................	1.05		94,500	
Supervision (fl45,000 ÷ 90,000 drums)	0.50		45,000	
Depreciation (fl135,000 ÷ 90,000 drums)	1.50		135,000	
Total cost	fl17.60	fl18.00	fl1,584,000	fl1,620,000
Difference in favour of making................................	fl0.40		fl36,000	

The company should purchase the new equipment and make the drums if 90,000 units per year are needed.

Problem 13-15 (continued)

3. Other factors which the company should consider include:

   a. Will volume in future years be increasing, or will it remain constant at 60,000 units per year? (If volume increases, then buying the new equipment becomes more desirable, as shown in the computations above.)

   b. Can quality control be maintained if the drums are purchased from the outside supplier?

   c. Will costs for materials and labour increase in future years, thereby increasing the cost of making the drums? (The supplier will be locked into an fl18 price.)

   d. Will the outside supplier be dependable in meeting shipping schedules?

   e. Can the company begin making the drums again, if the supplier proves to be undependable, or are there alternate suppliers?

   f. What is the labour outlook in the supplier's industry (e.g., are frequent labour strikes likely)?

   g. If the outside supplier's offer is accepted and the need for drums increases in future years, will the supplier have the added capacity to provide more than 60,000 drums per year?

Problem 13-17 (60 minutes)

1. The simplest approach to the solution is:

Gross margin lost if the store is closed		$(316,800)
Costs that can be avoided:		
Sales salaries	$70,000	
Direct advertising..	51,000	
Store rent...	85,000	
Delivery salaries	4,000	
Store management salaries		
($21,000 - $12,000)	9,000	
Salary of new manager..................................	11,000	
General office salaries	6,000	
Insurance on inventories ($7,500 x 2/3).........	5,000	
Utilities...	31,000	
Employment taxes	15,000*	287,000
Decrease in company profits if the North Store		
is closed		$ (29,800)

*Salaries avoided by closing the store:	
Sales salaries	$70,000
Delivery salaries	4,000
Store management salaries	9,000
Salary of new manager...................................	11,000
General office salaries	6,000
Total avoided...	100,000
Employment tax rate.......................................	× 15%
Employment taxes avoided..............................	$ 15,000

Problem 13-17 (continued)

Alternate Solution:

	North Store Kept Open	North Store Closed	Difference: Net Income Increase or (Decrease)
Sales...................................	$720,000	$ —	$(720,000)
Less cost of goods sold.............	403,200	—	403,200
Gross margin	316,800	—	(316,800)
Operating expenses:			
Selling expenses:			
Sales salaries......................	70,000	—	70,000
Direct advertising	51,000	—	51,000
General advertising	10,800	10,800	—
Store rent	85,000	—	85,000
Depreciation of store fixtures	4,600	4,600	—
Delivery salaries..................	7,000	3,000	4,000
Depreciation of delivery equipment	3,000	3,000	—
Total selling expenses	231,400	21,400	210,000
Administrative expenses:			
Store management salaries....	21,000	12,000	9,000
Salary of new manager	11,000	—	11,000
General office salaries............	12,000	6,000	6,000
Insurance on fixtures and inventory	7,500	2,500	5,000
Utilities	31,000	—	31,000
Employment taxes†.................	18,150	3,150	15,000*
General office—other	18,000	18,000	—
Total administrative expenses...........................	118,650	41,650	77,000
Total expenses	350,050	63,050	287,000
Net operating income (loss)	$ (33,250)	$(63,050)	$ (29,800)

*See the computation on the prior page.
† 15% (70,000 + 7,000 + 21,000 + 11,000 + 12,000) = $18,150

Problem 13-17 (continued)

2. Based on the data in (1), the North Store should not be closed. If the store is closed, then the company's overall net income will decrease by $29,800 per quarter.

3. Under these circumstances, the North Store should be closed. The computations are as follows:

Gross margin lost if the North Store is closed
(part 1)... $(316,800)
Gross margin gained from the East Store:
  $720,000 × 1/4 = $180,000; $180,000 x 45%* =
  $81,000 81,000
    Net loss in gross margin .... (235,800)
Less costs that can be avoided if the North Store is
  closed (part 1)... 287,000
Net advantage of closing the North Store .... $ 51,200

*The East Store's gross margin percentage is:
    $486,000 ÷ $1,080,000 = 45%

Problem 13-19 (45 minutes)

1. The $90,000 in fixed overhead costs charged to the new product is a common cost that will be the same regardless of whether the tubes are produced internally or purchased from the outside. Hence, they are not relevant. The variable manufacturing overhead per box of Chap-Off would be $0.50, as shown below:

Total manufacturing overhead cost per box of Chap-Off..	$1.40
Less fixed portion ($90,000 ÷ 100,000 boxes).............	0.90
Variable overhead cost per box	$0.50

The total variable costs of producing one box of Chap-Off would be:

Direct materials	$3.60
Direct labour...	2.00
Variable manufacturing overhead	0.50
Total variable cost per box...	$6.10

If the tubes for the Chap-Off are purchased from the outside supplier, then the variable cost per box of Chap-Off would be:

Direct materials ($3.60 × 75%)	$2.70
Direct labour ($2.00 × 90%)..	1.80
Variable manufacturing overhead ($0.50 × 90%).........	0.45
Cost of tube from outside	1.35
Total variable cost per box...	$6.30

Therefore, the company should reject the outside supplier's offer. A savings of $0.20 per box of Chap-Off will be realized by producing the tubes internally.

Problem 13-19 (continued)

Another approach to the solution would be:

Cost avoided by purchasing the tubes:
Direct materials ($3.60 × 25%)	$0.90
Direct labour ($2.00 × 10%)	0.20
Variable manufacturing overhead	
($0.50 × 10%)	0.05
Total costs avoided	$1.15*

Cost of purchasing the tubes from the outside......... $1.35

Cost savings per box by making internally............... $0.20

*This $1.15 is the cost of making one box of tubes internally, since it
represents the overall cost savings that will be realized per box of
Chap-Off by purchasing the tubes from the outside.

2. The maximum purchase price would be $1.15 per box. The company would not be willing to pay more than this amount, since the $1.15 represents the cost of producing one box of tubes internally, as shown in Part 1. To make purchasing the tubes attractive, however, the purchase price should be *less than* $1.15 per box.

Problem 13-19 (continued)

3. At a volume of 120,000 boxes, the company should buy the tubes. The computations are:

> Cost of making 120,000 boxes:
>> 120,000 boxes x $1.15 .... $138,000
>> Rental cost of equipment 40,000
>>> Total cost $178,000

> Cost of buying 120,000 boxes:
>> 120,000 boxes x $1.35 .... $162,000

> Or, on a total cost basis, the computations are:

> Cost of making 120,000 boxes:
>> 120,000 boxes x $6.10 .... $732,000
>> Rental cost of equipment 40,000
>>> Total cost $772,000

> Cost of buying 120,000 boxes:
>> 120,000 boxes x $6.30 .... $756,000

Thus, buying the boxes will save the company $16,000 per year.

Problem 13-19 (continued)

4. Under these circumstances, the company should make the 100,000 boxes of tubes and purchase the remaining 20,000 boxes from the outside supplier. The costs would:

Cost of making: 100,000 boxes x $1.15......................	$115,000
Cost of buying: 20,000 boxes x $1.35.........................	27,000
Total cost	$142,000

Or, on a total cost basis, the computation would be:

Cost of making: 100,000 boxes x $6.10......................	$610,000
Cost of buying: 20,000 boxes x $6.30.........................	126,000
Total cost	$736,000

Since the amount of cost under this alternative is $20,000 less than the best alternative in Part 3, the company should make as many tubes as possible and buy the remainder from the outside supplier.

5. a) The ability of the supplier to meet required delivery schedules.
   b) The quality of the tubes purchased from the supplier.
   c) Alternate uses of the capacity that would be used to make the tubes.
   d) Ability of the supplier to supply tubes if volume increases in future years.
   e) The problem of alternate sources of supply if the supplier proves undependable.

Problem 13-21 (45 minutes)

1.

	Debbie	Trish	Sarah	Mike	Sewing Kit
Direct labour cost per unit	$ 3.20	$2.00	$ 5.60	$ 4.00	$ 1.60
Direct labour hrs. per unit* (a).......................	0.40 hrs.	0.25 hrs.	0.70 hrs.	0.50 hrs.	0.20 hrs.
Selling price..................	$13.50	$5.50	$21.00	$10.00	$ 8.00
Less variable costs:					
Direct materials	4.30	1.10	6.44	2.00	3.20
Direct labour	3.20	2.00	5.60	4.00	1.60
Variable overhead......	0.80	0.50	1.40	1.00	0.40
Total variable costs....................	8.30	3.60	13.44	7.00	5.20
Contribution margin (b).	$ 5.20	$1.90	$ 7.56	$ 3.00	$ 2.80
Contribution margin per DLH (b) ÷ (a)	$13.00	$7.60	$10.80	$ 6.00	$14.00

*Direct labour cost per unit ÷ $8 per direct labour hour.

2.

Product	DLH Per Unit	Estimated Sales (units)	Total Hours
Debbie..	0.40 hrs.	50,000	20,000
Trish	0.25 hrs.	42,000	10,500
Sarah..	0.70 hrs.	35,000	24,500
Mike..	0.50 hrs.	40,000	20,000
Sewing Kit	0.20 hrs.	325,000	65,000
Total hours required.............			140,000

3. Since the Mike doll provides the lowest contribution margin per labour hour, its production should be reduced by 20,000 dolls (10,000 excess hours divided by 0.5 hrs. production time per doll = 20,000 dolls). Thus, production and sales of the Mike doll will be reduced to one-half of that planned, or 20,000 dolls for the year.

Problem 13-21 (continued)

4. Since the additional capacity would be used to produce the Mike doll, the company should be willing to pay up to $14 per hour ($8 usual rate plus $6 contribution margin per hour) for added labour time. Thus, the company could employ workers for overtime at the usual time-and-a-half rate of $12 per hour ($8 x 1.5 = $12), and still improve overall profit.

5. Additional output could be obtained in a number of ways including working overtime, adding another shift, expanding the workforce, contracting out some work to outside suppliers, and eliminating wasted labour time in the production process. The first four methods are costly, but the last method can add capacity at very low cost.

   Note: Some would argue that direct labour is a fixed cost in this situation and should be excluded when computing the contribution margin per unit. However, when deciding which products to emphasize, no harm is done by misclassifying a fixed cost as a variable cost—providing that the fixed cost is the constraint. If direct labour were removed from the variable cost category, the net effect would be to bump up the contribution margin per direct labour-hour by $8 for each of the products. The products will be *ranked* exactly the same—in terms of the contribution margin per unit of the constrained resource—whether direct labour is considered variable or fixed.

Problem 13-23 (30 minutes)

1. A product should be processed further so long as the incremental revenue from the further processing exceeds the incremental costs. The incremental revenue from further processing of the Grit 337 is:

Selling price of the silver polish, per jar	$4.00
Selling price of 250 grams of Grit 337 ($2.00 ÷ 4).....	0.50
Incremental revenue per jar..................................	$3.50

The incremental variable costs are:

Other ingredients..	$0.65
Direct labour...	1.48
Variable manufacturing overhead (25% × $1.48)...	0.37
Variable selling costs (7.5% × $4)........................	0.30
Incremental variable cost per jar.........................	$2.80

Therefore, the incremental contribution margin is $0.70 per jar ($3.50 – $2.80). The $1.60 cost per kilogram ($0.40 per 250 grams) required to produce the Grit 337 would not be relevant in this computation, since it is incurred regardless of whether the Grit 337 is further processed into silver polish or sold outright.

Problem 13-23 (continued)

2. Only the cost of advertising and the cost of the production supervisor are avoidable if production of the silver polish is discontinued. Therefore, the number of jars of silver polish that must be sold each month to justify continued processing of the Grit 337 into silver polish is:

Production supervisor...	$1,600
Advertising—direct	4,000
Avoidable fixed costs	$5,600

$$\frac{\text{Avoidable fixed costs, } \$5,600}{\text{Incremental CM per jar, } \$0.70} = \underline{8,000} \text{ jars per month}$$

Therefore, if 8,000 jars of silver polish can be sold each month, the company would be indifferent between selling it or selling all of the Grit 337 as a cleaning powder. If the sales of the silver polish are greater than 8,000 jars per month, then continued processing of the Grit 337 into silver polish would be advisable since the company's total profits will be increased. If the company can't sell at least 8,000 jars of silver polish each month, then production of the silver polish should be discontinued. To verify this, we show on the next page the total contribution to profits of sales of 7,000, 8,000 and 9,000 jars of silver polish, contrasted to sales of equivalent amounts of Grit 337 sold outright (i.e., 7,000 jars of silver polish would require the use of 1,750 kilograms of Grit 337 that otherwise could be sold outright as cleaning powder, etc.):

Problem 13-23 (continued)

	7,000 Jars of Polish; or 1,750 Kgs. of Grit 337	8,000 Jars of Polish; or 2,000 Kgs. of Grit 337	9,000 Jars of Polish; or 2,250 Kgs. of Grit 337
Sales of Silver Polish:			
Sales @ $4.00 per jar	$28,000	$32,000	$36,000
Less variable expenses:			
Production cost of Grit 337 @ $1.60 per kg	2,800*	3,200*	3,600*
Further processing and selling costs of the polish @ $2.80 per jar	19,600	22,400	25,200
Total variable expenses	22,400	25,600	28,800
Contribution margin	5,600	6,400	7,200
Less avoidable fixed costs:			
Production supervisor	1,600	1,600	1,600
Advertising	4,000	4,000	4,000
Total avoidable fixed costs	5,600	5,600	5,600
Total contribution to common fixed costs and to profits	$ -0-	$ 800	$ 1,600
Sales of Grit 337:			
Sales @ $2.00 per kg	$ 3,500	$ 4,000	$ 4,500
Less variable expenses:			
Production cost of Grit 337 @ $1.60 per kg	2,800*	3,200*	3,600*
Contribution to common fixed costs and to profits	$ 700	$ 800	$ 900

*This cost will be incurred regardless of whether the Grit 337 is further processed into silver polish or sold outright as cleaning powder; therefore, it is not relevant to the decision, as stated earlier. It is included in the computation above for the specific purpose of showing that it will be incurred under either alternative. The same thing could have been done with the depreciation on the mixing equipment.

© 2001 McGraw-Hill Ryerson Limited

Chapter 14

Capital Budgeting Decisions

Exercise 14-1 (20 minutes)

1. a. From Table 14C-3, the factor for 10% for 3 periods is 0.751. Therefore, the present value of the investment required is: $8,000 x 0.751 = $6,008.

    b. The Table 14C-3, the factor for 14% for 3 periods is 0.675. Therefore, the present value of the investment required is: $8,000 x 0.675 = $5,400.

2.

	Amount of Cash Flows		18%	Present Value of Cash Flows	
Year	A	B	Factor	A	B
1	$ 3,000	$12,000	0.847	$ 2,541	$10,164
2	6,000	9,000	0.718	4,308	6,462
3	9,000	6,000	0.609	5,481	3,654
4	12,000	3,000	0.516	6,192	1,548
				$18,522	$21,828

Investment project B is best.

3. The present value of the first option is $150,000, since the entire amount would be received immediately.

The present value of the second option is:

> Annual annuity: $14,000 x 7.469 (Table 14C-4).............. $104,566
> Lump-sum payment: $60,000 x 0.104 (Table 14C-3)...... 6,240
> Total present value... $110,806

Thus, she should accept the first option, which has a much higher present value.

On the surface, the second option appears to be a better choice since it promises a total cash inflow of $340,000 over the 20-year period ($14,000 x 20 = $280,000; $280,000 + $60,000 = $340,000), whereas the first option promises a cash inflow of only $150,000. However, the cash inflows under the second option are spread out over 20 years, causing the present value to be far less.

Exercise 14-3 (15 minutes)

	Year(s)	Amount of Cash Flows	14% Factor	Present Value of Cash Flows
Purchase of the shares .	Now	$(13,000)	1.000	$(13,000)
Annual cash dividends ..	1-3	420	2.322	975
Sale of the shares	3	16,000	0.675	10,800
Net present value				$ (1,225)

No, Kathy did not earn a 14% return on the Malti Company stock.

Exercise 14-5 (15 minutes)

Item	Year(s)	Amount of Cash Inflows	14% Factor	Present Value of Cash Flows
Project A:				
Cost of equipment....	Now	$(100,000)	1.000	$(100,000)
Annual cash inflows..	1-6	21,000	3.889	81,669
Salvage value of the equipment	6	8,000	0.456	3,648
Net present value				$ (14,683)
Project B:				
Working capital investment..............	Now	$(100,000)	1.000	$(100,000)
Annual cash inflows..	1-6	16,000	3.889	62,224
Working capital released	6	100,000	0.456	45,600
Net present value				$ 7,824

Project B is the better project. Project A is not acceptable at all, since it has a negative net present value.

Alternatively, the profitability indexes of the projects can be computed.

$$\text{Profitability index} = \frac{\text{Present value of cash inflows}}{\text{Investment required}}$$

Project A:

$$\text{Profitability index} = \frac{\$81,669 + \$3,648}{\$100,000} = \frac{\$85,317}{\$100,000} = 0.85$$

Project B:

$$\text{Profitability index} = \frac{\$62,224 + \$45,600}{\$100,000} = \frac{\$107,824}{\$100,000} = 1.08$$

Project B is preferred since its profitability index is higher and is greater than 1.0.

Exercise 14-7 (30 minutes)

1. Annual savings in part-time help $3,800
   Added contribution margin from expanded sales
   (1,000 dozen × $1.20) 1,200
   Annual cash inflows $5,000

2.

$$\text{Factor of the Internal Rate of Return} = \frac{\text{Investment Required}}{\text{Annual Cash Inflow}}$$

$$\frac{\$18,600}{\$5,000} = 3.720$$

Looking in Table 14C-4, and scanning along the six-year line, we can see that a factor of 3.720 falls between the 14% and 16% rates of return. By interpolation, the proper rate can be determined:

	Present Value Factors	
14% factor	3.889	3.889
True factor (above)	3.720	
16% factor		3.685
Difference	0.169	0.204

$$\text{Internal rate of return} = 14\% + \left(\frac{.169}{.204} \times 2\%\right)$$

Internal rate of return = 15.7%

Exercise 14-7 (continued)

3. Since the cash flows will not be even over the six-year life of the machine (there will be an extra $9,125 inflow in the sixth year), it will be necessary to use a trial-and-error approach in computing the internal rate of return. The extra cash inflow in the sixth year will increase the rate of return, so we need to adjust our trial rates upward from the 15.7% computed in Part 2. The proper return will turn out to be 22% (to the nearest whole percent):

Item	Year(s)	Amount of Cash Flows	22% Factor	Present Value of Cash Flows
Initial investment.......	Now	$(18,600)	1.000	$(18,600)
Annual cash inflows..	1-6	5,000	3.167	15,835
Salvage value...........	6	9,125	0.303	2,765
Net present value				$ -0-

Exercise 14-9 (30 minutes)

1. Note: All present value factors in the computation below have been taken from Table 14C-3, using a 12% discount rate.

Amount of the investment		$104,950
Less present value of Year 1 and Year 2 cash inflows:		
Year 1: $30,000 × 0.893................................	$26,790	
Year 2: $40,000 × 0.797................................	31,880	58,670
Present value of Year 3 cash inflow		$ 46,280

Therefore, the expected cash inflow for Year 3 would be:

$46,280 ÷ 0.712 = $65,000.

2. The equipment's net present value without considering the intangible benefits would be:

Item	Year(s)	Amount of Cash Flows	20% Factor	Present Value of Cash Flows
Cost of the equipment..	Now	$(2,500,000)	1.000	$(2,500,000)
Annual cost savings.....	1-15	400,000	4.675	1,870,000
Net present value				$ (630,000)

Therefore, the dollar value per year of the intangible benefits would have to be great enough to offset a $630,000 negative present value for the equipment. This dollar value can be computed as follows:

$$\frac{\text{Net Present Value,} \quad \$(630,000)}{\text{Factor for 15 Years,} \quad 4.675} = \$134,759$$

Exercise 14-9 (continued)

3.

$$\text{Factor of the internal rate of return} = \frac{\text{Investment in the project}}{\text{Annual cash inflow}}$$

$$\frac{\$106,700}{\$20,000} = 5.335$$

Looking in Table 14C-4, and scanning *down* the 10% column, we find that a factor of 5.335 equals 8 years. Thus, the equipment will have to be used for 8 years in order to yield a return of 10%.

As a follow-up question, the instructor may wish to ask the class how many years (approximately) the equipment would have to be used to yield a return of 14%, 18%, 20%, etc.

Exercise 14-11 (15 minutes)

1. The payback period would be:

$$\text{Payback Period} = \frac{\text{Investment Required}}{\text{Net Annual Cash Inflow}}$$

$$\frac{¥432,000}{¥90,000} = 4.8 \text{ years}$$

No, the equipment would not be purchased, since the payback period (4.8 years) exceeds the company's maximum payback time (4.0 years).

2. The simple rate of return would be:

$$\text{Simple Rate of Return} = \frac{\text{Cost Savings - Depreciation}}{\text{Initial Investment}}$$

$$\frac{¥90,000 - ¥36,000 \text{ *}}{¥432,000} = 12.5\%$$

*¥432,000 ÷ 12 years = \$36,000 per year.

No, the equipment would not be purchased, since the rate of return which it promises (12.5%) is less than the company's required rate of return (14%).

Note to the Instructor: This exercise provides a good opportunity to point out that the payback and simple rate of return methods may give incorrect signals to the manager in capital budgeting decisions. This can be done by computing the internal rate of return on the equipment in the problem, and seeing what signal it gives to the manager as to whether the equipment should be purchased. The factor for the internal rate of return would be:

$$\text{Factor of the Internal Rate of Return} = \frac{\text{Investment Required}}{\text{Net Annual Cash Inflow}}$$

$$\frac{¥432,000}{¥90,000} = 4.800$$

Exercise 14-11 (continued)

Looking in Table 14C-4, and reading along the 12-period line, we find that a 4.800 factor represents an internal rate of return of about 17%. Since the company's required return is 14%, the equipment should be purchased. However, notice above that if the manager relied on the simple rate of return to make the decision, the equipment would not be purchased since the simple rate of return is only 12.5%, and thus is less than the required return.

Problem 14-13 (20 minutes)

Item	Year(s)	Amount of Cash Flows	20% Factor	Present Value of Cash Flows
Cost of new equipment	Now	R(275,000)	1.000	R(275,000)
Working capital required......................	Now	(100,000)	1.000	(100,000)
Net annual cash receipts	1-4	120,000	2.589	310,680
Cost to construct new roads..........................	3	(40,000)	0.579	(23,160)
Salvage value of equipment	4	65,000	0.482	31,330
Working capital released	4	100,000	0.482	48,200
Net present value				R (7,950)

No, the project should not be accepted; it has a negative net present value at a 20% discount rate.

Problem 14-15 (30 minutes)

1. The net annual cost savings would be:

Reduction in labour costs	$108,000
Reduction in material waste	6,500
Total..	114,500
Less increased maintenance costs ($3,000 × 12)........	36,000
Net annual cost savings	$ 78,500

2. Using this cost savings figure, and other data from the text, the net present value analysis would be:

Item	Year(s)	Amount of Cash Flows	16% Factor	Present Value of Cash Flows
Cost of the machine.....	Now	$(500,000)	1.000	$(500,000)
Software and installation	Now	(80,000)	1.000	(80,000)
Salvage of the old equipment..................	Now	12,000	1.000	12,000
Annual cost savings (above)	1-12	78,500	5.197	407,965
Replacement of parts...	7	(45,000)	0.354	(15,930)
Salvage of the new machine....................	12	20,000	0.168	3,360
Net present value				$(172,605)

No, the automated welding machine should not be purchased. It has a negative net present value at a 16% discount rate.

3. The dollar value per year that would be required for the intangible benefits would be:

$$\frac{\text{Net Present Value,} \quad \$(172,605)}{\text{Factor for 12 Years,} \quad 5.197} = \$33,212$$

Thus, if management believes that the intangible benefits are worth at least $33,212 per year to the company, then the automated welding machine should be purchased.

Problem 14-17 (30 minutes)

1. The income statement would be:

Sales revenue		$300,000
Less variable expenses:		
Cost of ingredients (20% × $300,000)	$60,000	
Commissions (12.5% × $300,000).............	37,500	97,500
Contribution margin		202,500
Less operating expenses:		
Salaries	$70,000	
Rent ($3,500 × 12)...................................	42,000	
Depreciation	16,800*	
Insurance	3,500	
Utilities...	27,000	159,300
Net income		$ 43,200

  * $270,000 - $18,000 = $252,000; $252,000 ÷ 15 years = $16,800/year.

2. The formula for the simple rate of return is:

$$\text{Simple Rate of Return} = \frac{\text{Net Income}}{\text{Initial Investment}}$$

$$\frac{\$43,200}{\$270,000} = 16.0\%$$

Yes, the outlet should be opened since it promises a rate of return in excess of 12%.

Problem 14-17 (continued)

3. The formula for the payback period is:

$$\text{Payback Period} = \frac{\text{Initial Investment}}{\text{Net Annual Cash Inflow}}$$

$$\frac{\$270,000}{\$60,000\,*} = 4.5 \text{ years}$$

*$43,200 Net Income + $16,800 Depreciation = $60,000 Annual Cash Inflow.

According to the payback computation, the outlet should not be opened. The 4.5 years payback is greater than the maximum 4 years allowed. Payback and simple rate of return often given conflicting signals to the manager.

Problem 14-19 (50 minutes)

1. The net cash inflow from sales of the device for each year would be:

	Year			
	1	**2**	**3**	**4-12**
Sales in units	6,000	12,000	15,000	18,000
Sales in dollars (@ $35 each)..............	$ 210,000	$420,000	$525,000	$630,000
Less variable expenses (@ $15 each)..............	90,000	180,000	225,000	270,000
Contribution margin	120,000	240,000	300,000	360,000
Less fixed expenses:				
Salaries and other*	110,000	110,000	110,000	110,000
Advertising	180,000	180,000	150,000	120,000
Total fixed expenses	290,000	290,000	260,000	230,000
Net cash inflow (outflow).....................	$(170,000)	$ (50,000)	$ 40,000	$130,000

*Depreciation is not a cash expense and therefore must be eliminated from this computation. The analysis is:

($315,000 – $15,000 = $300,000) ÷ 12 years = $25,000 depreciation; $135,000 total expense – $25,000 depreciation = $110,000.

Problem 14-19 (continued)

2. The net present value of the proposed investment would be:

Item	Year(s)	Amount of Cash Flows	14% Factor	Present Value of Cash Flows
Investment in equipment	Now	$(315,000)	1.000	$(315,000)
Working capital needed	Now	(60,000)	1.000	(60,000)
Yearly cash flows (see above)	1	(170,000)	0.877	(149,090)
Yearly cash flows (see above)	2	(50,000)	0.769	(38,450)
Yearly cash flows (see above)	3	40,000	0.675	27,000
Yearly cash flows (see above)	4-12	130,000	3.338*	433,940
Salvage value of equipment	12	15,000	0.208	3,120
Release of working capital........................	12	60,000	0.208	12,480
Net present value				$ (86,000)

*Present value factor for 12 periods.........................	5.660
Present value factor for 3 periods...........................	2.322
Present value factor for 9 periods, starting 4 periods in the future	3.338

Since the net present value is negative, the company should not accept the device as a new product line.

Problem 14-21 (30 minutes)

1. The total-cost approach:

Item	Year(s)	Amount of Cash Flows	16% Factor	Present Value of Cash Flows
Purchase the new truck:				
Initial investment— new truck	Now	$(30,000)	1.000	$(30,000)
Salvage of the old truck.........................	Now	9,000	1.000	9,000
Annual cash operating costs	1-8	(6,500)	4.344	(28,236)
Salvage of the new truck.........................	8	4,000	0.305	1,220
Present value of the net cash outflows				$(48,016)
Keep the old truck:				
Overhaul needed now.	Now	$ (7,000)	1.000	$ (7,000)
Annual cash operating costs	1-8	(10,000)	4.344	(43,440)
Salvage of the old truck.........................	8	1,000	0.305	305
Present value of the net cash outflows				$(50,135)
Net present value in favour of purchasing the new truck				$ 2,119

The company should purchase the new truck, since it has the lowest present value of total cost.

Problem 14-21 (continued)

2. The incremental-cost approach:

Item	Year(s)	Amount of Cash Flows	16% Factor	Present Value of Cash Flows
Incremental investment—new truck............................	Now	$(23,000)*	1.000	$(23,000)*
Salvage of the old truck...........................	Now	9,000	1.000	9,000
Savings in annual cash operating costs...	1-8	3,500	4.344	15,204
Difference in salvage value in 8 years............	8	3,000	0.305	915
Net present value in favour of purchasing the new truck				$ 2,119

*$30,000 – $7,000 = $23,000. The $9,000 salvage value now of the old truck could also be deducted, leaving an incremental investment for the new truck of only $14,000.

Problem 14-23 (30 minutes)

The net annual cash inflow from rental of the property would be:

Net income, as shown in the problem......................	$32,000
Add back depreciation..	16,000
Net annual cash inflow	$48,000

Given this figure, the present value analysis would be as follows:

Item	Year(s)	Amount of Cash Flows	12% Factor	Present Value of Cash Flows
Keep the property:				
Annual loan payment..............	1-8	$ (12,000)	4.968	$(59,616)
Net annual cash inflow	1-15	48,000	6.811	326,928
Resale value of the property	15	230,000*	0.183	42,090
Present value of cash flows....				$ 309,402
Sell the property:				
Pay-off of mortgage	Now	$(90,000)	1.000	$(90,000)
Down payment received..............	Now	175,000	1.000	175,000
Annual payments received..............	1-15	26,500	6.811	180,492
Present value of cash flows....				$ 265,492
Net present value in favour of keeping the property				$ 43,910

*Land, $50,000 x 3 = $150,000, plus building, $80,000 = $230,000.

Thus, Professor Martinas should be advised to keep the property. Note that even if the property were worth nothing at the end of 15 years, it would still be more desirable to keep the property rather than sell it under the terms offered by the realty company.

Problem 14-25 (60 minutes)

1.

$$\text{Factor of the Internal Rate of Return} = \frac{\text{Investment in the Project}}{\text{Annual Cash Inflow}}$$

$$\frac{\$330,000}{\$80,000} = 4.125$$

From Table 14C-4, reading along the 9-period line, a factor of 4.125 falls between 18% and 20%. By interpolating:

18% factor...........	4.303	4.303
True factor..........	4.125	
20% factor...........		4.031
Difference	0.178	0.272

$$\text{Internal Rate of Return} = 18\% + \left(\frac{0.178}{0.272} \times 2\%\right)$$

$$\text{Internal Rate of Return} = 19.3\%$$

2.

$$\text{Factor of the Internal Rate of Return} = \frac{\text{Investment in the Project}}{\text{Annual Cash Inflow}}$$

We know the investment is $330,000, and we can determine the factor for an internal rate of return of 14% by looking in Table 14C-4 along the 9-period line. This factor is 4.946. Using these figures in the formula, we get:

$$\frac{\$330,000}{\text{Annual Cash Inflow}} = 4.946$$

Therefore, the annual cash inflow would be: $330,000 ÷ 4.946 = $66,721.

Problem 14-25 (continued)

3. a. 6-year useful life:

The factor for the internal rate of return would still be 4.125 [as computed in (1) above]. From Table 14C-4, reading along the 6-period line, a factor of 4.125 falls between 10% and 12%. By interpolating:

10% factor.....................	4.355	4.355
True factor.....................	4.125	
12% factor.....................		4.111
Difference.....................	0.230	0.244

Internal Rate of Return $= 10\% + \left(\dfrac{0.230}{0.244} \times 2\% \right)$

Internal Rate of Return $= 11.9\%$

b. 12-year useful life:

The factor of the internal rate of return would again be 4.125. From Table 14C-4, reading along the 12-period line, a factor of 4.125 falls between 22% and 24%. By interpolating:

22% factor.....................	4.127	4.127
True factor.....................	4.125	
24% factor.....................		3.851
Difference.....................	0.002	0.276

Internal Rate of Return $= 22\% + \left(\dfrac{0.002}{0.275} \times 2\% \right)$

Internal Rate of Return $= 22.0\%$

Problem 14-25 (continued)

The 11.9% return in part (a) is less than the 14% minimum return that Ms. Winder wants to earn on the project. Of equal or even greater importance, the following diagram should be pointed out to Ms. Winder:

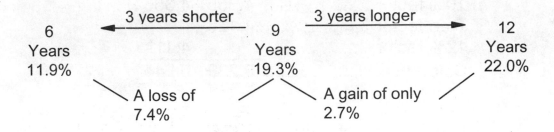

As this illustration shows, a *decrease* in years has a much greater impact on the rate of return than an *increase* in years. This is because of the time value of money; added cash inflows far into the future do little to enhance the rate of return, but loss of cash inflows in the near term can do much to reduce it. Therefore, Ms. Winder should be *very* concerned about any potential decrease in the life of the equipment, while at the same time realizing that any increase in the life of the equipment will do little to enhance her rate of return.

Problem 14-25 (continued)

4. a. The expected annual cash inflow would be:

$80,000 × 80% = $64,000.

$$\frac{\$330,000}{\$64,000} = 5.156 \text{ (rounded)}$$

From Table 14C-4, reading along the 9-period line, a factor of 5.156 falls between 12% and 14%. By interpolating:

12% factor	5.328	5.328
True factor	5.156	
14% factor		4.946
Difference	0.172	0.382

$$\text{Internal Rate of Return} = 12\% + \left(\frac{0.172}{0.382} \times 2\%\right)$$

Internal Rate of Return = 12.9%

b. The expected annual cash inflow would be:

$80,000 × 120% = $96,000.

$$\frac{\$330,000}{\$96,000} = 3.438 \text{ (rounded)}$$

From Table 14C-4, reading along the 9-period line, a factor of 3.438 falls between 24% and 26%. By interpolating:

24% factor	3.566	3.566
True factor	3.438	
26% factor		3.366
Difference	0.128	0.200

Problem 14-25 (continued)

$$\text{Internal Rate of Return} = 24\% + \left(\frac{0.128}{0.200} \times 2\%\right)$$

$$\text{Internal Rate of Return} = 25.3\%$$

Unlike changes in time, increases and decreases in *cash flows* at a given point in time have basically the same impact on the rate of return, as shown below:

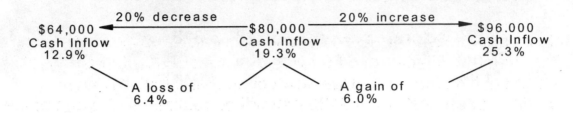

Problem 14-25 (continued)

5. Since the cash flows are not even over the 8-year period (there is an extra $135,440 cash inflow from sale of the equipment at the end of the eighth year), it will be necessary to use a trial-and-error approach to compute the internal rate of return. A good way to start is to estimate what the rate of return would be *without* the sale of equipment:

$$\frac{\$330,000 \text{ Investment}}{\$50,000 \text{ Annual Cash Inflow}} = 6.600 \text{ Factor}$$

Looking in Table 14C-4, and scanning along the 8-period line, we can see that a factor of 6.600 would represent an internal rate of return of less than 5%. If we now consider the fact that an additional cash inflow of $135,440 will be realized at the end of the eighth year, it becomes obvious that the true internal rate of return will be *greater* than 5%. By a trial-and-error process, and moving upward from 5%, we can eventually determine that the actual internal rate of return will be 10% (to the nearest whole percent):

Item	Year(s)	Amount of Cash Flows	10% Factor	Present Value of Cash Flows
Investment in the equipment..............	Now	$(330,000)	1.000	$(330,000)
Annual cash inflow...	1-8	50,000	5.335	266,750
Sale of the equipment..............	8	135,440	0.467	63,250
Net present value				$ -0-

Problem 14-27 (30 minutes)

1. The income statement would be:

Ticket revenue (50,000 x $3.60)		$180,000
Less operating expenses:		
Salaries	$85,000	
Insurance	4,200	
Utilities	13,000	
Depreciation	27,500 *	
Maintenance	9,800	
Total operating expenses		139,500
Net income		$ 40,500

  *$330,000 ÷ 12 years = $27,500 per year.

2. The simple rate of return would be:

$$\text{Simple Rate of Return} = \frac{\text{Net Income}}{\text{Initial Investment - Salvage from Old Equipment}}$$

$$= \frac{\$40,500}{\$330,000 - \$60,000 = \$270,000} = 15.0\%$$

Yes, the water slide would be constructed. Its return is greater than the specified hurdle rate of 14%.

3. The payback period would be:

$$\text{Payback Period} = \frac{\text{Initial Investment - Salvage from Old Equipment}}{\text{Net Annual Cash Inflow}}$$

$$= \frac{\$330,000 - \$60,000 = \$270,000}{\$68,000\,*} = 3.97 \text{ years (rounded)}$$

  *Net income, $40,500 + depreciation, $27,500 = $68,000.

Yes, the water slide would be constructed. The payback period is within the maximum 5 years required by Mr. Sharkey.

Problem 14-29 (40 minutes)

1. a.

Sales revenue		$300,000
Less variable production expenses (@ 20%) .		60,000
Contribution margin		240,000
Less fixed expenses:		
Advertising..	$ 40,000	
Salaries	110,000	
Utilities...	5,200	
Insurance	800	
Depreciation	31,500*	
Total fixed expenses		187,500
Net income...		$ 52,500

   * [$420,000 − (10% × $420,000)] ÷ 12 years = $31,500.

   b. The formula for the simple rate of return is:

$$\text{Simple Rate of Return} = \frac{\text{Incremental Revenue} - \text{Incremental Expenses, including Depreciation}}{\text{Initial Investment}} = \frac{\text{Net Income}}{}$$

$$\frac{\$52,500}{\$420,000} = 12.5\%$$

   c. The formula for the payback period is:

$$\text{Payback Period} = \frac{\text{Investment Required}}{\text{Net Annual Cash Inflow}}$$

$$\frac{\$420,000}{\$84,000*} = 5 \text{ years}$$

   *$52,500 net income + $31,500 depreciation = $84,000.

Problem 14-29 (continued)

2. a. A cost reduction project is involved here, so the formula for the simple rate of return would be:

$$\text{Simple Rate of Return} = \frac{\text{Cost Savings} - \text{Depreciation}}{\text{Initial Investment} - \text{Salvage from Old Equipment}}$$

The reduction in costs with the new equipment would be:

Annual costs, old equipment		$78,000
Annual costs, new equipment:		
Salary of operator	$16,350	
Maintenance	5,400	21,750
Annual savings in costs		$56,250

Thus, the simple rate of return would be:

$$\frac{\$56,250 - \$18,000* = \$38,250}{\$234,000 - \$9,000 = \$225,000} = 17\%$$

*$234,000 ÷ 13 years = $18,000

b. The formula for the payback period remains the same as in Part (1), except we must reduce the investment required by the salvage from sale of the old equipment:

$$\text{Payback Period} = \frac{\text{Investment Required} - \text{Salvage from Old Equipment}}{\text{Net Annual Cash Inflow}}$$

$$\frac{\$234,000 - \$9,000 = \$225,000}{\$56,250*} = 4 \text{ years}$$

*See Part (2a) above.

3. According to the company's criteria, machine B should be purchased. Machine A does not meet either the required minimum rate of return or the 4-year payback period.

Note: The internal rate of return on machine A is about 17%.

Chapter 15
Income Taxes in Capital Budgeting Decisions

Exercise 15-1 (15 minutes)

a.
Management development program cost	$100,000
Multiply by 1 – 30%	× 70%
After-tax cost	$ 70,000

b.
Increased contribution margin	$40,000
Multiply by 1 – 30%	× 70%
After-tax cash flow (benefit)	$28,000

c.

Year	Undepreciated Capital Cost	CCA	Tax Saving	PV Factor 8%	PV of Tax Savings
1	$210,000	31,500	9,450	.926	8,750.70
2	178,500	53,550	16,065	.857	13,767.71
3	124,950	37,485	11,246	.794	8,929.32

Exercise 15-3 (20 minuites)

Items and Computations	Year(s)	(1) Amount	(2) Tax Effect	(1) × (2) After-Tax Cash Flows	12% Factor	Present Value of Cash Flows
Project A:						
Investment in heavy trucks	Now	$(130,000)	—	$(130,000)	1.000	$(130,000)
Net annual cash inflows.............	1-9	25,000	1 – 0.30	17,500	5.328	93,240
CCA Tax Shield:						25,204

$$\frac{Cdt}{D+k} \times \frac{1+.5k}{1+k} - \frac{Sdt}{d+k} \times (1+.5k)^{-n}$$

$$\frac{130,000 \times 0.3 \times 0.3}{(0.3+0.12)} \times \frac{1.06}{1.12} - \frac{15,500 \times 0.3 \times 0.3}{(0.3+0.12)} \times (1.12)^{-9} = 25,204$$

Items and Computations	Year(s)	(1) Amount	(2) Tax Effect	(1) × (2) After-Tax Cash Flows	12% Factor	Present Value of Cash Flows
Salvage value of the trucks...........	9	15,000	—	15,000	0.361	5,415
Net present value...................						$ (6,141)
Project B:						
Investment in working capital	Now	$(130,000)	—	$(130,000)	1.000	$(130,000)
Net annual cash flows.............	1-9	25,000	1 – 0.30	17,500	5.328	93,240
Release of working capital	9	130,000	—	130,000	0.361	46,930
						$10,170

Problem 15-5 (25 minutes)

1. The net present value analysis would be:

Items and Computations	Year(s)	(1) Amount	(2) Tax Effect	(1) × (2) After-Tax Cash Flows	14% Factor	Present Value of Cash Flows
Investment in new trucks............	Now	$(350,00)	—	$(350,000)	1.000	$(350,000)
Salvage from sale of old trucks	Now	16,000	—	16,000	1.000	16,000
New annual cash receipts	1-7	105,000	1-040	63,000	4.039	254,457
Replacement of motors	4	(45,000)	—	45,000	0.552	(24,840)
Salvage from new trucks.............	7	18,000	—	18,000	0.354	6,372

CCA Tax Shield:

From net investment:

$$PV = \frac{Cdt}{D+k} \times \frac{1+.5k}{1+k} - Sdt \times (1+k)^{-n}$$

$$= \frac{334,000 \times 0.3 \times 0.4}{(0.3+0.16)} \times \frac{1+0.5 \times 0.16}{1.16} - \frac{18,000 \times 0.3 \times 0.4}{(0.3+0.16)} \times (1.16)^{-7}$$

$$= 87,130.44 \times 0.93104 - 4,695.65 \times$$

$$= \$81,122 - 1,662$$

$$= \$79,460$$

Problem 15-5 (continued)

Items and Computations	Year(s)	(1) Amount	(2) Tax Effect	(1) × (2) After-Tax Cash Flows	14% Factor	Present Value of Cash Flows

From replacement of motors:

$$PV = \frac{Cdt}{D+k} \times \frac{1 + .5k}{1 + k} - Sdt \times (1 + k)^{-n}$$

$$= \frac{45,000 \times 0.3 \times 0.4}{(0.3 + 0.16)} \times \frac{1 + 0.5 \times 0.16}{1.16} \times 0.16 \times (1.16)^{-7}$$

$$= 11,739 \times 0.93104 \times 0.552 \qquad\qquad = 6,033$$

Net present value $= \$(12,518)$

Since the project has a negative NPV, it shoould not be accepted

Problem 15-7 (45 minutes)

1. The net annual cash receipts under the contract would be:

Revenues from the contract	$ 450,00
Less out-of-pocket costs	280,000
Net annual cash receipts..................................	170,000

© 2001 McGraw-Hill Ryerson Limited

Exercise 15-7 (continued)

Items and Computations	Year(s)	(1) Amount	(2) Tax Effect	(1) × (2) After-Tax Cash Flows	14% Factor	Present Value of Cash Flows
Investment in special equipment....	Now	$(600,000)	—	$(600,000)	1.000	$(600,000)
Working capital needed............	Now	(115,000)	—	(115,000)	1.000	(115,000)
New annual cash receipts(above)..	1-8	170,000	1 – 0.30	119,000	4.639	552,041
CCA Tax Shields						98,824

$$\frac{Cdt}{D+k} \times \frac{1+.5k}{1+k} - \frac{Sdt}{d+k} \times (1+.5k)^{-n}$$

$$\frac{600,000 \times 0.2 \times 0.3}{(0.2+0.14)} \times \frac{1.07}{1.14} - \frac{9,000 \times 0.2 \times 0.3 \times (1.14)^{-8}}{(0.2+0.14)}$$

$$= 105,882.35 \times 0.938596 - 1,588.23 \times 0.3506$$

$$= 99380.75 - 556.83$$

$$= \underline{\underline{98,824}}$$

Salvage value of the equipment.....	8	9,000	—	9,000	0.351	3,159
Release of working capital	8	115,000	—	115,000	0.351	40,365
Net present value.......................						$ (20,611)

The contract should *not* be accepted, since it does not provide the minimum 14% rate of return.

Problem 15-7 (continued)

2)

Items and Computations	Year(s)	(1) Amount	(2) Tax Effect	(1) × (2) After-Tax Cash Flows	14% Factor	Present Value of Cash Flows
Investment in special equipment	Now	$(600,000)	—	$(600,000)	1.000	$(600,000)
Working capital needed............	Now	(115,000)	—	(115,000)	1.000	(115,000)
New annual cash receipts (above) .	1-8	170,000	1 – 0.30	119,000	4.639	552,041
CCA Tax Shields						247,060

$$\frac{Cdt}{D+k} \times \frac{1+.5k}{1+k} - \frac{Sdt}{d+k} \times (1+.5k)^{-n}$$

$$\frac{600{,}000 \times 0.5 \times 0.3}{(0.2+0.14)} \times \frac{1.07}{1.14} - \frac{9{,}000 \times 0.5 \times 0.3 \times (1.14)^{-8}}{(0.2+0.14)} \times 0.3506$$

$$=264{,}705.88 \times 0.938596 - 3{,}970.59 \times 0.3506$$

$$=248{,}451.88 - 1{,}392.09$$

$$=\underline{\underline{247{,}060}}$$

Items and Computations	Year(s)	(1) Amount	(2) Tax Effect	(1) × (2) After-Tax Cash Flows	14% Factor	Present Value of Cash Flows
Salvage value of equipment..........	8	9,000	—	9,000	0.351	3,159
Release of working capital	8	115,000	—	115,000	0.351	40,365
Net present value.................						$ 127,625

The contract should be accepted, since it provides a return greater than the minimum 14% rate of return.

Problem 15-7 (continued)

3. The rate of return in Part 1 because of the use of accelerated depreciation that provides earlier recognition of tax savings because of a higher CCA rate. Thus, simply the choice of a depreciation method can make a difference between a project being acceptable or unacceptable.

Problem 15-9 (60 minutes)

1.

		Year			Total
	1	2	3	4-10	1-10
Tonnes extracted..........	90,000	145,000	240,000	180,000	1,735,000
Contribution margin per tonne					
($7 − $3 = $4).............	× $4	× $4	× $4	× $4	
Total contribution margin	$360,000	$580,000	$960,000	$720,000	
Less fixed costs for salaries, etc.	450,000	450,000	450,000	450,000	
Net cash receipts (outflow)	$ (90,000)	130,000	$510,000	$270,000	

2. See the present value computations that begin on the next page.

No, the project should not be undertaken; it has a negative net present value at an 18% discount rate.

Problem 15-9 (continued)

Items and Computations	Year(s)	(1) Amount	(2) Tax Effect	(1) × (2) After-Tax Cash Flows	14% Factor	Present Value of Cash Flows
Cost of special equipment............	Now	$(600,000)	—	$(800,000)	1.000	$(800,000)
Working capital needed...............	Now	(75,000)	—	(75,000)	1.000	(75,000)
Net cash receipts (above)............	1	(90,000)	1 − 0.30	(63,000)	0.847	53,361
Net cash receipts (above)............	2	130,000	1 − 0.30	91,000	0.718	65,338
Net cash receipts (above)............	3	510,000	1 − 0.30	357,000	0.609	217,413
Net cash receipts (above)............	4 - 10	270,000	1 − 0.30	189,000	2.320*	438,480
CCA Tax Shields........................						127,555

$$PV = \frac{Cdt}{D+k} \times \frac{1+.5k}{1+k} - \frac{Sdt}{d+k} \times (1+k)^{-n}$$

$$= \frac{800{,}000 \times 0.25 \times 0.3}{(0.25+0.18)} \times \frac{1+0.5 \times 0.18}{1.18} - \frac{40{,}000 \times 0.25 \times 0.3}{(0.25+0.18)} \times (1.18)^{-10}$$

$$= 139{,}534 \times 0.9237 - 6{,}977 \times 0.191$$

Problem 15-9 (continued)

Items and Computations	Year(s)	(1) Amount	(2) Tax Effect	(1) × (2) After-Tax Cash Flows	14% Factor	Present Value of Cash Flows
Filling and leveling of land	10	$(250,000)	1 − 0.30	$(175,000)	0.191	$(33,425)
Salvage value of the equipment	10	40,000		40,000	0.191	7,640
(5% × $800,000)						
Working capital released	10	75,000		75,000	0.191	14,325
Net present value						$ 15,687

Yes, the project should not be undertaken; it has a positive net present value at an 185 discount rate.

* Factor for an annuity of 10 years at 18%	4.494
Factor for an annuity of 3 years at 18%	2.174
Difference	2.320

Problem 15-11 (45 minutes)

Alternative 1

Items and Computations	Year(s)	(1) Amount	(2) Tax Effect	(10 × (2) After-Tax Cash Flows	8% Factor	Present Value of Cash Flows
Investment in the bonds............	Now	$(225,000)	—	$(225,000)	1.000	$(225,000)
Salary at the university.............	1-12	75,000	1-36	48,000	7.536	361,728
Interest on bonds (12.5% of 225,000)...	1-12	28,125	1-0.36	18,000	7.536	135,648
Maturity of the bonds	12	225,000	—	225,000	0.397	89,325
Net present value.....................						$ 361,701

Problem 15-11 (continued)

Alternative 2

Items and Computations	Year(s)	(1) Amount	(2) Tax Effect	(10 × 2) After-Tax Cash Flows	8% Factor	Present Value of Cash Flows
Investment in the business	Now	$(225,000)	—	$(225,000)	1.000	$(225,000)
Net annual cash receipts (872,500 - $760,000 = $112,500	1-12	112,500	1-36	72,000	7.536	542,592
Present value of tax shield	1.12					19,152
.Payment to break the lease	12	(2,500)	1-0.36	(1,600)	0.397	(635)
Working capital released................	12	145,000	—	145,000	0.397	57,565
Net present value.......................						393,674
Net present value in favour of alternative 2						$31,973

CCA tax shield:

$$PV = \frac{Cdt}{D+k} \times \frac{1 + .5k}{1+k} - \frac{Sdt}{d+k} \times (1+k)^{-n}$$

$$= \frac{80,000 \times 0.2 \times 0.36}{(0.25 + 0.16)} \times \frac{1 + 0.5 \times 0.08}{1.08} - \frac{0 \times 0.2 \times 0.36}{(0.2 + 0.08)} \times (1.08)^{-12}$$

$$= 20,571 \times 0.931 - 0 = 19,152$$

Problem 15-13 (60 minutes)

1.

Buy the new trucks:

Items and Computations	Year(s)	(1) Amount	(2) Tax Effect	(10 × (2) After-Tax Cash Flows	12% Factor	Present Value of Cash Flows
Investment in the trucks	Now	$(650,000)	—	$(650,000)	1.000	$(650,000)
Sale price received on old trucks	Now	85,000	—	85,000	1.000	85,000
Annual cash operating costs	1-7	(110,000)	1-0.30	(77,000)	4.564	(351,428)
PV of CCA tax shield						10,223
Salvage value of the new trucks	7	60,000	—	60,000	0.452	27,120
Present value of cash flows						$(779,085)

Keep the old trucks:

Items and Computations	Year(s)	(1) Amount	(2) Tax Effect	(10 × (2) After-Tax Cash Flows	12% Factor	Present Value of Cash Flows
Repairs needed	1	$(170,000)	1-0.30	$(119,000)	0.893	$(106,267)
Annual cash operating costs	1-7	(200,000)	1-0.30	(140,000)	4.564	(638,960)
Salvage value of the old trucks	7	15,000	—	15,000	0.452	6,780
Present value of cash flows						(738,477)
Net present value in favour of keeping the old trucks						$40,638

Problem 15-13 (continued)

2. The solution by the incremental-cost approach would be as follows:

Items and Computations	Year(s)	(1) Amount	(2) Tax Effect	(10 × (2)) After-Tax Cash Flows	12% Factor	Present Value of Cash Flows
Investment in the new trucks	Now	$(650,000)	—	$(650,000)	1.000	$(650,000)
Repairs avoided on the old truck	1	170,000	1-0.30	119,000	0.893	102,267
Sale price received on old trucks.....	Now	85,000	—	85,000	1.000	85,000
Savings in annual cash operating costs ($200,000 - $110,000)	1-7	90,000	1-0.30	63,000	4.564	287,532
PV of CCA tax shield						110,223
Difference i salvage value in seven years ($60,000 – 15,000).....	7	45,000	—	45,000	0.452	20,340
Net present value.....						$(40,638)

$$PV = \frac{Cdt}{d+k} \times \frac{1+.5k}{1+k} - \frac{Sdt}{d+k} \times (1+k)^{-n}$$

$$= \frac{565,000 \times 0.3 \times 0.3 \times 1.06}{(0.3+0.12)} \times \frac{1}{1.12} - \frac{45,000 \times 0.3 \times 0.3 \times (1+0.1)^{-7}}{(0.3+0.12)}$$

$$= (\$114,582 \times 0.9464) - (\$9,642.86 \times 0.452) = \$110,223$$

Problem 15-15 (50 minutes)

	Investment 1	Investment 2	Investment 3
A. Initial outlay	$(50,000)	$(25,000)	$(75,000)
B. Salvage value of old machine	5,000	—	—

C. Tax shield on new machine

$$\frac{cdt}{d+k} \times \frac{1+.5k}{1+K}$$

1. $\dfrac{50,000 \times .2 \times .4}{.2 + .16} \times \dfrac{1 + .5 \times .16}{1 + .16}$ 10,345

2. $\dfrac{25,000 \times .3 \times .4}{.3 + .16} \times \dfrac{1 + .5 \times .16}{1 + .16}$ 6,072

3. $\dfrac{75,000 \times .35 \times .4}{.35 + .16} \times \dfrac{1 + .5 \times .16}{1 + .16}$ 19,168

D. Lost tax shield on old machine

$\dfrac{sdt}{d+k} \times \dfrac{5,000(.20)(.40)}{(.16) + (.20)}$ (1,111)   —   —

E. Lost tax shield on new machine

$\dfrac{sdt}{d+k}$ (PV factor)

1. $\dfrac{7,000\,(.20)(.40)}{(.16 + .20)}$ (.641)   (997)

2. NIL

3. $\dfrac{6,000(.35)(.40)}{(.16 + .35)}$ .641   (1,056)

Problem 15-15 (continued)

	Investment 1	Investment 2	Investment 3
F. Savings or income value (annuity factor)			
1. 33,000(2.246)(.60)	44,471		
2. (9,000 + 4,800)(3.274)(.60).................		27,109	
3. [125,000(.1) + 145,000(.2) + 165,000(.3) + 185,000(.4)] (0.60)(2.246)(0.35)..............................			77,824
G. Present value of salvage on new machine			
1. 7,000 × .641...	4,487		
2. NIL			
3. 6,000 × .641...			3,846
H. Miscellaneous cash flows (700 × .60)......		(420)	
Net present value	$ 12,195	$ 7,761	$ 24,782

Either the first and second investment should be made (i.e., investment = $50,000 + $25,000 = $75,000) or investment 3 should be made. Since the third investment has a higher net present value than investments 1 and 2 put together (i.e., $12,195 + $7,761 = $19,956 which is less than $24,782), the third investment should be made.

(SMAC Adapted)

Problem 15-17 (30 minutes)

1. Pessimistic

($500 × 6.811 − $15,000	=	−$11,595
($2,000 × 6.811 − $15,000	=	−$1,378

   Most likely

($3,500 × 6.811 − $15,000	=	8,839
($3,300 × 6.811) − $15,000	=	7,476

   Optimistic

($4,500 × 6.811 − $15,000	=	15,650
($3,900 × 6.811) − $15,000	=	11,563

2. Expected NPV—project A

   (.15 × $500) + (.7 × $3,500) + (.15 × $4,500) = $3,200.

   This yearly expected value of $3,200 is then multiplied by the 12 percent annuity factor of 6.811 to give $21,795—From this amount we deduct the $15,000 investment to give an NPV of $6,795.

   Expected NPV—project B

   (.15 × $2,000) + (.7 × $3,300) + (.15 × $3,900) = $3,195.

   This yearly expected value is multiplied by the 12 percent annuity factor of 6.811 to give $21,761—From this amount we deduct the $15,000 investment to give $6,761.

   A difference of $34 in the expected values of projects A and B seems immaterial. On the basis of expected value alone, a manager would be indifferent in choosing between the projects.

Problem 15-17 *(continued)*

3. *Project A*

i	E_i	$\bar{E}$	$(E_i-\bar{E})$	$(E_i-\bar{E})^2$	P_i	$(E_i-\bar{E})^2 p_i$
1	500	3,200	−2,700	7,290,000	.15	1,093,500
2	3,500	3,200	300	90,000	.70	63,000
3	4,500	3,200	1,300	1,690,000	.15	253,500
					variance =	$1,410,000

Standard deviation = $\sqrt{\$1{,}410{,}000}$ = $1,187

Project B

1	2,000	3,195	−1,195	1,428,025	.15	214,204
2	3,300	3,195	105	11,025	.70	7,718
3	3,900	3,195	705	497,025	.15	74,554
					variance =	$ 296,476

Standard deviation = $\sqrt{\$296{,}476}$ = $545

Coefficient of variation:

	A	B
$\dfrac{\text{standard deviation}}{\text{expected value}}$ =	$\dfrac{\$1{,}187}{\$3{,}200}$ = .37;	$\dfrac{\$545}{\$3{,}195}$ = .17

4. Project A is more risky than project B as evidenced by both the higher standard deviation and a larger coefficient of variation. The calculation of the coefficient of variation really was not necessary because it does not provide any additional information than the standard deviation when the expected values are the same which is essentially true for this problem.

Which project one would actually select depends on whether one is a risk taker or is risk adverse. A risk taker may select project A in the hope of higher returns while a risk adverter would probably choose project B with less variability in its returns.

Chapter 16
Service Department Costing: An Activity Approach

(See Next Page for Exercise 16-1 Chart)

Exercise 16-1 (20 minutes)

	Service Departments			Operating Departments		
	A	B	C	1	2	Total
Overhead costs	$140,000	$105,000	$48,000	$275,000	$430,000	$998,000
Allocation:						
Department A: (5%; 20%; 45%;	(140,000)	7,000	28,000	63,000	42,000	
Department B: (1/8; 2/8; 5/8)		(112,000)	14,000	28,000	70,000	
Department C: (1/3; 2/3)			(90,000)	30,000	60,000	
Total overhead costs after allocations	$ -0-	$ -0-	$ -0-	$396,000	$602,000	$998,000

* Typically, allocations can either be shown in percentages, in fractions, or as a rate per unit of activity. Department A allocations, for example, have been shown as percentages above, but they could have been shown as 1/20; 4/20; 9/20; and 6/20 or they could have been shown as $200 per employee. Usually fractions will be used if percentages result in odd decimals. Both percentages and fractions are used above for sake of illustration.

Supporting computations:

Department A allocated to:

Dept. B	35 emp.	5%	
Dept. C	140 "	20	
Dept. 1	315 "	45	
Dept. 2	210 "	30	
	700 emp.	100%	

Department B allocated to:

Dept. C	2,000 sq. m.	1/8
Dept. 1	4,000 sq. m.	2/8
Dept. 2	10,000 sq. m.	5/8
	16,000 sq. m.	8/8

Department C allocated to:

Dept. 1	30,000 hrs.	1/3
Dept. 2	60,000 hrs.	2/3
	90,000 hrs.	3/3

Exercise 16-3 (10 minutes)

	Northern Plant	Southern Plant
Variable costs:		
120,000 tonnes × $0.25	$ 30,000	
60,000 tonnes × $0.25		$ 15,000
Fixed costs:		
70% × $300,000..	210,000	
30% × $300,000..		90,000
Total allocated costs	$240,000	$105,000

Exercise 16-5 (20 minutes)

1.

	Restaurant			
	Rick's Harbourside	Imperial Garden	Ginger Wok	Total
Percentage of 1999 sales	32%	50%	18%	100%
Allocation of 1999 fixed administrative expenses (based on the above percentages)	$ 640,000	$1,000,000	$360,000	$2,000,000

2.

1999 allocation (above)	$ 640,000	$1,000,000	$360,000	$2,000,000
1998 allocation	800,000	750,000	450,000	2,000,000
Increase (decrease in allocation	$(160,000)	$ 250,000	$ (90,000)	$ -0-

The manager of the Imperial Garden undoubtedly will be upset about the increased allocation of fixed administrative expense forced on his/her restaurant, but he/she will feel powerless to do anything about it. Such increased allocations may be viewed by some managers as a penalty for an outstanding performance.

3. As stated in the text, sales dollars ordinarily are not a good base for allocating fixed costs. The problem is that sales dollars vary from period to period, and as a result can cause one department or division to be allocated costs because of what happens in *other* departments or divisions. In our illustration above, two restaurants remained static, and as a result, forced a greater allocation of costs onto the one restaurant that showed improvement during the period.

Exercise 16-7 (15 minutes)

1.

	Janitorial Services	Radiology	Pediatrics	OB Care	General Hospital
Cost to be allocated	$ 375,000	$590,000			
Allocation:					
Janitorial Services:					
(4%; 20%; 16%; 60%)	(375,000)	15,000	$ 75,000	$ 60,000	$225,000
Radiology: (3/10; 2/10; 5/10)		(605,000)	181,500	121,000	302,500
Total overhead costs after allocations ..	$ -0-	$ -0-	$256,500	$181,000	527,500

Supporting computations:

Janitorial Services

Radiology...............	600 sq. m.	4%
Pediatrics	3,000 sq. m.	20
OB Care...............	2,400 sq. m.	16
General Hospital	9,000 sq. m.	60
	15,000 sq. m.	100%

Radiology:

Pediatrics..............	9,000 X-rays	3/10
OB Care...............	6,000 X-rays	2/10
General Hospital.......	15,000 X-rays	5/10
	30,000 X-rays	10/10

2. The allocations would be the same as in Part 1, since budgeted fixed costs are always allocated to consuming departments. Thus, $6,000 of the actual fixed costs in Janitorial Services and $10,000 of the actual fixed costs in Radiology would not be allocated to other departments.

Problem 16-9 (30 minutes)

1.

	Auto Division	Truck Division
Variable costs:		
$3 × 35,000 meals...............	$105,000	
$3 × 20,000 meals...............		$60,000
Fixed costs:		
65% × $40,000....................	26,000	
35% × $40,000....................		14,000
Total cost allocated................	$131,000	$74,000

The variable costs are allocated according to the budgeted rate per meal, multiplied by the budgeted number of meals which will be served in each division during the month. The fixed costs are allocated in predetermined lump-sum amounts based on the peak-period need for meals in each division.

© 2001 McGraw-Hill Ryerson Limited

Problem 16-9 (continued)

2.

	Auto Division	Truck Division
Variable costs:		
$3 × 20,000 meals...............	$60,000	
$3 × 20,000 meals...............		$60,000
Fixed costs:		
65% × $40,000....................	26,000	
35% × $40,000....................		14,000
Total cost allocated.................	$86,000	$74,000

Notice that the variable costs are allocated according to the budgeted rate per meal and not according to the actual rate. Also notice that the fixed costs are again allocated in predetermined, lump-sum amounts, based on budgeted fixed costs. Any difference between budgeted and actual costs is not allocated, but rather is treated as a spending variance in the cafeteria:

	Variable	Fixed
Total actual costs for the month....................	$128,000	$42,000
Total cost allocated above...........................	120,000	40,000
Spending variance—not allocated................	$ 8,000	$ 2,000

Problem 16-9 (continued)

3. Actual variable costs $128,000
    Actual fixed costs 42,000
      Total actual costs....................................... $170,000

    One-half of the cost, or $85,000, would be allocated to each division, since an equal number of meals was served in each division during the month.

4. There are two main criticisms: First, the spending variances should not be allocated, because this forces the inefficiencies of the service department onto the using departments. Second, the fixed costs should *not* be allocated according to month by month usage of services, because this causes the allocation to one division to be affected by what happens in another division.

5. Their strategy probably will be to underestimate their peak period requirements in order to force a greater proportion of any allocation onto other departments. Top management can control ploys of this type by careful follow-up, with rewards being given to those managers who estimate accurately, and severe penalties assessed against those managers who underestimate their peak period requirements.

    For example, departments whose managers underestimate their peak period requirements may be denied access to the cafeteria once their estimates have been exceeded.

Problem 16-11 (30 minutes)

1. Beginning-of-year allocations of variable costs are based on the budgeted rate multiplied by the budgeted level of activity. Fixed costs are allocated in lump-sum amounts based on the peak-period needs of the using departments. The computations are:

	Forming Department	Assembly Department	Total
Variable costs:			
$0.40 × 160,000 machine-hours	$ 64,000		
$0.40 × 80,000 machine-hours		$32,000	$ 96,000
Fixed costs:			
70% × $150,000	105,000		
30% × $150,000		45,000	150,000
Total cost allocated..........	$169,000	$77,000	$246,000

2. a. End-of-year allocations of variable costs are based on the budgeted rate multiplied by the actual level of activity. Fixed costs are again allocated in predetermined lump-sum amounts based on budgeted costs. The computations are:

	Forming Department	Assembly Department	Total
Variable costs:			
$0.40 × 190,000 machine-hours	$ 76,000		
$0.40 × 70,000 machine-hours		$28,000	$104,000
Fixed costs:			
70% × $150,000	105,000		
30% × $150,000		45,000	150,000
Total cost allocated..........	$181,000	$73,000	$254,000

Problem 16-11 (continued)

b. Any amount above the budgeted variable cost per machine-hour and the budgeted total fixed cost would not be allocated to the other departments. The amount not allocated would be:

	Variable Cost	Fixed Cost	Total
Actual cost incurred during the year	$110,000	$153,000	$263,000
Cost allocated (above)	104,000	150,000	254,000
Cost not allocated (spending variance)	$ 6,000	$ 3,000	$ 9,000

As indicated above, the costs not allocated represent spending variances that should be borne by the Maintenance Department.

© 2001 McGraw-Hill Ryerson Limited

Problem 16-13 (60 minutes)

1. and 2.

	Bldg. & Grounds	Admin- istration	Equip. Maint.	Fabrication	Finishing
Variable costs to be allocated	R -0-	R22,200	R16,900		
Administration @ R20 per employee:					
30 × R20		(600)	600		
450 × R20		(9,000)		R 9,000	
630 × R20		(12,600)			R12,600
Equipment maintenance @ R0.10 per MH:					
70,000 × R0.10			(7,000)	7,000	
105,000 × R0.10			(10,500)		10,500
Totals	R -0-	R -0-	R -0-	R16,000	R23,100

Problem 16-13 (continued)

	Bldg. & Grounds	Administration	Equip. Maint.	Fabrication	Finishing
Fixed costs to be allocated..........	R88,200	R60,000	R24,000		
Bldg. & Grounds @ R30 per sq. m.:					
50 × R30	(1,500)	1,500			
140 × R30	(4,200)		4,200		
1,200 × R30	(36,000)			R36,000	
1,550 × R30	(46,500)				R46,500
Administration:					
3% × R61,500		(1,845)	1,845		
38% × R61,500		(23,370)		23,370	
59% × R61,500		(36,285)			36,285
Equipment Maintenance					
40% × R30,045			(12,018)	12,018	
60% × R30,045			(18,027)		18,027
Totals	-0-	-0-	-0-	71,388	100,812
Total Allocated Costs..........	R -0-	R -0-	R -0-	87,388	123,912
Other flexible budget costs at the planned activity level				566,000	810,000
Total overhead costs (a)				R653,388	R933,912
Budgeted machine hours (b)..........				70,000	105,000
Predetermined overhead rate (a) ÷ (b).....				R 9.33	R 8.89

Problem 16-13 (continued)

Computation of allocation rates:

Variable Administration:

$$\frac{\text{Variable costs, R22,200}}{30 + 450 + 630 = 1{,}110} = \text{R20 per employee}$$

Variable Equipment Maintenance:

$$\frac{\text{Variable costs, R16,900 + R600}}{70{,}000 + 105{,}000 = 175{,}000} = \text{R0.10 per MH}$$

Fixed Bldg. & Grounds:

$$\frac{\text{Fixed costs, R88,200}}{50 + 140 + 1{,}200 + 1{,}550 = 2{,}940} = \text{R30 per sq. m.}$$

Fixed Administration:

Department fixed costs..........................	R60,000
Allocated from Bldg. & Grounds	1,500
Costs to be allocated............................	R61,500

Employees at full capacity:

Equipment Maintenance....................	45	3%
Fabrication	570	38
Finishing...	885	59
Total...	R1,500	100%

Fixed Equipment Maintenance:

Department fixed costs......................	R24,000
Allocated from Bldg. & Grounds.........	4,200
Allocated from Administration	1,845
Costs to be allocated..........................	R30,045

Allocation percentages are given in the problem.

Problem 16-13 (continued)

3.

	Equip. Maint.	Fabrication	Finishing	Total
Variable cost allocation:				
32 employees x R20......	R640			R 640
460 employees x R20......		R9,200		9,200
625 employees x R20......			R12,500	12,500
Total cost allocated............				R22,340
Actual variable administration cost				R23,800
Total cost allocated— above				22,340
Spending variance—not allocated...........................				R 1,460

Problem 16-15 (50 minutes)

a. i. Direct Method

Accounting dept. (AD) to Consulting: to AC 3/4 or $6,000
                                        to LC 1/4 or $2,000
Legal dept. (LD) to Consulting: to AC 1/5 or $2,000
                                 to LC 4/5 or $8,000

Income Statements

	Accounting Consulting	Legal Consulting
Revenue......................	$30,000	$20,500
Individual costs	(6,000)	(14,000)
Allocated AD, LD..........	(8,000)	(10,000)
Net income...................	$16,000	$ (3,500)

a. ii. Reciprocal/Cross Allocation Method

AD = 8,000 + .5LD and LD = 10,000 + .2AD
AD = $14,444 and LD = $12,889
Allocating, AD to AC, $8,666; to LC, $2,889
          LD to AC, $1,289; to LC, $5,156

Income Statements

	Accounting Consulting	Legal Consulting
Revenue......................	$30,000	$20,500
Individual costs	(6,000)	(14,000)
Allocated AD, LD..........	(9,955)*	(8,045)*
Net income...................	$14,045	$ (1,545)

---

*$8,666 + $1,289 = $9,955

**$2,889 + $5,156 = $8,045

Problem 16-15 (continued)

b.   *MEMORANDUM*

DATE: Date of examination
TO: Managing Partner
FROM: Independent Consultant
SUBJECT: Performance of Consulting Service

The memorandum should note the following points:

i. Only one month of activity has taken place; therefore, results will be very difficult to analyze. No comparisons are possible. Consequently, any analysis will be highly subjective and, recommendations should be handled carefully.

ii. The performance of the individual departments is different under the different approaches of cost allocation.

iii. The overall performance is satisfactory and since this "one-stop shopping" arrangement is in a sense a joint product set-up, the overall is more important than the artificial measurement of the parts.

iv. Some cost control procedures may be initiated, but these should be handled carefully, since we are dealing with professional staff and we would not want to suppress the creative element in their work. Therefore, the use of standard costing in such an organization may not be warranted.

(SMAC Solution, adapted)

Chapter 17
"How Well Am I Doing? Financial Statement Analysis

Exercise 17-1 (15 minutes)

1. The trend percentages are:

	Year 5	Year 4	Year 3	Year 2	Year 1
Sales	125.0	120.0	115.0	110.0	100.0
Cash	60.0	80.0	96.0	130.0	100.0
Accounts receivable	190.0	170.0	135.0	115.0	100.0
Inventory	125.0	120.0	115.0	110.0	100.0
Total	142.1	133.7	120.3	112.6	100.0
Current liabilities	160.0	145.0	130.0	110.0	100.0

2. Sales: The sales are increasing at a steady and consistent rate.

Assets: The most noticeable thing about the assets is that the accounts receivable have been increasing at a rapid rate—far outstripping the increase in sales. This disproportionate increase in receivables is probably the chief cause of the decrease in cash over the five-year period. The inventory seems to be growing at a well-balanced rate in comparison with sales.

Liabilities: The current liabilities are growing more rapidly than the total current assets. The reason is probably traceable to the rapid buildup in receivables in that the company doesn't have the cash needed to pay bills as they come due.

Exercise 17-3 (25 minutes)

1. Gross margin percentage:

$$\frac{\text{Gross margin,}\ \$127{,}500}{\text{Sales,}\ \ \ \ \ \ \ \ \ \ \ \$420{,}000} = 30.4\%\ \text{(rounded)}$$

2. Current ratio:

$$\frac{\text{Current assets,}\ \ \ \$115{,}000}{\text{Current liabilities,}\ \$\ 50{,}000} = 2.3\ \text{to}\ 1$$

3. Acid-test ratio:

$$\frac{\text{Quick assets,}\ \ \ \ \ \ \$41{,}500}{\text{Current liabilities,}\ \$50{,}000} = 0.83\ \text{to}\ 1$$

4. Debt-to-equity ratio:

$$\frac{\text{Total liabilities,}\ \ \ \ \ \ \ \ \ \ \ \ \ \ \ \ \$130{,}000}{\text{Total shareholders' equity,}\ \$170{,}000} = 0.76\ \text{to}\ 1\ \text{(rounded)}$$

5. Accounts receivable turnover:

$$\frac{\text{Sales on account,}\ \ \ \ \ \ \ \ \ \ \ \ \ \ \ \ \$420{,}000}{\text{Average accounts receivable,}\ \$\ 30{,}000} = 14\ \text{times}$$

$$\frac{365\ \text{days}}{14\ \text{times}} = 26\ \text{days (rounded)}$$

6. Inventory turnover:

$$\frac{\text{Cost of goods sold,}\ \$292{,}500}{\text{Average inventory,}\ \ \ \$\ 65{,}000} = 4.5\ \text{times}$$

$$\frac{365\ \text{days}}{4.5\ \text{times}} = 81\ \text{days to turn (rounded)}$$

7. Times interest earned:

$$\frac{\begin{array}{l}\text{Earnings before interest}\\ \text{and income taxes,}\ \ \ \ \ \ \ \ \$38{,}000\end{array}}{\text{Interest expense,}\ \ \ \ \ \ \ \ \ \ \$\ 8{,}000} = 4.75\ \text{times}$$

8. Book value per share:

$$\frac{\text{Shareholders' equity,}\ \ \ \ \ \ \ \ \ \$170{,}000}{\text{Common shares outstanding,}\ \ \ \ 6{,}000} = \$28.33/\text{share}$$

(rounded)

Exercise 17-5 (20 minutes)

1. Return on total assets:

$$\text{Return on Total Assets} = \frac{\text{Net Income} + [\text{Interest expense} \times (1 - \text{Tax rate})]}{\text{Average Total Assets}}$$

$$\frac{\$21,000 + [\$8,000 \times (1 - 0.30)]}{1/2 \,(\$280,000 + \$300,000)} = \frac{\$26,600}{\$290,000} = 9.2\% \text{ (rounded)}$$

2. Return on common shareholders' equity:

$$\text{Return on Common Shareholders' Equity} = \frac{\text{Net Income} - \text{Preferred Dividends}}{\text{Average Common Shareholders' Equity}}$$

$$\frac{\$21,000}{1/2 \,(\$161,600 + \$170,000)} = \frac{\$21,000}{\$165,800} = 12.7 \text{ (rounded)}$$

3. Financial leverage was positive, since the rate of return to the common shareholders (12.7%) was greater than the rate of return on total assets (9.2%). This positive leverage is traceable in part to the company's current liabilities, which may have no interest cost, and in part to the bonds payable, which have an after-tax interest cost of only 7%.

   10% interest rate $\times$ (1 − 0.30) = 7%.

Exercise 17-7 (15 minutes)

1. Current assets (Kr90,000 + Kr260,000 + Kr490,000 +
   Kr10,000)... Kr850,000
   Current liabilities (Kr850,000 ÷ 2.5)............................ 340,000
   Working capital Kr510,000

2.

$$\text{Acid-Test Ratio} = \frac{\text{Cash + Marketable Securities + Accounts Receivable}}{\text{Current Liabilities}}$$

$$\frac{\text{Kr90,000 + 0 + Kr260,000}}{\text{Kr340,000}} = 1.03 \text{ (rounded)}$$

3. a. Working capital would not be affected:

   Current assets (Kr850,000 – Kr40,000)................... Kr810,000
   Current liabilities (Kr340,000 – Kr40,000)............... 300,000
   Working capital.. Kr510,000

   b. The current ratio would rise:

   $$\text{Current Ratio} = \frac{\text{Current Assets}}{\text{Current Liabilities}}$$

   $$\frac{\text{Kr810,000}}{\text{Kr300,000}} = 2.7 \text{ to } 1$$

Problem 17-9 (30 minutes)

1. a. Computation of working capital:

Current assets:	
Cash...	$ 50,000
Marketable securities...................................	30,000
Accounts receivable, net..............................	200,000
Inventory	210,000
Prepaid expenses..	10,000
Total..	500,000
Current liabilities:	
Accounts payable	150,000
Notes due in one year	30,000
Accrued liabilities..	20,000
Total..	200,000
Working capital..	$300,000

b. Computation of the current ratio:

$$\frac{\text{Current assets,} \quad \$500,000}{\text{Current liabilities,} \quad \$200,000} = 2.5 \text{ to } 1$$

c. Computation of the acid-test ratio:

$$\frac{\text{Cash + Marketable securities + Accounts receivable}}{\text{Current liabilities}} \quad \frac{\$280,000}{\$200,000} = 1.4 \text{ to } 1$$

Problem 17-9 (continued)

2.

Transaction	The Effect on		
	Working Capital	Current Ratio	Acid-Test Ratio
(a) Issue of capital stock for cash ...	Increase	Increase	Increase
(b) Sold inventory at a gain............	Increase	Increase	Increase
(c) Write-off of uncollectible accounts	None	None	None
(d) Declaring of a cash dividend	Decrease	Decrease	Decrease
(e) Payment of accounts payable ...	None	Increase	Increase
(f) Borrowing on a short-term note.	None	Decrease	Decrease
(g) Sold inventory at a loss............	Decrease	Decrease	Increase
(h) Purchase of inventory on account	None	Decrease	Decrease
(i) Payment of short-term notes	None	Increase	Increase
(j) Purchase of equipment for cash	Decrease	Decrease	Decrease
(k) Sold marketable securities at a loss	Decrease	Decrease	Decrease
(l) Collection of accounts receivable...............................	None	None	None

Problem 17-11 (45 minutes)

		This Year	Last Year
1. a.	Net income	$280,000	$196,000
	Less preferred dividends	20,000	20,000
	Net income to common (a)	$260,000	$176,000
	Average number of common shares (b)	50,000	50,000
	Earnings per share (a) ÷ (b)...................	$5.20	$3.52
b.	Common dividend per share (a)............	$ 1.80	$ 1.50
	Market price per share (b)	$40.00	$36.00
	Dividend yield ratio (a) ÷ (b)...................	4.5%	4.2%
c.	Common dividend per share (a)	$1.80	$1.50
	Earnings per share (b)..........................	$5.20	$3.52
	Payout ratio (a) ÷ (b).............................	34.6%	42.6%
d.	Market price per share (a)	$40.00	$36.00
	Earnings per share (b)..........................	$ 5.20	$ 3.52
	Price-earnings ratio (a) ÷ (b).................	7.7	10.2

Investors regard Sabin Electronics less favourably than other firms in the industry, as evidenced by the fact that they are willing to pay only 7.7 times current earnings for a share of Sabin's shares, as compared to 12 times current earnings for the average of all shares in the industry. If investors were willing to pay 12 times current earnings for Sabin's shares, it would be selling for about $62.40 per share (12 × $5.20), rather than for only $40 per share. The fact that the price-earnings ratio is going down (from 10.2 last year to 7.7 this year) while the dividend yield is holding somewhat constant suggests that investors are buying the shares primarily for its dividend yield, rather than for long-term appreciation. The lower price-earnings ratio may also reflect the company's weakened financial position.

Problem 17-11 (continued)

	This Year	Last Year
e. Shareholders' equity..............................	$1,600,000	$1,430,000
Less preferred shares	250,000	250,000
Common shareholders' equity (a)	$1,350,000	$1,180,000
Number of common shares (b)..............	50,000	50,000
Book value per share (a) ÷ (b)...............	$27.00	$23.60

Notice that market value is above book value for both years. However, this does not necessarily indicate that the shares are overpriced. As stated in the text, market value is an indication of investors' perceptions of future earnings and/or dividends, whereas book value is a result of already completed transactions and is geared to the past.

2. a. Net income	$ 280,000	$ 196,000
Add after-tax cost of interest paid:		
[$72,000 × (1 – 0.30)].......................	50,400	50,400
Total (a)	$ 330,400	$ 246,400
Average total assets (b).......................	$2,730,000	$2,380,000
Return on total assets (a) ÷ (b)............	12.1%	10.4%
b. Net income	$ 280,000	$ 196,000
Less preferred dividends	20,000	20,000
Net income remaining for common (a).	$ 260,000	$ 176,000
Average total shareholders' equity.......	$1,515,000	$1,379,500
Less average preferred share..............	250,000	250,000
Average common equity (b).................	$1,265,000	$1,129,500
Return on common equity (a) ÷ (b)......	20.6%	15.6%

Problem 17-11 (continued)

   c. Leverage is positive in both years, since the return on common equity is greater than the return on total assets. This positive financial leverage is due to three factors: the preferred shares, which has a dividend rate of only 8%; the bonds, which have an after-tax interest cost of only 8.4% [12% interest rate × (1 − 0.30) = 8.4%]; and the accounts payable, which may bear no interest cost.

3. The authors would recommend purchase, at least on a speculative basis. The share's downside risk seems small, since it is now selling for only 7.7 times earnings to 12 times earnings for the average firm in the industry. In addition, its earnings are strong and trending upward, and its return on common equity (20.6%) is extremely good. Its return on total assets (12.1%) compares well with that of the industry. The risk, of course, is whether the company can get its cash problem under control. Conceivably, the cash problem could worsen, leading to an eventual reduction in profits through inability to operate, a discontinuance of dividends, and a precipitous drop in the market price of the company's shares. This does not seem likely, however, since the company has borrowing capacity available, and can easily control its cash problem through more careful management of accounts receivable and inventory. The client must understand, of course, that there is risk in the purchase of any shares; the risk seems well justified in this case since the upward potential of the shares is great if the company gets its problems under control.

Problem 17-13 (20 minutes)

1.   LYDEX COMPANY
                        Comparative Balance Sheets

	This Year	Last Year
Current assets:		
Cash	5.6%	8.5%
Marketable securities	—	2.0
Accounts receivable, net	15.8	12.1
Inventory	22.8	16.1
Prepaid expenses	1.4	1.2
Total current assets	45.6	39.9
Plant and equipment, net	54.4	60.1
Total assets	100.0%	100.0%
Current liabilities	22.8%	18.5%
Note payable, 10%	21.1	20.2
Total liabilities	43.9	38.7
Shareholders' equity:		
Preferred stock, 60000, $2.40 no par	10.5	12.1
Common stock, 75000 no par	35.1	40.3
Retained earnings	10.5	8.9
Total shareholders' equity	56.1	61.3
Total liabilities and equity	100.0%	100.0%

Problem 17-13 (continued)

2.

LYDEX COMPANY
Comparative Income Statements

	This Year	Last Year
Sales	100.0%	100.0%
Less cost of goods sold	80.0	79.3
Gross margin	20.0	20.7
Less operating expenses.........................	10.1	12.5
Net operating income..............................	9.9	8.2
Less interest expense.............................	2.3	2.4
Net income before taxes.........................	7.6	5.8
Less income taxes (30%)	2.3	1.7
Net income	5.3%	4.0%*

* Due to rounding, figures may not fully reconcile down a column.

3. The company's current position has declined substantially
between the two years. Cash this year represents only 5.6% of
total assets, whereas it represented 10.5% last year (cash +
marketable securities). In addition, both accounts receivable and
inventory are up from last year, which helps to explain the
decrease in the cash account. The company is building
inventories, but not collecting from customers. (See Problem 17-12
for a ratio analysis of the current assets.) Apparently a part of the
financing required to build inventories was supplied by short-term
creditors, as evidenced by the increase in current liabilities.

Looking at the income statement, as noted in the solution to the
preceding problem there has been a slight deterioration in the
gross margin percentage. Ordinarily, the increase in sales (and in
inventories) should have resulted in an increase in the gross
margin percentage since fixed manufacturing costs would be
spread across more units. Note that the other operating expenses
are down as a percentage of sales—possibly because many of
them are likely to be fixed.

Problem 17-15 (40 minutes)

Effect on Ratio	Reason for Increase, Decrease, or No Effect
1. Decrease	Declaring a cash dividend will increase current liabilities, but have no effect on current assets. Therefore, the current ratio will decrease.
2. Increase	A sale of inventory on account will increase the quick assets (cash, accounts receivable, marketable securities) but have no effect on the current liabilities. For this reason, the acid-test ratio will increase. The same effect would result regardless of whether the inventory was sold at cost, at a profit, or at a loss. That is, the acid-test ratio would increase in all cases; the only difference would be the amount of the increase.
3. Increase	The interest rate on the bonds is only 8%. Since the company's assets earn at a rate of 10%, positive leverage would come into effect, increasing the return to the common shareholders.
4. Decrease	A decrease in net income would mean less income available to cover interest payments. Therefore, the times-interest-earned ratio would decrease.
5. Increase	Payment of a previously declared cash dividend will reduce both current assets and current liabilities by the same amount. An equal reduction in both current assets and current liabilities will always result in an increase in the current ratio, so long as the current assets exceed the current liabilities.
6. No Effect	The dividend payout ratio is a function of the dividends paid per share in relation to the earnings per share. Changes in the market price of a share have no effect on this ratio.
7. Increase	A write-off of inventory will reduce the inventory balance, thereby increasing the turnover in relation to a given level of sales.

Problem 17-15 (continued)

Effect on Ratio	Reason for Increase, Decrease, or No Effect
8. Decrease	Sale of inventory at a profit will increase the assets of a company. The increase in assets will be reflected in an increase in retained earnings, which is part of shareholders' equity. An increase in shareholders' equity will result in a decrease in the ratio of assets provided by creditors as compared to assets provided by owners.
9. Decrease	Extended credit terms for customers means that customers on the average will be taking longer to pay their bills. As a result, the accounts receivable will "turn over," or be collected, less frequently during a given year.
10. Decrease	A common share dividend will result in a greater number of shares outstanding, with no change in the underlying assets. The result will be a decrease in the relative book value per share.
11. No Effect	Book value per share is dependent on historical costs of already completed transactions as reflected on a company's balance sheet. It is not affected by current market prices for the company's stock.
12. No Effect	Payments on account reduce cash and accounts payable by equal amounts; thus, the net amount of working capital is not affected.
13. Decrease	The stock dividend will increase the number of common shares outstanding, thereby reducing the earnings per share.
14. Decrease	Payments to creditors will reduce the total liabilities of a company, thereby decreasing the ratio of total debt to total equity.

Problem 17-15 (continued)

Effect on Ratio	Reason for Increase, Decrease, or No Effect
15. Decrease	A purchase of inventory on account will increase current liabilities, but will not increase the quick assets (cash, accounts receivable, marketable securities). Therefore, the ratio of quick assets to current liabilities will decrease.
16. No Effect	Write-off of an uncollectible account against the Allowance for Bad Debts will have no effect on total current assets. For this reason, the current ratio will remain unchanged.
17. Increase	The price-earnings ratio is obtained by dividing the market price per share by the earnings per share. If the earnings per share remains unchanged, and the market price goes up, then the price-earnings ratio will increase.
18. Decrease	The dividend yield ratio is obtained by dividing the dividend per share by the market price per share. If the dividend per share remains unchanged and the market price goes up, then the yield will decrease.

Problem 17-17 (40 minutes)

1.

	This Year	Last Year
a. Current assets	$ 4,800,000	$ 2,500,000
Current liabilities	2,500,000	1,000,000
Working capital	$ 2,300,000	$ 1,500,000
b. Current assets (a)	$ 4,800,000	$ 2,500,000
Current liabilities (b)	$ 2,500,000	$ 1,000,000
Current ratio (a) ÷ (b)	1.92 to 1	2.5 to 1
c. Quick assets (a)	$ 1,700,000	$ 1,200,000
Current liabilities (b)	$ 2,500,000	$ 1,000,000
Acid-test ratio (a) ÷ (b)	0.68 to 1	1.2 to 1
d. Sales on account (a)	$20,000,000	$15,000,000
Average accounts receivable (b)	$ 1,150,000	$ 700,000
Accounts receivable turnover (a) ÷ (b)	17.4 times	21.4 times
Average collection period:		
365 ÷ turnover	21.0 days	17.1 days
e. Cost of goods sold (a)	$13,000,000	$ 9,000,000
Average inventory (b)	$ 2,100,000	$ 1,100,000
Inventory turnover (a) ÷ (b)	6.2 times	8.2 times
Average sale period: 365 ÷ turnover	58.9 days	44.5 days
f. Net operating income (a)	$ 1,740,000	$ 1,440,000
Interest expense (b)	$ 240,000	$ 240,000
Times interest earned (a) ÷ (b)	7.25 times	6.0 times
g. Total liabilities (a)	$ 4,500,000	$ 3,000,000
Total shareholders' equity (b)	$ 5,470,000	$ 4,900,000
Debt-to-equity ratio (a) ÷ (b)	0.82 to 1	0.61 to 1

Problem 17-17 (continued)

2. The following comments can be made relative to the company's current financial condition:

a. The working capital is increasing, but both the current ratio and the acid-test ratio have deteriorated significantly over the last year. (This shows the danger of relying on working capital alone in assessing the well-being of a company.) With an acid-test ratio of only 0.68 to 1, it is not surprising that the company is having difficulty paying its bills. The company may be only months away from being forced into bankruptcy.

b. The company is taking 5 days longer to collect an account than the average for the industry. Equally significant, the collection period has increased over the last year. This is the result either of poor collection efforts or sales to customers who are poor credit risks.

c. The company is taking nearly 19 days longer to turn its inventory than the average for the industry. And the average sale period has increased significantly over the last year. Slow turnover of inventory is usually indicative of inventory shares that are too large or include too many unsalable goods.

d. The company's earning power is very strong, as evidenced by its excellent times-interest-earned ratio.

e. The company's 0.82 to 1 debt-to-equity ratio is already above the industry average of 0.70 to 1, even without the proposed $500,000 loan.

3. Despite the problems noted in (2) above, the authors would approve the loan. With the help of the $500,000 in new funds, the company should have breathing room to tighten up the collection of its accounts receivable and to reduce its inventory to a more manageable size. If the receivables and inventory are brought under control, then several hundred thousand dollars should become available either to pay off the loan or to further strengthen the company's current financial condition. This is not a hopeless situation; it is simply a situation where a good company has allowed control over certain key assets to slip over the last year or so.

Problem 17-19 (60 minutes or longer)

PEPPER INDUSTRIES
Income Statement
For the Year Ended March 31

		Key to Computation
Sales	$4,200,000	—
Less cost of goods sold	2,730,000	(h)
Gross margin	1,470,000	(i)
Less operating expenses	930,000	(j)
Net operating income	540,000	(a)
Less interest expense	80,000	—
Net income before taxes	460,000	(b)
Less income taxes (30%)	138,000	(c)
Net income	$ 322,000	(d)

PEPER INDUSTRIES
Balance Sheet
March 31

Current assets:		
Cash	$ 70,000	(f)
Accounts receivable, net	330,000	(e)
Inventory	480,000	(g)
Total current assets	880,000	(g)
Plant and equipment	1,520,000	(q)
Total assets	$2,400,000	(p)
Current liabilities	$ 320,000	—
Bonds payable, 10%	800,000	(k)
Total liabilities	1,120,000	(l)
Shareholders' equity:		
Common shares, 140,000 no par	700,000	(m)
Retained earnings	580,000	(o)
Total shareholders' equity	1,280,000	(n)
Total liabilities and equity	$2,400,000	(p)

Problem 17-19 (continued)

Computation of missing amounts (other computational sequences are possible):

a. $\dfrac{\text{Earnings before interest and taxes}}{\text{Interest expense, \$80,000}}$ = 6.75 times interest earned.

Therefore, the earnings before interest and taxes for the year must be $540,000.

b. $540,000 − $80,000 = $460,000.

c. $460,000 × 30% tax rate = $138,000 income tax expense.

d. $460,000 − $138,000 = $322,000.

e. $\dfrac{\text{Sales on account, \$4,200,000}}{\text{Average accounts receivable balance}} = \dfrac{\text{Accounts receivable}}{\text{turnover, 14.0 times.}}$

Therefore, the average accounts receivable balance for the year must have been $300,000. Since the beginning balance was $270,000, the ending balance must have been $330,000.

f.

$\dfrac{\text{Cash + marketable securities + current receivables}}{\text{Current liabilities, \$320,000}} = \dfrac{\text{1.25 to 1}}{\text{acid - test ratio.}}$

Therefore, the total quick assets must be $400,000. Since there are no marketable securities and since the accounts receivable are $330,000, the cash must be $70,000.

g. $\dfrac{\text{Current assets}}{\text{Current liabilities, \$320,000}}$ = 2.75 to 1 current ratio.

Therefore, the current assets must total $880,000. Since the quick assets (cash and accounts receivable) total $400,000 of this amount, the inventory must be $480,000.

Problem 17-19 (continued)

h.

$$\frac{\text{Cost of goods sold}}{\text{Average inventory, } 1/2(\$360,000 + \$480,000) = \$420,000} = \text{Inventory turnover, 6.5 times.}$$

Therefore, the cost of goods sold for the year must be $2,730,000.

i. $4,200,000 – $2,730,000 = $1,470,000 gross margin.

j. $1,470,000 gross margin – $540,000 net operating income = $930,000 operating expenses.

k. Since the interest expense for the year was $80,000 and the interest rate was 10%, the bonds payable must total $800,000.

l. $320,000 + $800,000 = $1,120,000.

m.

$$\frac{\text{Net income - Preferred dividends, } \$322,000}{\text{Average number of common shares outstanding}} = \begin{array}{l} \$2.30 \text{ earnings} \\ \text{per share.} \end{array}$$

Therefore, there must be 140,000 common shares outstanding. Since the shares have a $5 noted value per share, the total common shares must be $700,000.

n. $\dfrac{\text{Total liabilities, } \$1,120,000}{\text{Shareholders' equity}} = 0.875 \text{ debt - to - equity ratio.}$

Therefore, the total shareholders' equity must be $1,280,000.

o. Total shareholders' equity, $1,280,000 – Common shares, $700,000 = $580,000 Retained earnings.

Problem 17-19 (continued)

p. $1,120,000 Liabilities + $1,280,000 Shareholders' equity = $2,400,000 Total. This answer can also be obtained through the return on total assets ratio:

$$\frac{\text{Net income} + [\text{Interest expense} \times (1 - \text{Tax rate})]}{\text{Average total assets}} = \text{Return on total assets.}$$

$$\frac{\$322,000 + [\$80,000 \times (1 - 0.30)] = \$378,000}{\text{Average total assets}} = 18.0\% \text{ Return on total assets.}$$

Therefore the average total assets must be $2,100,000. Since the total assets at the beginning of the year were $1,800,000, the total assets at the end of the year must have been $2,400,000 (which would also equal the total of the liabilities and the shareholders' equity).

q. Total assets $2,400,000 – $880,000 Current assets = $1,520,000 Plant and equipment.

Problem 21 (25 minutes)

1. Net income to the common shareholders:

	Method A	Method B	Method C
Income before interest and taxes............................	$170,000	$170,000	$170,000
Deduct interest expense: 8% × $500,000	—	—	40,000
Income before taxes	170,000	170,000	130,000
Deduct income taxes (30%).................................	51,000	51,000	39,000
Net income	119,000	119,000	91,000
Deduct preferred dividends: 8% × $500,000	—	40,000	—
Net income remaining for common shareholders	$119,000	$ 79,000	$ 91,000

2. Return on common equity:

Net income remaining for common shareholders (a)...	$ 119,000	$ 79,000	$ 91,000
Common shareholders' investment (b)......................	$1,000,000	$500,000	$500,000
Return on common equity (a) ÷ (b)	11.9%	15.8%	18.2%

3. Methods B and C provide a greater return on common equity than Method A because of the effect of positive leverage in the company. Methods B and C each contain sources of funds that require a fixed annual return on the funds provided. Apparently, this fixed annual cost is less than what is being earned on the assets in the company, with the difference going to the common shareholders.

   Method C, which involves the use of debt, provides more leverage than Method B, which involves the use of preferred shares, due to the fact that the interest on the debt is tax deductible, whereas the dividends on the preferred shares are not.

Problem 17-23 (30 minutes)

Requirement 1. Cost saving

		Existing		Proposed
Material costs		$140,000		$120,000
Labour	6000 * $18	108,000	4500 * $20	90,000
Overhead		80,000		110,000
Total cost		$328,000		$320,000
Cost saving		$8,000		

Requirement 2

Value added in total is the extra profit generated from the cost saving or $8,000.

Value added per dollar of input is $8,000/$328,000 or 2.4 cents per dollar of input based on the original cost of the project.

For the $30,000 additional overhead, management expects to save $18,000 in labour and $20,000 in materials. Thus the value added per dollar of new costs would be $38,000/$30,000 or $1.27 per dollar of new costs.

Appendix A
Pricing Products and Services

Exercise A-1 (20 minutes)

1. Maria makes more money selling the ice cream cones at the lower price, as shown below:

	$1.89 Price	**$1.49 Price**
Unit sales	1,500	2,340
Sales..............................	$2,835.00	$3,486.60
Cost of sales @ $0.43.....	645.00	1,006.20
Contribution margin.........	2,190.00	2,480.40
Fixed expenses	675.00	675.00
Net operating income	$1,515.00	$1,805.40

2. The price elasticity of demand, as defined in the text, is computed as follows:

$$\varepsilon_d = \frac{\ln(1+\%\text{ change in quantity sold})}{\ln(1+\%\text{ change in price})}$$

$$= \frac{\ln\left(1+\left(\dfrac{2,340-1,500}{1,500}\right)\right)}{\ln\left(1+\left(\dfrac{1.49-1.89}{1.89}\right)\right)}$$

$$= \frac{\ln(1+0.56000)}{\ln(1-0.21164)}$$

$$= \frac{\ln(1.56000)}{\ln(0.78836)}$$

$$= \frac{0.44469}{-0.23780} = -1.87$$

Exercise A-1 (continued)

3. The profit-maximizing price can be estimated using the following
   formula from the text:

$$\text{Profit-maximizing price} = \left(\frac{\varepsilon_d}{1+\varepsilon_d}\right)\text{Variable cost per unit}$$

$$= \left(\frac{-1.87}{1+(-1.87)}\right)\$0.43$$

$$= 2.1494 \times \$0.43 = \$0.92$$

This price is much lower than the prices Maria has been
charging in the past. Rather than immediately dropping the
price to $0.92, it would be prudent to drop the price a bit and
see what happens to unit sales and to profits. The formula
assumes that the price elasticity is constant, which may not be
the case.

Exercise A-3 (5 minutes)

Sales (300,000 units × $15)	$4,500,000
Less: desired return on investment (12% × $5,000,000)	600,000
Target cost for 300,000 units	$3,900,000

Target cost per unit = $3,900,000 ÷ 300,000 = $13 per unit

Problem A-5 (30 minutes)

1. The postal service makes more money selling the souvenir sheets at the lower price, as shown below:

	$7 Price	$8 Price
Unit sales	100,000	85,000
Sales...............................	$700,000	$680,000
Cost of sales @ $0.80.....	80,000	68,000
Contribution margin.........	$620,000	$612,000

2. The price elasticity of demand, as defined in the text, is computed as follows:

$$\varepsilon_d = \frac{\ln(1 + \%\text{ change in quantity sold})}{\ln(1 + \%\text{ change in price})}$$

$$= \frac{\ln\left(1 + \left(\dfrac{85,000 - 100,000}{100,000}\right)\right)}{\ln\left(1 + \left(\dfrac{8 - 7}{7}\right)\right)}$$

$$= \frac{\ln(1 - 0.1500)}{\ln(1 + 0.1429)}$$

$$= \frac{\ln(0.8500)}{\ln(1.1429)}$$

$$= \frac{-0.1625}{0.1336}$$

$$= -1.2163$$

Problem A-5 (continued)

3. The profit-maximizing price can be estimated using the following formula from the text:

$$\text{Profit-maximizing price} = \left(\frac{\varepsilon_d}{1+\varepsilon_d}\right)\text{Variable cost per unit}$$

$$= \left(\frac{-1.2163}{1+(-1.2163)}\right)\$0.80$$

$$= 5.6232 \times \$0.80 = \$4.50$$

This price is much lower than the price the postal service has been charging in the past. Rather than immediately dropping the price to $4.50, it would be prudent for the postal service to drop the price a bit and observe what happens to unit sales and to profits. The formula assumes that the price elasticity of demand is constant, which may not be true.

The critical assumption in these calculations is that the percentage increase (decrease) in quantity sold is always the same for a given percentage decrease (increase) in price. If this is true, we can estimate the demand schedule for souvenir sheets as follows:

Price*	Quantity Sold[§]
$8.00	85,000
$7.00	100,000
$6.13	117,647
$5.36	138,408
$4.69	162,833
$4.10	191,569
$3.59	225,375
$3.14	265,147
$2.75	311,937
$2.41	366,985

* The price in each cell in the table is computed by taking 7/8 of the price just above it in the table. For example, $6.13 is 7/8 of $7.00 and $5.36 is 7/8 of $6.13.

Problem A-5 (continued)

§ The quantity sold in each cell of the table is computed by multiplying the quantity sold just above it in the table by 100,000/85,000. For example, 117,647 is computed by multiplying 100,000 by the fraction 100,000/85,000.

The profit at each price in the above demand schedule can be computed as follows:

Price (a)	Quantity Sold (b)	Sales (a) × (b)	Cost of Sales $0.80 × (b)	Contribution Margin
$8.00	85,000	$680,000	$68,000	$612,000
$7.00	100,000	$700,000	$80,000	$620,000
$6.13	117,647	$721,176	$94,118	$627,058
$5.36	138,408	$741,867	$110,727	$631,140
$4.69	162,833	$763,687	$130,267	$633,420
$4.10	191,569	$785,433	$153,255	$632,178
$3.59	225,375	$809,096	$180,300	$628,796
$3.14	265,147	$832,562	$212,117	$620,445
$2.75	311,937	$857,827	$249,550	$608,277
$2.41	366,985	$884,434	$293,588	$590,846

Problem A-5 (continued)

The contribution margin is plotted below as a function of the selling price:

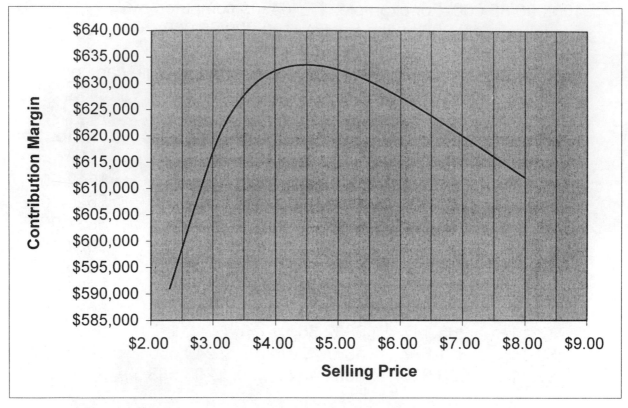

The plot confirms that the profit-maximizing price is about $4.50.

Problem A-5 (continued)

4. If the postal service wants to maximize the contribution margin and profit from sales of souvenir sheets, the new price should be:

$$\text{Profit-maximizing price} = \left(\frac{\varepsilon_d}{1+\varepsilon_d}\right)\text{Variable cost per unit}$$

$$= \left(\frac{-1.2163}{1+(-1.2163)}\right)\$1.00$$

$$= 5.6232 \times \$1.00 = \$5.62$$

Note that a $0.20 increase in cost has led to a $1.12 ($5.62 – $4.50) increase in selling price. This is because the profit-maximizing price is computed by multiplying the variable cost by 5.6232. Since the variable cost has increased by $0.20, the profit-maximizing price has increased by $0.20 × 5.6232, or $1.12.

Some people may object to such a large increase in price as "unfair" and some may even suggest that only the $0.20 increase in cost should be passed on to the consumer. The enduring popularity of full-cost pricing may be explained to some degree by the notion that prices should be "fair" rather than calculated to maximize profits.

Problem A-7 (45 minutes)

1. Projected sales (100 machines × $4,950 per machine). $495,000
    Less desired profit (15% × $600,000)............................   90,000
    Target cost for 100 machines... $405,000

    Target cost per machine ($405,000 ÷ 100 machines).... $4,050
    Less National Restaurant Supply's variable selling cost
       per machine   650
    Maximum allowable purchase price per machine.......... $3,400

2. The relation between the purchase price of the machine and
    ROI can be developed as follows:

$$ROI = \frac{\text{Total projected sales} - \text{Total cost}}{\text{Investment}}$$

$$= \frac{\$495,000 - (\$650 + \text{Purchase price of machines}) \times 100}{\$600,000}$$

Problem A-7 (continued)

The above formula can be used to compute the ROI for various purchase prices. The ROIs for purchase prices between $3,000 and $4,000 (in increments of $100) can be computed as follows:

Purchase price	ROI*
$3,000	21.7%
$3,100	20.0%
$3,200	18.3%
$3,300	16.7%
$3,400	15.0%
$3,500	13.3%
$3,600	11.7%
$3,700	10.0%
$3,800	8.3%
$3,900	6.7%
$4,000	5.0%

* Computed using the formula ROI =

$$\frac{\$495,000 - (\$650 + \text{Purchase price}) \times 100}{\$600,000}$$

Problem A-7 (continued)

Using the above data, the relation between purchase price and ROI can be plotted as follows:

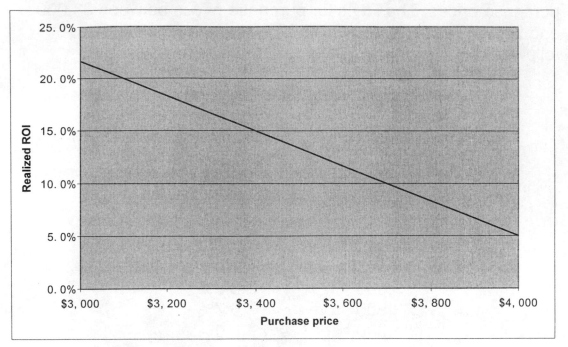

3. A number of options are available in addition to simply giving up on adding the new sorbet machines to the company's product lines. These options include:

- Check the projected unit sales figures. Perhaps more units could be sold at the $4,950. However, management should be careful not to indulge in wishful thinking just to make the numbers come out right.
- Modify the selling price. This does not necessarily mean increasing the projected selling price. Decreasing the selling price may generate enough additional unit sales to make carrying the sorbet machines more profitable.
- Improve the selling process to decrease the variable selling costs.
- Rethink the investment that would be required to carry this new product. Can the size of the inventory be reduced? Are the new warehouse fixtures really necessary?
- Does the company really need a 15% ROI? Does it cost the company this much to acquire more funds?

Problem A-9 (45 minutes)

1. Supporting computations:

Number of hours worked per year:
    20 workers x 40 hrs. x 50 weeks = 40,000 hrs.

Number of surfboards produced per year:
    40,000 ÷ 2 hrs. per surfboard = 20,000 surfboards.

Standard cost per surfboard: $1,600,000 ÷ 20,000 surfboards = $80.

Fixed manufacturing overhead cost per surfboard:
    $600,000 ÷ 20,000 surfboards = $30.

Manufacturing overhead per surfboard: $5 variable + $30 fixed = $35.

Direct labour cost per surfboard: $80 − ($27 + $35) = $18.

Given the computations above, the completed standard cost card would be as follows:

	Standard Quantity or Hours	Standard Price or Rate	Standard Cost
Direct materials........	6 board feet	$ 4.50 per board foot	$27
Direct labour	2 hours	9.00 per hour*	18
Manufacturing overhead	2 hours	17.50 per hour**	35
Total standard cost per surfboard			$80

  *$18 ÷ 2 hrs. = $9 per hr.
 **$35 ÷ 2 hrs. = $17.50 per hr.

Problem A-9 (continued)

2. a.

$$\text{Markup Percentage} = \frac{\left[\frac{\text{Required ROI}}{\times \text{Investment}}\right] + \text{SG \& A}}{\text{Volume in Units} \times \text{Unit Product Cost}}$$

$$= \frac{(18\% \times \$1,500,000) + \$1,130,000}{20,000 \text{ units} \times \$80}$$

$$= \frac{\$1,400,000}{\$1,600,000}$$

$$= 87.5\%$$

b.
Direct materials	$ 27
Direct labour	18
Manufacturing overhead	35
Total cost to manufacture	80
Add markup: 87.5%	70
Target selling price	$150

c.
Sales (20,000 boards × $150)	$3,000,000
Less cost of goods sold (20,000 boards × $80)	1,600,000
Gross margin	1,400,000
Less selling, general, and administrative expense	1,130,000
Net income	$ 270,000

$$\text{ROI} = \frac{\text{Net operating Income}}{\text{Sales}} \times \frac{\text{Sales}}{\text{Average Operating Assets}}$$

$$= \frac{\$270,000}{\$3,000,000} \times \frac{\$3,000,000}{\$1,500,000}$$

$$= 9\% \times 2$$

$$= 18\%$$

Problem A-9 (continued)

3. Supporting computations:

Total fixed costs:

Manufacturing overhead......................................	$ 600,000
Selling, general, and administrative [$1,130,000 − (20,000 boards × $10 = $200,000) = $930,000]	930,000
Total fixed costs...	$1,530,000

Variable costs per unit:

Direct materials	$27
Direct labour...	18
Variable manufacturing overhead	5
Variable selling	10
Variable cost per unit..	$60

To achieve the 18% ROI, the company would have to sell at least the 20,000 units assumed in part (2) above. The break-even volume can be computed as follows:

$$\text{Break-even point in units sold} = \frac{\text{Fixed expenses}}{\text{Unit contribution margin}}$$

$$= \frac{\$1,530,000}{\$150 - \$60}$$

$$= 17,000 \text{ units}$$

Appendix B
Cost of Quality

Exercise B-1 (10 minutes)

1.

		Prevention Cost	Appraisal Cost	Internal Failure Cost	External Failure Cost
a.	Product testing..............		X		
b.	Product recalls				X
c.	Rework labour and overhead....................			X	
d.	Quality circles	X			
e.	Downtime caused by defects			X	
f.	Cost of field servicing....				X
g.	Inspection of goods.......		X		
h.	Quality engineering	X			
i.	Warranty repairs				X
j.	Statistical process control..........................	X			
k.	Net cost of scrap...........			X	
l.	Depreciation of test equipment....................		X		
m.	Returns and allowances arising from poor quality				X
n.	Disposal of defective products......................			X	
o.	Technical support to suppliers	X			
p.	Systems development...	X			
q.	Warranty replacements				X
r.	Field testing at customer site		X		
s.	Product design..............	X			

Exercise B-1 (continued)

2. Prevention costs and appraisal costs are incurred in an effort to keep poor quality of conformance from occurring. Internal and external failure costs are incurred because poor quality of conformance has occurred.

Problem B-3 (60 minutes)

1.

FLOREX COMPANY
Quality Cost Report

	This Year		Last Year	
	Amount	**Percent***	**Amount**	**Percent***
Prevention costs:				
Quality engineering............	$ 570,000	0.76	$ 420,000	0.56
Systems development.......	750,000	1.00	480,000	0.64
Statistical process control .	180,000	0.24	—	—
Total.............................	1,500,000	2.00	900,000	1.20
Appraisal costs				
Inspection	900,000	1.20	750,000	1.00
Product testing..................	1,200,000	1.60	810,000	1.08
Supplies used in testing....	60,000	0.08	30,000	0.04
Depreciation of testing				
equipment......................	240,000	0.32	210,000	0.28
Total.............................	2,400,000	3.20	1,800,000	2.40
Internal failure costs:				
Net cost of scrap...............	1,125,000	1.50	630,000	0.84
Rework labour....................	1,500,000	2.00	1,050,000	1.40
Disposal of defective				
products...........................	975,000	1.30	720,000	0.96
Total.............................	3,600,000	4.80	2,400,000	3.20
External failure costs:				
Cost of field servicing........	900,000	1.20	1,200,000	1.60
Warranty repairs	1,050,000	1.40	3,600,000	4.80
Product recalls	750,000	1.00	2,100,000	2.80
Total.............................	2,700,000	3.60	6,900,000	9.20
Total quality cost..................	$10,200,000	13.60	$12,000,000	16.00

* As a percentage of total sales.

2. See the graph on the following page.

© 2001 McGraw-Hill Ryerson Limited

Problem B-3 (continued)

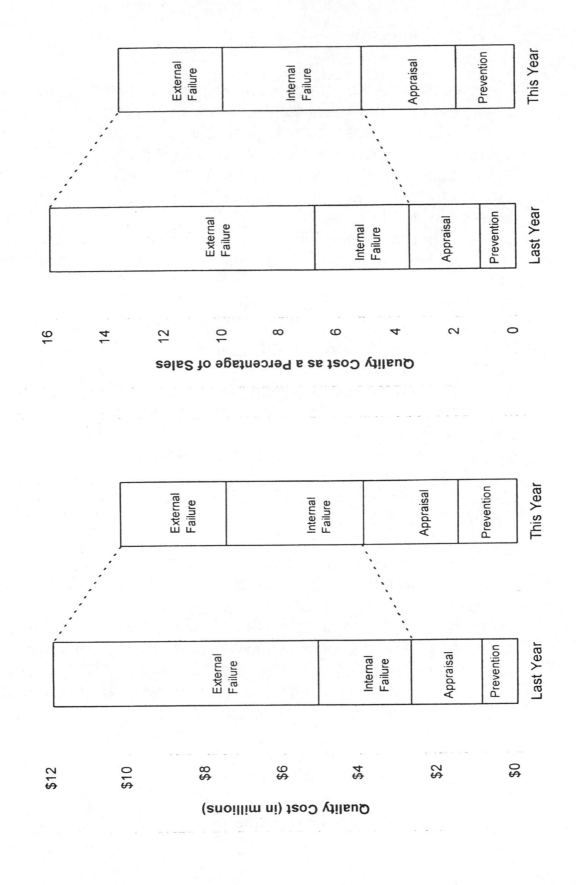

Problem B-3 (continued)

3.   The overall impact of the company's increased emphasis on quality over the past year has been positive in that total quality costs have decreased from 16% of sales to 13.6% of sales. Despite this improvement, the company still has a poor distribution of quality costs. The bulk of the quality costs in both years is traceable to internal and external failure, rather than to prevention and appraisal. Although the distribution of these costs is poor, the trend this year is toward more prevention and appraisal as the company has given more emphasis on quality.

Probably due to the increased spending on prevention and appraisal activities during the past year, internal failure costs have increased by one half, going from $2.4 million to $3.6 million. The reason internal failure costs have gone up is that, through increased appraisal activity, defects are being caught and corrected before products are shipped to customers. Thus, the company is incurring more cost for scrap, rework, and so forth, but it is saving huge amounts in field servicing, warranty repairs, and product recalls. External failure costs have fallen sharply, decreasing from $6.9 million last year to just $2.7 million this year.

If the company continues its emphasis on prevention and appraisal—and particularly on prevention—its total quality costs should continue to decrease in future years. Although internal failure costs are increasing for the moment, these costs should decrease in time as better quality is designed into products. Appraisal costs should also decrease as the need for inspection, testing, and so forth decreases as a result of better engineering and tighter process control.

Problem B-5 (45 minutes)

1. A percentage analysis of the company's quality cost report is presented below:

	This Year			Last Year		
	Amount	Percentage*		Amount	Percentage*	
Prevention costs:						
Machine maintenance	$ 120	2.5 %	20.3 %	$70	1.7 %	10.4 %
Training suppliers	10	0.2	1.7	—	0.0	0.0
Quality circles	20	0.4	3.4	—	0.0	0.0
Total...............	150	3.1	25.4	70	1.7	10.4
Appraisal costs:						
Incoming inspection	40	0.8	6.8	20	0.5	3.0
Final testing	90	1.9	15.3	80	1.9	11.9
Total...............	130	2.7	22.0	100	2.4	14.9
Internal failure costs:						
Rework	130	2.7	22.0	50	1.2	7.5
Scrap	70	1.5	11.9	40	1.0	6.0
Total...............	200	4.2	33.9	90	2.1	13.4
External failure costs:						
Warranty repairs.............	30	0.6	5.1	90	2.1	13.4
Customer returns	80	1.7	13.6	320	7.6	47.8
Total...............	110	2.3	18.6	410	9.8	61.2
Total quality cost...	$ 590	12.3 %	100.0 %	$670	16.0 %	100.0 %
Total production cost.....................	$4,800			$4,200		

* Percentage figures may not add down due to rounding.

Problem B-5 (continued)

From the above analysis it would appear that Mercury, Inc.'s program has been successful.

Total quality costs have declined from 16.0% to 12.3% as a percentage of total production cost. In dollar amount, total quality costs went from $670,000 last year to $590,000 this year.

External failure costs, those costs signaling customer dissatisfaction, have declined from 9.8% of total production costs to 2.3%. These declines in warranty repairs and customer returns should result in increased sales in the future.

Appraisal costs have increased from 2.4% to 2.7% of total production cost.

Internal failure costs have increased from 2.1% to 4.2% of production costs. This increase has probably resulted from the increase in appraisal activities. Defective units are now being spotted more frequently before they are shipped to customers.

Prevention costs have increased from 1.7% of total production cost to 3.1% and from 10.4% of total quality costs to 25.4%. The $80,000 increase is more than offset by decreases in other quality costs.

2. The initial effect of emphasizing prevention and appraisal was to reduce external failure costs and increase internal failure costs. The increase in appraisal activities resulted in catching more defective units before they were shipped to customers. As a consequence, rework and scrap costs increased. In the future, an increased emphasis on prevention should result in a decrease in internal failure costs. And as defect rates are reduced, resources devoted to appraisal can be reduced.

3. To measure the cost of not implementing the quality program, management could assume that sales and market share would continue to decline and then calculate the lost profit. Or, management might assume that the company will have to cut its prices to hang on to its market share. The impact on profits of lowering prices could be estimated.